Real Estate Ownership, Investment and Due Diligence 101

By Professor and Investor Leonard P. Baron, MBA, CPA and Team of Expert Co-Authors

Thank you for your purchase and your consideration! Send us any feedback you feel would improve the book. Good Luck!

- LOCATION
- LABOR MARKET STRONG
STABLE AREAS
GOOD NEIGHBORHOOD
GOOD SCHOOLS
GOOD TENANT
GOOD CASH FLOW

BUYER BEWARE

REAL ESTATE IS BUYER BEWARE - DO YOU KNOW OF WHAT TO "BEWARE"?

In using this guide one must understand and accept that real estate is ALWAYS HIGH RISK, THERE IS NO RISK FREE PROPERTY, and YOU CAN NEVER ELIMINATE REAL ESTATE RISK!

And a percentage of users of this material who do all the due diligence in this book and every due diligence task and procedure ever known to man will still lose money on real estate transactions and ownership. It is inevitable! And unfortunately that may end up being you.

The more time, work, and effort you do to educate yourself, working hard to understand, lower and/or mitigate those risks before you buy...the better chances you have of having a good and profitable real estate ownership experience.

So, you should use the material herein as a general overview guide, but there are many issues we don't cover herein, many issues we don't know, and many issues we've never even heard about. In conjunction with this guide, to better protect yourself on all the due diligence you need to do, you should research and talk to others in your local jurisdiction, like real estate owners, possibly a lawyer, CPA, financial advisor, your real estate sales professional, mortgage lender, home inspector and/or other inspectors you deem necessary, a contractor or two, a plumber, electrician, the city or county building, code compliance, assessor, zoning or development departments, your escrow agent, the title insurance officer, and HOA expert, your homeowners insurance agent and any other agents, officers, inspectors, consultants, advisors, your family, friends, etc. – anyone else who you believe can help better advise you on buying and owning real estate.

PLEASE REALIZE WE ARE NOT TRYING TO SCARE YOU OR DISSUADE YOU FROM BUYING PROPERTY. THE GOAL IS TO INSPIRE YOU TO REALLY CONSIDER THE REAL AND SIGNIFICANT RISKS THAT ARE INHERENT IN REAL ESTATE AND HELP YOU HELP YOURSELF MAKE SMART AND SAFE PURCHASES.

SO PLEASE, FOR YOUR OWN GOOD, RELAX, READ, ENJOY, LEARN, TAKE YOUR TIME, STUDY ALL THE CONCEPTS AND ISSUES, AND TAKE THE SIGNIFICANT TIME TO FOCUS AND EMPLOY WHAT YOUR LEARN WHEN YOU ARE READY TO ACTUALLY PURCHASE PROPERTY.

YOU CAN DO IT, GOOD LUCK.

Leonard P. Baron

Email for Access to www.ProfessorBaron.com website documents, checklists, spreadsheets that support the book – leonard@professorbaron.com.

We do not sell, give away, or share your email address. We take your privacy seriously.

Amazon and Kindle Books

The Textbook Can Be Purchased at ProfessorBaron.com and at Amazon dot Com:

By Searching "Professor Leonard Baron"

TABLE OF CONTENTS – ABRIDGED
MATCHES PROFESSORBARON.COM SITE

TABLE OF CONTENTS

MATCHES PROFESSORBARON.COM SITE

Foreward

REASON FOR THIS COURSE

This Course was created to assist real estate buyers, whether for a personal residence or investment property, in being a little bit smarter about buying the "right" property for themselves. The way to be smarter is by doing your due diligence - your homework - to reduce the chances of something going wrong.

INDEPENDENT, NEUTRAL, UNBIASED AND CONCISE

The authors are also an independent, neutral and unbiased source of information. This will help a buyer obtain a clearer picture of the vitally important issues in any real estate deal. And the course also gets straight to the point – the top issues you must consider and review in your buying process.

EXPERIENCED AUTHORS

The authors are industry professionals in real estate investing and analysis, mortgage financing, real property brokerage and sales, property and liability insurance, homeowner's association financial analysis and home inspections. They have decades of combined experience in real estate investment and ownership. They cumulatively own about 50 properties including condos, townhomes, single family homes, duplexes, plus other commercial real estate that was acquired over the past 20 to 30 years. Additionally, they have been involved in over 1000 transactions either as principals, brokers, advisors, insurers, inspectors, financers, and others issues.

LOST THE RISK, NOT YOUR SHIRT!

What the authors are teaching in this manual is all the items upon which they have already learned the hard lessons on and lost money upon in the past. Losing money on property issues teaches one the most expensive and the most valuable lessons an individual will ever learn. By studying and employing the concepts in this book, you will learn those valuable lessons while hopefully avoiding making the expensive mistakes the authors have made in the past.

Buyers should realize that there are probably between 300 and 600 pages of documents - See website for Document List - that one needs to read and understand, plus home inspections, insurance choices, analysis, checklists, etc. that go along with purchasing real estate. The authors are here to help buyers decipher, understand, analyze, and advise on these. Your job is to read, study, learn and understand the concepts that this guide presents and do the procedures you need to do to help yourself make those better decisions.

SHOULD PEOPLE EVEN BUY REAL ESTATE?

If you learn all the due diligence in this course and all the risks, you might shake your head and wonder why anyone would ever buy real estate? The reason people buy real estate is simple - they hope to earn wealth. And that can be you. But to earn that wealth, you need to take the right prudent steps to increase your chances of being successful in your acquisitions. You do this by reducing many of the inherent, but generally straightforward, risks related to buying and owning property.

LONG TERM INVESTING RECOMMENDED

Real estate is also a long term deal. Reading this guide will teach individuals many lessons that illustrate why short term ownership is high risk and prone to failure. While it is possible for one to earn wealth with short term ownership, the chances of success are very low. With transaction costs, cost over runs, delays, trying to make money by any fancy get rich quick scheme can prove very illusive.

Buy for the long haul. That will give you the highest chances of long term financial security and success. Anyone reading this sentence can earn long term wealth on real estate with hard work, a good real estate education, common sense and determination. And hard work. Let us repeat again – and hard work!

Get Rich Quick Schemes - For individuals who believe there is quick and easy money in real estate and that one can buy foreclosures or fixer uppers and quickly flip them for significant profits, this course will highly discourage people from trying that strategy.

The chances of earning significant wealth with real estate over short periods of time, even with the right due diligence, is very, very low. And the chances of losing wealth with short term, get rich quick attempts, is very, so very high.

The authors prefer the low risk and earn significant wealth over time strategy. If you like the sound of that, the material in this guide should be very useful to you.

This is equivalent to a college level course so study the material over a couple of months.

Remember, real estate is the largest purchase you will ever make in life and it has significant financial, stress and time consumption risk. Take your time, do your homework, you have years to get rich on real estate….there is no rush. Our hope is to help you be smarter about buying property so you really can accumulate wealth over the long haul and enjoy the spoils of your hard work down the road.

CHAPTER 1

DUE DILIGENCE TO REDUCE YOUR RISK

DUE DILIGENCE CHECKLIST AT BOTTOM OF CHAPTER. YOUR WHOLE BUYING PROCESS REVOLVES AROUND FINDING WHAT YOU BELIEVE IS A FAIR DEAL AND THEN DOING THE TASKS (a.k.a. Hard Work) NEEDED TO CONFIRM IT IS A FAIR DEAL AND REDUCE YOUR RISK ON THAT ACQUISITION.

DUE DILIGENCE is the process of "doing your homework" to assess the inherent risks in real estate transactions and ownership and then performing the tasks that reduce those risks....BEFORE YOU BUY.

The information that you learn by doing your due diligence will help you to lessen the uncertainty involved in your purchase. This will lower the risk of something

Due Diligence Property Acquisition Checklist

going wrong and costing you a lot of money and hence reducing your home equity or investment returns. Personal residences are investments too and you do not want to encounter "surprises" from your new home.

HOT TIP OF THE BOOK: Anyone can say, "I'm going to buy real estate to earn wealth" and go out and buy a personal residence or investment property that has all kinds of significant risk issues because they didn't do the hard work to educate themselves on those issues and mitigate, or reduce the risk of, those issues by avoiding certain properties. I would guesstimate that the vast majority of those people never end up earning that wealth that they hoped to attain. If you want to be one of the few that greatly improve your chances of long term wealth via real estate ownership, we suggest you educate yourself and do the hard work needed to hopefully attain your goals.

HOT TIP OF THE CHAPTER: You are make the most expensive, riskiest, and most complicated purchase of your life. This book will give you tools that will hopefully help you to reduce your risk. The book is equivalent to the work required to be done in a university level course. Take several months to read, study, review and material and hopefully you will make a smart and safe purchase that will provide you with long term wealth.

Due Diligence Example: A simple to understand due diligence example we all know is to hire an experienced home inspector to review the physical condition of the property you are interested in buying. If the inspector says, "there is a major foundation problem that will probably cost $25,000 or more to fix" you will be glad you were fully aware of this issue BEFORE you purchased the property. At that point you will assess whether or not it is smart to cancel the deal or ask for a significant price reduction.

While the vast majority of purchasers know to hire a home inspector there are many other vital due diligence tasks that one should review, perform and analyze before buying property. Other risks are issues like title issues, or the financial shape of the homeowners association, or are there insurance issues...and of course one of the most important – what will my cash flows and investment returns be on my purchase?...or, would it be better to rent for a while rather than own a property?

Due diligence takes time, energy, and effort but real estate purchases are the largest purchases you will ever make. So you must be diligent and work hard to reduce your risk...as failure to do your homework could end up being a drain on your finances for years, or DECADES, to come.

SOME RISK IS UNAVOIDABLE – We DO NOT know all the things that can be done to reduce risk – there are situations that can and will come up in the future that we cannot even contemplate right now or may be occurring right now that we just do not know. No one has the knowledge, experience or foresight to be able to identify and mitigate every risk issue.

However, we do know a LOT of the due diligence one can do so let us start off on the right foot protecting ourselves by reducing our risk by doing the proper due diligence on the things we know how to do.

Here are the items that we suggest you do and there is a chapter or information in this course on each one:

1. <u>Desired Property Location and Type</u> – Determine, based on what you can afford after being qualified by a mortgage lender, what areas of town or neighborhoods or condo or townhome complexes are the target areas or properties that best fit your home or investment acquisition criteria. You should know where you want to own property so you can concentrate on finding available properties in those areas. You should spend at least several months learning areas, pricing, rents, local amenities before you start seriously looking to buy. Do you want to own property next to parks, near retail stores, in the best school district, in a condominium or townhome complex or outside of town. If you narrow down your areas of interest, you will be able to concentrate your efforts on buying the "RIGHT" property that fits your criteria.

   - Listed Above and on Checklist
   - Review this Memorandum with other items and issues related to what you want in a property – Desired Property Location and Type Memorandum (Chapter 2)

2. <u>Schedule You Cash Inflows And Outflows On The Property</u>: You need to have a full understanding of the reasonably and conservatively estimated cash flows on your target purchase to make sure it makes sense to buy that particular asset – whether for investment rental property or for personal residence.

   - Chapter 3 – Investor Rental Cash Flows
   - Chapter 4 - Homebuyer Tips – Rent Vs. Own
   - Chapter 6 – Income Taxes - Impact on Cash Flow

Here's a GREAT tip from one of our EXPERTS:

Real estate is an **ASSET** in these two cases:

   1. Personal Residence – you can comfortably afford the payments;
   2. Investment Property – the rental income pays all the expenses.

Real Estate is a **LIABILITY** in these two cases:

   1. Personal Residence – you cannot afford the payments;
   2. Investment Property – the rental income does not pay all the expenses.

   3. <u>Mortgage Loans Due Diligence</u> – (aka know what you are signing on to). Learn how mortgages work, how much you can afford, how to secure fair terms, how to review your Good Faith Closing

Estimate and HUD-1 statement, how to analyze any point vs. rate options that you have and understand any other terms like prepayment, escrowing, etc. Learn what mortgages to avoid, e.g., negative amortization, ARMS, subprime, balloon payment, Alt-A loans.

- Chapter 7 – Home Mortgage Financing for Property

4. <u>Property Valuation and Comparable Market Sales Analysis</u>: Comparing the offering price of the property you desire to buy with other comparable properties will help you confirm the price you are paying is in line with the market. There are many many factors that determine a property value, e.g., condition, building square footage, lot size, view, area, etc., no two properties are alike. But comparing the price of the property you plan to buy with other recent sales or properties listed for sale in the near vicinity, and reconciling the differences, should help you get a comfortable feeling about the fair price for your property. You may buy the property for less, or for more, as one needs to look at all the factors involved to determine what is the right price to pay. And never walk away from the RIGHT property over a few thousand dollars; you will never find the perfect property or deal. The appraisal and valuation chapter will give you some help as will having your real estate agent prepare a Comparable Market Analysis (CMA) for you on your target property.

- Chapter 17 – Appraisal – Property Valuation

5. <u>Homeowners Association (HOA) Financial Condition Due Diligence</u>: This is for condominium, townhome, planned unit developments (PUD) or any other type of property where the individual unit owners share the costs of operating the public and/or common areas of the community. This particular task is extremely confusing, time consuming and unfortunately very tough to do based on different state's rules and laws, accounting statements and non-standardized forms. Regardless, it is VITAL to do to weed out the communities with obviously troubling issues related to the HOA financial condition and/or management and litigation issues.

- Chapter 8 – Homeowners Association Finances

6. <u>Property and Liability Insurance</u>: This is an issue that seems simple to understand in general terms, we all need insurance. But the specifics and issues related to reducing your risk by having the proper insurance are NOT simple to understand nor simple to make sure are properly in place on your property. Understanding the components and types of insurance and what they DO cover and what they DO NOT cover will go a long way in protecting you personally and covering your ASSets.

- Chapter 10 - Property and Liability Insurance

7. <u>Title due diligence and Limited Liability Companies LLCs</u>: Title insurance is one of the parts of buying property that most people hardly hear about or understand. And the risk of loss on a title issue is very low – but the potential losses are huge. So gaining an understanding of what you need to review on the "preliminary" title policy is important and reviewing the final issued policy. Equally important is the way in which you hold title to your property. We only discuss the basics as it can be different in each state and any complex issues on how to hold title need to be reviewed with your title agent and/or attorney.

- Chapter 11 – Title Insurance and Holding Title
- Chapter 12 – LLCs and Asset Protection

8. <u>Tax Issues Due Diligence</u>: Federal Income Taxes (FIT) are a significant cash flow issue that can greatly enhance your returns on investment properties, reduce your actual cash outflow on personal residences...or FIT may do nothing for you. For the vast majority of people filing taxes ("filers") their taxes are relatively simple and straightforward...it is the Internal Revenue Service's (IRS) forms, like that 1040, that make taxes seem complicated. This chapter will simplify taxes so that (again for the vast majority of filers) they can be clearly understood and used in your cash flow assumptions.

   If you are in the minority of filers - typically wealthier people or self employed - with varied sources of income and many deductions, or are typically subject to the Alternative Minimum Tax (AMT) then this chapter will give you the basics. Regardless of your tax situation, you should always consult a professional tax advisor for assistance. However your knowing these basics will help you better understand your tax advisor's advice and information.

   - Chapter 6 – <u>Income Taxes Impact on Cash Flows</u>

9. <u>Property Condition Due Diligence</u>: Having a home inspection by a competent professional is only one-half the battle. The other half is taking the time to talk to the inspector, ask questions, take notes, and really get a solid feel for the costs and expenses involved in bringing your property to the standards that you need or desire – whether a rental property or personal residence. During the inspection is not the time to be trying to figure out if your couch will fit in the living room or what color to paint the kitchen. But it is the time to figure out if the kitchen needs to be painted and what will that cost?

   We have included a fairly comprehensive checklist for you to use during the inspection – study it beforehand. Make sure you let your inspector know before you hire him/her that you want the inspection to be done "with you" NOT just "for you". An inspection is money well spent!

   - Chapter 9 – Home Inspections and Fix Up Costs

10. <u>Renting and Managing your Rental Property</u>: See Chapter 13

11. <u>Other Items and Issues</u>: Chapter 14, 15, 16, 18 and Articles

Here is a checklist to use for keeping track of the due diligence process during your purchase:

<u>DueDiligenceChecklist.pdf</u>

NEXT YOU WILL SEE THE INFORMATION IN THE DUE DILIGENCE CHECKLIST. THE DOWNLOADABLE CHECKLIST AT

WWW.PROFESSORBARON.COM

IS FORMATTED BETTER FOR CLEAR VIEWING AND EASY USE. WE RECOMMEND YOU DOWNLOAD AND PRINT THAT CHECKLIST AS SOON AS POSSIBLE AND USE IT IN CONJUNCTION WITH YOUR DUE DILIGENCE PROCESS.

For website www.ProfessorBaron.com access please email access@ProfessorBaron.com and you will be emailed instructions.

Due Diligence Property Acquisition Checklist

ProfessorBaron.com

A Smarter Way to Buy Real Estate

Buying Real Estate is the largest and riskiest purchase you will ever make in life.
Experienced buyers do their homework to protect themselves from the inherent risks.
You can also protect yourself, you just need to know what to do and how to do it.

Download the latest version of the checklist at www.ProfessorBaron.com to study these concepts
early on in the process and use once you begin offering on properties.

Property, Transaction and Contingencies Information

Property Address: _____

County Assessor
Parcel Number: _____

My Agent / Phone # _____

Seller's Agent / Phone # _____

Seller and/or Bank Involved in Sale _____

Escrow Agent/Company/Phone # _____

Transaction Document Coordinator _____

Price: _____

Downpayment: _____

Closing Costs: _____

Rehabilitation Estimate: _____

TOTAL CASH EQUITY TO CLOSE ESCROW: _____

Financing Details: _____

_____

I have a copy of my contract? Counter-Offers? Bank Addendums? Bank's Short Sale Letter(s)?

If Short Sale read "Don't get stuck
Paying extra at closing on your Short
Sale" before making offers - Chapter 5

Contract Ratification/Signed Date: _____

Escrow Begins Date: _____

Contingency Removal Dates	DATE	NOTES/Extensions?	CONTRACT ADVICE: The seller may say NO on any/all of these below, but worth a TRY!
Home Inspection / Document Review			Keep this contingency alive until you receive and inspect the HOA
Loan/Financing			Try to keep the loan contingency in effect until the loan is "Funded".
Appraisal			If the appraisal comes in low, try to re-negotiate the price down.
Other			
Contract Closing Date			Penalty/Day Late Closing?

	YES	NO	Not Applicable

1 **Desired Property Location and Type - See notes in Chapter 1**

Have I seen at least ten to twenty properties so I know what the market has to offer?
    If not, go ahead and offer but keep shopping until you have reviewed enough properties
    that you are confident you are getting a fair deal. Read the Valuation Chap 17.

Is this the neighborhood and/or community where I want to own?
    Do I know the areas well enough to make that decision?
    Have I talked to my friends/family/neighbors about this area?
    Have I driven around this area during the day, night, weekend to see what it is like?
    Can I afford this property with all my other bills?

Are the amenities I desire nearby (parks, schools, retail, Starbucks? etc)?
Or are they far far away as I would prefer?
    Is this the right school district for me?

Other Important Issues (You fill in):

    -
    -
    -

Is this a property that I plan to own for at least 5+ years and hopefully longer?
-- Five years will hopefully allow your costs on sale to be covered by the appreciation in value.
    If not, read the beginning of Chapter 4 - Rent vs. Own.

No property will ever be perfect, but is this close to the RIGHT property for ME?

2 **Schedule Your Cash Inflows and Outflows on the Property - Chapters 3, 4, 6**

Is this a rental property? Do my cash flows make good sense based on my investment
    criteria. Particularly important - am I being conservative based on my research as
    to costs to make the property rental ready, the market rents, vacancy and property expenses?
    Will the property provide a positive cash flow to me?
    Have I done enough INDEPENDENT and VERIFIABLE research to know I am being conservative?

Is this a personal residence? Have I penciled out my cash flows rent vs. own and
    am I comfortable with the numbers - not just what can I finance/borrow, but can I
    afford to pay the mortgage on this property and still pay my other bills?
Do I understand my Federal Income Tax benefits picture?

The answer better be yes to: "Can I comfortably afford the payments"

3 **Mortgage Loan/Financing - Chapter 7**   Lender Name/Contact Info: _____

    (If paying cash, many items will be NOT Applicable, but I still need to review the GFE for title and escrow costs).

When purchasing property it is critical to shop mortgage lenders. Interview at least two lenders
    and obtain Good Faith Closing Estimates (GFE) (or at least Preliminary Cost Worksheets) from the
    lenders. Review their GFE/offers and select the one your are most comfortable working
    with on your purchase. Did I do this?

See Article "Dissecting a GFE Costs to Comparison Shop" - Chapter 7.
I have separated out the three parts of the GFE so I can analyze the most
    important numbers on the GFE and I have reviewed them for reasonableness?

When getting ready to lock my loan, I requested some Rate vs. Points options and done a payback period
analysis on my options so I can make the best decision?

I have received an email lender confirming rate, points and terms we agreed upon for locking my loan?

Avoid anything other than a 30 year fixed rate amortizing mortgage - or a 15 year mortgage if the payments are affordable. Otherwise, I may need to refinance the loan several years down the road and go through all the hassle and stress and pay thousands a

Additionally, I may not be able to obtain new financing in the future and could lose the property.

I have avoided doing things that are detrimental to my credit score while I am in
  the buying process, like adding to my credit card balances, forgetting to pay bills or
  buying a new automobile?
    (Note: I know my loan could be rejected at the last minute if I hurt my FICO score)

I have kept my lender apprised of where I am in the purchasing process?

I have diligently submitted AND resubmitted documents as requested by the lender?

I have discussed the following items with my lender: prepayment penalties, escrowing
  taxes and insurance, putting a little more money down to try to get a better interest rate
  on my mortgage.

I have requested time to review the loan documents before I sign them?
  I will do this as my loan gets closer to being approved.
  I need to understand what I am signing.
Do the terms agree to my GFE Terms? You are not obligated on the loan until you sign these documents and your loan is "funded".

4   <u>Property Valuation and Comparable Market Sales Analysis - Chapter 17</u>

I have shopped lots of properties and I know the areas where I plan to buy. I do have a good feel for the value of the property I plan to offer upon. Regardless:

I have reviewed recent sales of comparable properties and determined how they compare
  to the property I plan to purchase?

I have adjusted the pricing to reflect the condition of better or lesser properties, square
  footage of property, square footage of lot, view premiums, traffic/busy street negatives, etc.

I had my real estate agent prepare "comps" for my review. I want ALL the sales and listings that are recent, nearby and comparable so I can do my own analysis as to whether or not I feel the price is in line (not just the ones that appear comparable to m

NOTE: Fair Returns on Investment Valuation - Prices can flucuate a lot in the current
  market and I will not reject a property if the investment returns are good (positive cash flows)
  just because a similar property sold for less. I know the lender may not feel the same as
  lending is based on current comparable sales. So it may be a good deal but the appraisal
  may come in low. In that case I may need to put down more equity to close, hopefully I
  will be able to get the cash equity needed to make the deal close.

  AND, If the appraisal comes in low, I will go back to the seller and try to get the price down,
    that may or may NOT work and then I will make my decision to move foreward or not.

Real estate is a long term deal, so reasonable short term fluctuations in price or value should not be a big concern of mine, I am buying the RIGHT property for the long haul.

NEVER WALK AWAY FROM THE RIGHT DEAL OVER A FEW THOUSAND DOLLARS. GOOD PROPERTIES ARE HARD TO FIND.

---

5   **Homeowners Association Due Diligence & Special Condo Issues - Chapter 8**   HOA Name and Contact Info: _____

This is going to be one of the most confusing and difficult parts of the due diligence process but you need to try to weed out obvious major problems. First and foremost you need to try to get the documents to review them and that is going to be time con

Have I run through the HOA Due Diligence Checklist from that Chapter?

Am I comfrotable with the HOA situation? Financial, Legal, Operational?

NOTE: Two of the Expert Authors hate and avoid properties that are in Common Interest Developments - so governed by HOAs, so condos, townhomes, co-ops, PUDs. There are lots of potential issues with HOAs as noted extensively in the Chapter. From unruly b

The Professor, on the other hand, owns some property in HOA governed communities and is perfectly fine with it since he did his due diligence to reduce his risk on the many issues. In fact he loves the fact that he can just pay a monthly HOA fee and the e

You need to figure out what works for YOU!

---

6   **Property and Liability Insurance Chapter 10**   Insurance Agent Name/Contact Info: _____

I have requested and received some quotes from national insurance carriers for my property?
> (I will do this right after I get a property into escrow, or before)

I have factored these costs into my financial analysis - whether personal residence or rental property?

I have discussed and made sure with my insurance agent that there is an adequate amount to cover the structure for damages and for my liability? I understand each item on my policy and other optional coverages I can obtain. I was also careful NOT to over

I know what is NOT covered by my insurance, and I also know what is NOT covered by the HOA insurance if it is a condominium or townhome community?

Condo/Townhome Interior Policy Coverage - I understand why this is just a smart move?

I assessed whether or not I need earthquake insurance, flood insurance, renters insurance, or an umbrella policy? I also discussed and considered building code upgrade, coverage for lost rents or for special valuable items, like jewelry or artwork?

I have reviewed a C.L.U.E. report on my property showing any past insurance claims?

I have discussed raising my deductible to reduce my premiums and whether this makes sense for me?

Insurance is one of those parts of owning real estate I know people do not think too much about until there is a disaster. I am glad I know I have the right coverage in place and for an adequate amount.

7 <u>Title, Escrow and Title Insurance</u>   Title Insurance Agent and Phone Number:
    <u>Due Diligence – Chapters 11, 12</u>   _____

Title issues are a low risk item. Rarely is there an issue. However, I know when there is an issue it is serious with large financial implications. I will discuss this with my title insurance representative and real estate agent.

Deed Type Receiving - If not a grant or general warranty deed, discuss with title agent and attorney.

NHD Disclosure Report - Did I review this report in full? This is a 60 or more page report (CA) that details property issues like: Is it in a flood zone, earthquake area, landslide, near farms or military bases or chemically contaminated sites. Did I

PRELIMINARY TITLE POLICY ITEMS
I DID read through the "exclusions" to the policy and asked questions if anything sounds strange?
For the items that are excluded as to coverage, I fully understand what each means.
Escrow, the Seller or Title Agent need to clear any strange/vital items off the policy before I close escrow.

Have I considered having a survey done of the property if this is typical for the area? If yes, have I walked the property with and reviewed the survey?

Holding Title - I understand the different ways to hold title and have selected the way to hold title that makes the most sense for my situation. I should consider consulting with a real estate attorney on this issue.

Date Received?

Did I Follow Up after Closing to get the Copy of Final Title Policy and Review Exclusions Again?
   --- This typically will take several months to receive - ask title agent why.

---

8 <u>Tax Issues Due Diligence - Chapter 6</u>

Personal Residence, I have penciled out my tax savings for my itemized deduction?
       So I do fully understand Schedule A and Marginal Tax Rates and my MT Bracket?

Rental Property, I have penciled out my operating statement estimate for my passive activity losses (if any) to shield income and reduce my taxes? I have determined whether or not I can use that passive activity losses or income based on IRS rules about

I have consulted with a tax attorney or CPA on this issue if needed?

If I am doing a 1031/1033 exchange or personal residence gain exclusion, am I complying with the IRS rules to make sure I do it correctly? I have enlisted the help of a competent advisor for this task?

I know I had better have the properties I plan to buy already under contact for a 1031 exchange, or close, before I even close escrow on the property I am selling - time is very very very tight on these!

---

9 <u>Property Condition Due Diligence -</u>   Home Inspector Name/Contact Info:
           <u>Chapter 9</u>   _____

REVIEW THE HOME INSPECTION CHECKLIST IN <u>DETAIL</u> WHEN YOU START THE BUYING PROCESS - JUST SO YOU ARE FAMILIAR WITH THE ITEMS AND ISSUES. ALSO YOU SHOULD DO YOUR OWN INSPECTION AND REVIEW THE CHECKLIST IN DETAIL AT LEAST ONCE IN THE DAYS <u>BEFORE</u> YOUR ACTUAL

I have run through the home inspection checklist with my property inspector and/or a contractor...several times.

I have obtained bids and estimates to fix what needs to be fixed on the property?

I have prepared a conservative budget and have had an experienced person review it?

My real estate agent has requested of the seller to credit me some money for repairs or fix the item? I may get nothing, and then I will decide whether or not to move forward with the purchase.			

I have added a generous generous "contingency" amount to my COST estimates, like 33.3% to 50.0% or more depending on how detailed an estimate I created and with what experts I did the estimating? I realize I cannot just say it will ONLY cost "that much"	Yes, I know it will take longer and cost more than anticipated. Possibly a LOT more. I have reserves to cover cost overruns.

10   Renting and Managing your Property - Chapter 13

IS it already rented, review Article "Reviewing an existing lease and keeping the tenants"

This is for rental properties before the purchase is made. Follow the Webbook Chapter for after your purchase closes escrow.

I am preparing my schedule and budget for rehabbing my property while I am still in escrow. I will give sufficient time to complete my rehabiliation and will start the advertising to rent my property several weeks before I believe it will be ready.			
I will read up on the local leasing laws, disclosures, obtain a lease document, determine how I am going to do a credit report and check criminal records for prospective tenants.			
I have at least reviewed the credit application provided on the site and will use a comprehensive application and review it thoroughly.			
I have had my insurance agent run a CUE report on my propective tenant if they can - as long as allowed in my state.			
I will do the hard work upfront on the leasing process to get a good tenant who will hopefully stay for many years so I do not have to do the leasing process each year. I realize every time I have to re-lease the property to a new tenant I probably will			

11 Other Issues - Do I plan to do or try any of these?

If yes, have I read the appropriate chapters or information and really thought this through?

If I plan to	Review the Following
Get Rich Quickly on Real Estate (hahaha!)	README File Article "Strategies to Earn Significant Wealth on Real Estate with No Risk"
Buy Foreclosures at the Courthouse Steps	Chapter 5
Buy Fancy Prize Properties	Chapter 3 Article - Prizes vs. Income Producing Assets
Flipping Properties	Chapter 14
Fixer Uppers	Chapter 14
Buy Apartment Buildings	Chapter 15
Second Home	Chapter 16
Vacation Rental	Chapter 16
Land	Chapter 18
Build a Home	Chapter 18
Buy Moderately Priced Boring Properties to rent out	GREAT JOB.... You "Get" it! Article "Prizes vs. Income Producing Assets

MAKE SURE YOU DOWNLOAD THE MOST UP TO DATE DUE DILIGENCE CHECKLIST FROM WWW.PROFESSORBARON.COM WHEN YOU ARE READY TO BUY PROPERTY.

EMAIL ACCESS@PROFESSORBARON.COM FOR ACCESS TO THE WEBSITE.

We don't sell or distribute your email, we only use it for your website access and send out about one newsletter email per month – and you can unsubscribeto it if you so choose.

Chapter 2

The Purchasing Process Explained

This is just a general explanation of the process for a typical transaction. Some of the items and issues may be slightly different depending upon the property and the state within which you reside. However, this will give you a feel for what you are about to do and help keep you on track in the progression of your real estate endeavors.

The start of the process involves two really important items which you do during the first few weeks of your property search.

```
Purchasing Steps

First - Financing & Real Estate Agent

1    Desired Property Type & Location
2    Shop for Property
3    Offering on Property
4    Offer Accepted/Signed by Seller
5    Mortage Loan Moving Forward
6    Moving Forward Steps
7    Closing Escrow/Own Property

     Congratulations!
```

• Financing - You need to determine the maximum purchase price of the property you can finance. So can you afford a $120,000 property or a $250,000 property? You will need to go to a bank, lender, credit union or mortgage broker to get qualified based on your income, assets, credit score and cash downpayment. Review Chapter 7 – Mortgage Financing for Property for help with this vital due diligence task. Get pre-approved or pre-qualified by the lender so that when you make offers on properties you will be able to include a letter from the lender stating that you can afford the property and obtain financing. Submitting this letter with your offer(s) will increase the chances that a seller accepts your offer to purchase as they will have greater confidence you are able to finance and close escrow on the purchase of their property.

If you are not ready to buy or the lender tells you that you cannot afford what you would like based on your income or credit factors, have the lender advise you on how to get your "house in order" so that you are the most creditworthy you can be when the time is ready to buy real estate down the road. That may involve paying off debt, saving more money for a downpayment, and/or correcting negative items on your credit report, etc.

• Real Estate Agent – You also need to select a real estate professional so they can start providing listings of available properties for sale and assisting you to determine what areas, locations, and condominium or townhome complexes fit within your buying and financing ability. You will of course shop on line too on Redfin.com, Trulia.com, Yahoo.com, Zillow.com, Google.com but you will need a real estate professional to make offers on properties. See the ARTICLE on Selecting a Real Estate Agent for help with this due diligence task. In Chapter 5 you will learn that you need to use a real estate agent to have access to shop the local multiple listing service (MLS) properties so it makes sense to start talking to a few agents upfront in the process.

Article: Selecting a Real Estate Agent

Selecting a Real Estate Professional to Assist You In Your Purchase

First and foremost, you should work hard to find a good real estate professional that you feel will do a great job helping you find a property. Then stick with that individual during the process. Dropping and changing agents usually does you little additional good in your search and probably is detrimental to the process. If you stick with one agent, they will have confidence that all their hard work finding you the right property will pay off. And that is probably going to get you the best overall results in your search for your new home or a quality investment property.

Real estate agents work hard for their money and we suggest make your life and their lives easier assuring them that you will stick with them throughout the process – and they'll do a great job for you!

So below we are going to give some advice and guidance on selecting an agent – not everyone is going to agree with our opinions, but we are on your side and hopefully our recommendations will be beneficial to you.

1. The most important item to remember is that a real estate professional's job is to show you property, help guide you in the process and try to get a property you like into escrow (or "under contract") and close the transaction. They are not going to do all your due diligence for you and a smart buyer would not want that. You cannot outsource protecting yourself, that is your job. The agent will assist you, but there is too much to do and only you can "make the call" on issues and items that could make you comfortable to move forward with the purchase. Or uncomfortable enough where you decide to terminate your purchase.

The other item to remember is that a real estate professional earns a living by closing real estate deals and getting paid commissions. Most will work hard to protect you and advise you on issues and problems, but not all. You are the one who needs to dot your "i's" and cross your "t's" and mitigate as much risk as possible. Once you close escrow on the property, any issues are your problem.

2. Agent selection. There are several things to look for and consider in selecting the real estate professional to represent you in a transaction. Experience is key as real estate is a learn by doing process. We suggest that an experienced agent should be closing at least five property transactions per year. Every transaction is complex and each agent, just like the authors, obtain new and relevant "training" on each deal. If a newer agent is being guided by an experienced agent, that can help a lot – newer professionals have to get experience somewhere.

So an agent who closes at least five deals per year, or more, and preferably for several years in a row, is probably a safer bet for you. One issue with real estate sales professionals is that most states do not require much training, practical experience or cost to become an agent. So there are many part time agents who only do one or two deals per year. And it is unlikely they are going to be experienced enough to really do a great job for you, let alone help you protect yourself.

For those part time agents we apologize for pointing out that fact – but agents should really do enough transactions to learn the process really well or they should not be doing real estate sales – in the Professor's opinion. It would really be best for everyone if it was much harder to be a real estate sales professional so only the best trained full time professionals were advising buyers on the largest purchases they will ever make. Enough on that…

So, the more experience, training and real estate education a professional has the better chance they will serve you well and be helpful to you the buyer.

So ask the agent how many transactions they closed in the past 12 months and several years. If they have not closed that many, ask who is guiding them as they learn the business and what professional training have they had to prepare them to assist you. Again, closed transactions count.

You also want to get some references from the recently closed transactions and call those references to ask how the agent performed for them.

Also, make sure they have the time and take the time to show you lots of properties and will offer on properties that you want to offer upon. If they have too many clients at once, service to you may suffer. So make your best judgment.

3. Location, location, location. That's right, real estate people use those three words to describe the most important thing in real estate. And when you interview an agent for the job of representing you, you should find out how well they know the location, location, location of which you want to purchase property. Some agents are going to be familiar with the entire county and can talk to you about each neighborhood in which you are potentially interested to buy.

If you do not know where you want to buy you need to figure that out early in the process based on what you can afford and what amenities are important to you. Then make sure your agent knows those areas well.

If the agent has no familiarity with where you want to buy and where you can afford property, you should find an agent that does. Different streets, different neighborhoods, different communities can look similar to the untrained eye. However, they can be very very different and you need a professional who is well versed in the local areas where they are going to sell you property.

Note: We would select an experienced competent trustworthy agent who does not know an area all that well over a lesser experienced agent who does know the area. So interview and make your best choice.

4. Will they help you protect yourself? This is the largest purchase you are ever going to make and your real estate professional should be well versed in and advise you on how to better do your due diligence. Real estate professionals know that helping you protect yourself is a smart way to gain your trust AND your business. Independent information is hard to find in real estate, but agents who work hard to give you accurate, unbiased information and help ensure you are doing everything you can to protect yourself seem to earn an extraordinary amount of business – as they should.

Again, it is your job to protect yourself, but agents should know and be able to advise you on how to do it. So take your due diligence checklist with you to the interview and ask some questions pertaining to items like these:

- If you are going to buy into an HOA governed community, the agent should be able to give you basic advice on HOA financial analysis.
- If you are buying investment property, they should be able to help you pencil out a deal and calculate the investment returns it is expected to generate.
- They should be able to advise you on basic financing and help you review a Good Faith Estimate from your lender.
- Advise you on the basics on what property and liability insurance covers.
- Why and what you need to review on the preliminary title policy.
- Any other issues and items on the checklist.

Buying real estate is the largest and riskiest purchase you will ever make. The agent you use should be someone you trust and feel can do a great job getting a property under contract for you. They should help you through the process and advise you on how to better protect yourself so you make a smart purchase.

An agent who has a good handle on these issues and experience is going to be a good choice to represent you. So interview several, find the best qualified, and stick with them through the process!

End of Article

THE PROCESS OF BUYING REAL ESTATE

1. Determine Desired Property Type and Location – Once you know the range of what you can afford and have selected an agent, you need to determine what areas are where you can afford and would like to buy. You also should determine what type of property you would like to buy, single family residence (SFR), townhome, condominium, co-op, or another type. There are many factors you should consider as you make decisions on your target property acquisition, see the attached memorandum for help Desired Property Location and Type Memorandum.

Article: Desired Property Location and Type

Below are some items and issues you should consider in making your decision on the location, type and size of property you would most like to buy. Think the items though and other issues that are of a concern to you. Only you can decide what works best, and hopefully you can find something in your price range that makes sense.

- Personal Residence or Investment Property?
- Quiet Area or Busy and Urban areas?
- Retail, Parks, Medical nearby?
- School Districts, Proximity to Work or Employment Centers?
- Downtown, Suburbia, or in the Country?
- Investment Property – How does it Cashflow?
- Personal Residence Is it better to Rent or Own in my desired Location?
- Maintenance – Do I want to be responsible for yard, driveway, sidewalks (detached home) and have few restrictions on what I can build, which means the neighbors have few restrictions too.
- Maintenance – Do I want to avoid being responsible for yard, etc. (condo, townhome, PUD) and live in a highly restricted property, which means the neighbors are restricted too.
- How many bedrooms, baths, square footage, garage, big lot, small lot, newer or older house?
- Other Factors should be discussed with Family, Friends, Real Estate Agent and others.

You really need to think through the most important issues and items that positively or negatively appeal to you about owning real estate and owning a particular type, style, size and location. It is a long term commitment so think it through carefully. Your agent should give you guidance, but family, friends and others are also good for providing helpful advice. You should take one to three months to learn the areas, go look at properties, drive neighborhoods, understand property types and characteristics, know communities, and learn the general areas where you would like to buy.

There may be many areas that are suitable for you and the greater the population of properties that fit your needs and price range, the better the chances you will find and be able to purchase the "right" property for you. As you get a good feeling about where you want to own real estate, it will help you and your agent to focus on those areas so you are not driving all over the county chasing properties that do not suit your needs. During the entire buying process you will probably add and delete areas and communities as you drive, investigate and learn the different areas.

However, knowing where you want to buy and what is comfortable and suits your needs, is one of the most important tasks your can do to reduce your risk on owning real estate. Take several months and look at twenty or more properties as you form your desired location(s) and property type(s). Experienced buyers know the areas, complexes, cities where they want to acquire additional real estate.

End of Article

MAKE SURE YOU UNDERSTAND THAT YOU WILL NEVER FIND THE PERFECT PROPERTY. BUT WITH A LOT OF HARD WORK YOU CAN FIND ONE THAT IS CLOSE TO WHAT YOU WANT AND THAT IS THE "RIGHT" ONE FOR YOU. AND NEVER WALK AWAY FROM THE "RIGHT" PROPERTY OVER A FEW THOUSAND DOLLARS, YOU MAY NOT FIND ANOTHER "RIGHT" ONE FOR QUITE A WHILE AND YOU WILL HAVE TO DO ALL THE TIME CONSUMING AND HARD WORK OVER AGAIN!

2. Shop for Property – Once you know your price range and where and the type of property you plan to own, you are ready to shop. You should expect to look for a couple or more months as you drive areas, go to open houses, review online listings and have your agent give you property tours. Unless you do sufficient research and actually go look inside properties for sale, you will not get a feel for what is the "right" property for you.

Tools to help you Shop:

• Real Estate Broker or Agent – Interview several agents and select one to work with and stick with that agent during the process. Avoid using multiple Realtors. If you commit to an agent, they will commit to you and work even harder than they already do to get a property for you. Once you select your agent have them provide a copy of the local association of real estate broker's standard purchase contract for your review…at your convenience.

• Multiple Listing Service – MLS Data – Most local areas have a real estate association that maintains lists of available properties for sale in the area. A real estate agent will have access to these listings. Most of the listings are also online these days, but access to properties is typically available only through your agent. Once you know the area you like based on either your cash flow projections or just the area if you are buying a personal residence have the agent run the MLS for all the "active" properties in that area and give you the list. Also, have them set the MLS system to automatically email you properties, new listings when they come online, or any changes to the existing listings when made. This way you have the most up to date information as quickly as all the other potential buyers in the marketplace. You could and should use Redfin.com, Ziprealty.com or any other online service you like to assist in you effort to learn about the properties available in your market.

• Online Websites – Use online tools like Google Maps, Bing.com Maps, Yahoo Maps, Redfin.com, Trulia.com, ZipRealty.com, Zillow.com, and any and all other tools you can find to assist in your quest to find the "right" property for you.

• Shopping Properties – For the areas you desire to buy property, get to know the locations and/or complexes really well. You are going to spend a lot of money and you need to be comfortable buying property there. Make sure you look at many many properties as you need to educate yourself on the market, size, bedrooms, bathrooms, cost, neighborhood, etc. The more the better in your effort to find a suitable property for you.

• Comparable Sales – Comparable Market Analysis – Once you are really focused on the area you like and a few potential target homes or condos, have the agent query ALL the properties that sold in that general area in the past six months or year.

You do not want to just get a comparable market report with the properties that are similarly priced to the property you are considering purchasing. You want ALL the sales and available property data so you can review all the sales that compare to your target purchase. Use Redfin for this too and Zillow and Trulia. Remember, you are spending hundreds of thousands of dollars so it is worth your time to know the market inside and out. Your agent may be able to prepare a Comparable Market Properties report that maps all the properties and features on a map for you in the areas you like. Study it to better learn the market.

• Driving the area – Drive the area to see what amenities – retail shops, parks, schools, entertainment – are in the vicinity that are important to you.

3. Offering on a Property – Once you find a property that you feel is "right" for you, it is time to make an offer to purchase. We recommend having the real estate agent give you a copy of the offering contract well before you are going to make an offer so you can read through it and understand what you are signing. Also, keep your lender informed that you are close to making your offer so that the financing process that you initiated before you started looking can get moving quickly.

• Offer on Several – If you like multiple places, offer on all of them and hope that you get one offer ACCEPTED. Some sellers or banks will take longer to get back to you. Short sales can take months, so do not wait for a response, keep offering. If you get one under contract, which means the seller signs your offer, you can cancel the others and move forward with the one you believe is the "right" one for you. See Chapter 5 – Foreclosures, Short Sales, REO, MLS. Try not to drive your agent bonkers by making offers on properties you do not really want . It wastes your time too!

4. Offer Accepted/Signed by Seller - Now you are "IN ESCROW" – You may have a few counter offers back and forth before you both finalize the agreement. NOTE: If this is a SHORT SALE, the process is a little different while you wait for the bank or lender to approve your offer that the seller already accepted. See Chapter 5 for details – and Read the article in that chapter – Don't Get Stuck Paying Extra at Closing on Your Short Sale. Once your offer on a short sale is approved by the bank the normal process continues. On a regular sale, or with the short sale approved by the bank, you are now "in escrow" and will pay a refundable earnest money deposit (EMD)– usually 1.00% of the purchase price. You are now getting close to having "at risk" money. This means you can lose your EMD or more if you do not comply with the conditions and timelines in your contract.

Arbitration and Mediation Clauses. In many states' contracts there are standardized arbitration and mediation clauses that a buyer and seller can agree to in case there is a dispute over the contract. So if there is a dispute and both parties have signed these clauses, they can avoid going to court and settle it with a typically much less expensive dispute resolution mechanism.

• See Chapter 19 for Information on these important issues. And consult an attorney if needed.

• **Contingencies** – Most contracts have something called contingencies – like a home inspection contingency, financing contingency, appraisal contingency, or HOA document review contingency. These are usually completely negotiable between the seller and you the buyer. Contingency means the written contract you and the seller have signed has some items that are still not 100% agreed upon and finalized – but they are likely to get resolved. One example is a home inspection – Chapter 9. Your offer will give you the right to have a qualified inspector investigate the condition of the property and report back to you on what he or she finds. You usually will have 10-17 days to resolve and remove this contingency. If you find items that need to be fixed, you would request the seller fix them or credit you money at closing. So your real estate agent, in conjunction with you, would make this request in writing by the end of the "study" period, the seller will respond in writing, and you both will agree upon a resolution.

The seller may offer to complete everything you want fixed, give you money, say take the property "AS IS" or cancel the agreement. Then you would decide whether you want to proceed, negotiate more if you are still within your contracted timeframe, or cancel the purchase. If you do come to an agreement to move forward - once you both sign off on that resolution, you would "remove" this contingency from the contract. So that would mean one of the still outstanding issues is not outstanding any longer and you can move forward to clear other contact items and issues.

— IMPORTANT INFORMATION ON CONTINGENCIES — Legal rules on contingencies vary state to state. So check with your real estate agent to understand the rules in your state. Typically any and all contingencies can be negotiated out, in, or in any way by agreement between the seller and buyer so make sure you are comfortable with what you agree to on contingencies and timeframes. Typically once the contingency period passes (or you remove the contingency from the contract) your EMD becomes non-refundable. Make sure you are aware of the contingency dates and terms so you can request extensions or cancel the purchase and get your EMD returned if you need.

If you are buying from a bank (or short sale), read their counteroffer addendum(s) or "Short Sale Bank Letter" carefully as it may shorten the contingency periods that you offered in your contract. Removing the contingencies or letting the dates simply pass could mean that you agree that you are satisfied with all the items and issues related to these inspections and review. If you are not satisfied with any of them then request for additional time to review what you need. The seller may say NO and tell you to accept the state of the property and move forward with the contract or terminate the contract. Most sellers will approve reasonable and short extensions. If they will not, you will have to choose on whether to move forward or cancel the deal.

- **Typical Contingencies**

1. Home Inspection – Chapter 9 –This keeps your option open to cancel the contract if you feel the items needing repair in the house add up to too much money or if the seller will not credit you some monies for those needed repairs.

2. Homeowners Association Analysis Contingency– Chapter 8 - Unfortunately you will usually have to get the home inspection done ($200 - $400) and pay for an appraisal ($350 - $550) before you get these HOA documents. If the condition of the HOA or litigation on the complex makes you decide to cancel the contract, you are probably out all the money – and maybe money you paid for the condominium documents too. That is unfortunately part of the risk you take in buying property in a community governed by an HOA.

3. Appraisal Contingency – This contingency is to determine if the property will appraise at your contracted price. A bank will lend money – your mortgage – based off the lower of the purchase price or the appraisal. So, if the property does not appraise at the contracted price, you will either have to come up with additional funds at closing, get the seller to agree to reduce the price, or cancel the deal. Your lender can explain this in detail.

4. Loan/Financing Contingency – This is a contingency so that if for any reason the loan fails and you are not able to close escrow on the property, you would get your EMD back – hence it would not be forfeited to the

seller. In your offer make it contingent until the loan is "Funded" – hopefully the seller will agree to that term – or at least not notice that you checked that box (in the California Association of Realtors (CAR) contract) to keep this contingency open. The seller may cross out this term or a bank addendum may delete it and if you can't negotiate it back in and your loan fails on the last day – you may lose your EMD.

5. Insurance Contingency - This is NOT in the contract, but you must call your insurance agent immediately to make sure that there is not an insurance issue with the property you have in escrow (typically in the CUE database) that would preclude your being able to obtain insurance for the property. At this point it would also be smart to get an estimate of the cost of the policy that you are going to buy to make sure it is reasonable. And make sure your policy is paid through escrow so it is in place the second you close escrow. If you are paying for it directly to the insurance company, so outside of escrow, make sure it starts the day before you close escrow – and if you close escrow early make sure it is in place before you close!

6. Termite Inspection Contingency – This isn't a contingency, but it is similar. Most regular contracts have a termite clause that the seller has a termite inspection done and pays for some of the repairs and/or fumigation. This is negotiable between the seller and buyer but the seller usually pays for it and some, but not necessarily all repairs. Discuss this with your real estate agent when you are making your offer.

AGAIN, any and all contingencies are governed by the terms that you agree to in the purchase contract. So make sure you read and fully understand what you are agreeing to with the seller. If you agree to remove a contingency, like the right to back out of the purchase if it doesn't appraise (Chapter 17) for at least as much as the purchase price, and then it doesn't appraise for the purchase price, you will have to come up with additional cash at closing or if you cancel the deal you will lose your EMD... so pay attention to and understand the contingencies.

5. Mortgage Loan – Moving Forward – Once you are in escrow move forward with your Mortgage Financing immediately. Mortgage rates change every day so have your lender provide you with the current rates, points and terms so you can "lock" your loan rate and points (do the payback period analysis in Chapter 7) and get an email from the lender with the agreed upon rate, points and terms of your locked loan. The lender will require updated paperwork, documents, paystubs, bank statements, etc. so work hard to get them what they need to make sure your loan moves smoothly and quickly through the system. There will be lots of paperwork here. You must pay for the appraisal ($350 - $550 for Single Family Homes) and if the deal fails you are out that money.

Sometimes agreeing to an impound account to escrow taxes and insurance or signing a "pre-payment penalty" will reduce your interest rate. Explore these options and make your best choice. Prepayment penalties are okay if you plan to hold the home for a at least a five plus years – and of course we do not recommend buying real estate if you do not plan to hold it for at least five years – the longer the better.

Note: Do not buy any cars, furniture, run up credit card debts or forget to pay bills on time during this process. The bank will pull an updated credit report a few days before you close. If there are new items it could cause your financing to fail and you may lose your EMD and the property.

6. Moving Forward – As your lender works on the mortgage bank or lender requirements, as you work through the due diligence tasks and your contingency removals, you are getting closer to closing escrow and being the proud owner of a good and lower risk property – if you read, understood and did the tasks in this book to lower your risk.

7. Closing Escrow and Owning the Property – As the process gets close to your ownership, the lender may have final conditions for closing, e.g., updated bank statements or employment verifications. Rarely does financing fund on the day it is scheduled. Don't stress out. Plan ahead for this. Get all the last minute lender requests and re-requests for paperwork over to the lender ASAP. You will own the property in just a few days.

Loan documents and escrow instructions will be prepared. Make sure to read them before you sign. Make sure they match what you agreed upon with your mortgage lender.

Then you will sign the loan and escrow documents, you will wire in your portion of the closing funds, the mortgage lender will fund the loan to the escrow company within a short timeframe and all will be in order. The escrow agent will prepare the deed transfer and it will be recorded at the county courthouse. Funds will be distributed to the seller, agents, title company, insurance company, notary, etc. by the escrow office. And you should receive the keys!

Congratulations, you just joined the world of real estate ownership. Some risk on property ownership is unavoidable, but you SIGNIFICANTLY reduced your risk by doing the hard work upfront, taking your time, and doing the proper due diligence, great job – your parents will be proud!

And your folks will be most excited that you probably will not have to ask them for money to bail you out of a bad real estate deal!

Ed's House Above – Paid Off!

Co-Author's House – Not Paid Off but on Schedule...Looking forward to April 30, 2035!

CHAPTER 3

INVESTOR RENTAL CASH FLOWS

Penciling out a simple cash flow statement for a real estate investment is the easiest way to significantly reduce your financial risk in acquiring a property. This is the starting point for any rental property analysis. With about a one to two hour investment of your time to study this chapter and learn the simple and straightforward analysis tools we give you, you can quickly analyze your target real estate deals. We will make it very simple!

By doing this analysis you will be able to determine what your initial returns could potentially be on buying a certain property. You will put your pencil to your paper with some conservative operating estimates of rental income and expenses that you believe you can achieve. And with your penciled out information, you will be able to weed out poor real estate investment choices.

Long Term Annual Returns % Estimates - Different Asset Types And - General Risk Profile			
Bank CD	Bonds	Diversified Stocks	Real Estate
1.500%	4.500%	7.500%	?? **
Low Risk	Semi-Low Risk	Semi-High Risk	High Risk

** Depends on How Good of a Deal You Buy!

So, everything in this chapter leads Investors to the Investment Analysis Spreadsheet that you will use to look at real estate deals. We note the basics herein and then you will start using the spreadsheet and instructions or you can do the calculations by hand with the .PDF file if you prefer to work that way. It is the same analysis either way and you need to be really comfortable analyzing the numbers to understand the investment returns.

The simple analysis tool for PRE-Tax calculations will help you better understand how the money flows and give you a good feel for healthy investment cash flows. After you learn this analysis and use it, you will then graduate to using the AFTER Tax spreadsheet that you will learn how to use in Chapter 6. But let's start with this Chapter and the simple concepts herein.

The most important reason to pencil out your deal is so you know whether the property is going to pay for itself - THIS IS GOOD - or if you are going to keep paying for it each month - THIS IS BAD -and for how many years? We recommend only buy properties that are cash flow positive!

CASH FLOW POSITIVE OR CASH FLOW NEGATIVE?

The most important overall concept in real estate is to determine what your cash flow picture looks like on an investment. There are really two possibilities:

1. Positive Operating Cash Flows - Recommended! - (PAYS FOR ITSELF) – Estimate the rents generated from the property and subtract reasonable and conservatively estimated expenses to be paid. For example:

POSITIVE CASH FLOWS	
Rental Income Monthly	$1,400
Expenses (Taxes,Mortgage,Repairs)	$(1,150)
Monthly Net Cash Flow	$250
Annual Cash Flow - Positive	$3,000

2. Negative Operating Cash Flows - <u>Not Recommended!</u> - (YOU PAY MONTHLY FOR IT) - The strategy here is that value increases or appreciation over time will more than compensate for all the negative cash flows along the way. Negative Cash Flows, if you invest in a negative cash flow deal, could continue for years and maybe even a decade.

NEGATIVE CASH FLOWS	
Rental Income Monthly	$1,400
Expenses (Taxes,Mortgage,Repairs)	$(1,600)
Monthly Net Cash Flow	$(200)
Annual Cash Flow - Negative	$(2,400)

NEGATIVE CASH FLOW PROPERTY MEANS YOU NEED TO USE YOUR PERSONAL FUNDS TO COVER THE NEGATIVE $2,400 PER YEAR CASH FLOWS – YOUR HOPE IS THAT OVER TIME THE CASH FLOWS BECOME POSITIVE AND/OR THE PROPERTY WILL HAVE LONG TERM APPRECIATION.

This chapter will run your through the types of properties you should be targeting, doing your market research to help you best verify rents, vacancy and expenses, helping you learn how to use our simple spreadsheet to pencil out your deals – Attached Investment Analysis Spreadsheet below, and why doing this simple analysis will significantly reduce your financial risk and really increase your returns.

INVESTMENT STRATEGY

Our investment strategy deals primarily with number one above – earning your return based on Positive operating cash flows from the property. Any long term appreciation on your Positive cash flowing property and the pay down of principal due to the amortization of the loan (See Amortization Article to Understand – Chapter 7) is the "Icing on the Cake". First let's make sure the property throws off the positive cash flows we need to buy and eat (pay for) the cake instead of the CAKE EATING US!

To get a feel for the SMART investment strategy - Right now click herein to: Read the Article on Prizes vs. Moderately Priced Properties

Article: Prizes vs. Income Producing Assets – and this applies to commercial properties too!

When you buy real estate, you are going to invest your hard earned cash into the property. It will be either a downpayment where you also take out a mortgage to buy the property, or you may pay all cash for it.

Before you put down all that money (EQUITY CASH) you want to project whether you will have positive cash flow or whether you will have negative cash flow.

Prize Assets - Properties people brag about like the Beach House - are LIABILITIES – NOT ASSETS. These are properties where the market rents less all the expenses typically generate negative cash flows. The hope is that over many years as rents rise the property will eventually generate positive cash flows. Hence, a buyer is looking more for long term increases in property value, or appreciation, than looking for ongoing free cash flows. Avoid these!

Income Producing Assets are typically properties where the market rents less all expenses typically generate positive cash flows. One might call these boring moderately priced properties. One should also earn long term increases in property value appreciation, but your investment returns are less dependent on property value increases.

For example: Look at the following two properties where you put down 25% equity and hence your mortgage is 75%. The important item is how much CASH EQUITY you invest and how much of a rate of return you earn on that.

CASH FLOW ANALYSIS - PRIZES VS. INCOME PRODUCING ASSETS		
	INCOME ASSET Moderately Priced Condo in Suburbia	PRIZE ASSET Fancy Condo in Ritzy Area of City
Purchase Price	$150,000	$500,000
Mortgage 75%	$112,500	$375,000
Equity Cash	$37,500	$125,000
Income Statement		
Rent/Month	$1,295	$2,500
Expenses	$(350)	$(1,100)
Mortgage	$(675)	$(2,250)
Net CF/Month	$270	$(850)
Net CF/Year	$3,240	$(10,200)
Cash on Cash Returns	8.64%	-8.16%

These are real examples from the current marketplace in a California coastal city. How does that NEGATIVE (8.16%) look to you. Let's call it, IN THE RED! It doesn't look very good to us. And if you buy into a deal like this, after a while you will agree that paying out each month to cover negatives on rental property is not "The American Dream".

IF YOU ALREADY BOUGHT PRIZE PROPERTIES IN THE PAST AND STILL OWN THEM, DON'T WORRY, YOU ARE NOT THE ONLY ONE. THE AUTHOR AND SEVERAL CO-AUTHORS ALSO BOUGHT SOME SO CALLED PRIZES BACK IN THE DAY AND STILL OWN THEM – BUT WE ALL CAN DO A LITTLE BETTER ANALYSIS NOW AND WILL ONLY PICK UP INCOME PRODUCING PROPERTIES GOING FORWARD! HOPEFULLY OURS WILL TURN POSITIVE ONE OF THESE YEARS!

Funny story here. Our attorney investor and contributor was editing this article and on the prior paragraph about the negative cash flow properties and he noted, "You may also want to consider a short sale here" to get rid of this liability. The professor's thoughts are, "Thanks for pointing that out! I know, because I pay out each month!!!". But again, we all get a little smarter and learn with each property we buy!

Back to the financial numbers - so, in this case, you can see how a moderately priced property (Income Producing Asset) throws off positive cash flows and even better, a rate of return of 8.64% – we like that – IN THE BLACK. You can also see that for Prizes – the rents are just not enough to cover the high expenses of a fancy property.

The other issue with prize properties points to the idea that one always wants to keep their property in decent condition and fix problems so that tenants are generally happy with their home. If you are positive a few hundred dollars a month, spending a couple hundred dollars to fix something to keep your property in good shape is not a big deal. If you are negative hundreds of dollars per month, it is a big deal and you might let the problem drag on, possibly causing more damage, and probably making your tenant unhappy, and probably making your tenant care less about your property. And, if you the owner does not care to fix issues, the tenant make take the same attitude and might not even alert you to issues. Just something to think about.

OVERALL, the end result is that Prizes typically have low or negative cash flows while moderately priced properties have much better cash flows.

We can assure you that owning BORING properties with positive cash flows - so the property can support itself - is much more stress free and hence lower risk than owning properties where you need to pay into them each month to cover the negative cash flows.

The end result is that in Chapter 3 you will teach yourself how to find property prices, rents, and expenses and you will PENCIL OUT your own deal.

Let's RECAP –

Prize properties are no PRIZE!
Moderately priced BORING properties– are the real PRIZES! $$$$$$

End of Article

The appreciation in value strategy – number two way above – means that you will have negative or minimal positive cash flows, so you are hoping for long term appreciation. Many people unknowingly, until they close escrow and start taking in rent and paying bills, use this strategy. But from experience we can assure you that appreciation in value does not pay the mortgage bills and other expenses, but positive cash flow does pay the bills.

Therefore, you want your properties to support themselves by having sufficient rental income pay the bills.

In reality your investment returns are going to come from a combination of cash flows, long term appreciation and the paying off of your mortgage loan due to the normal amortization process of the mortgage. However, you want your deal to make sense on a cash flow basis up front so down the road you still own the property to realize that appreciation.

CASH FLOW ANALYSIS AND FORECAST

In doing your analysis, the most important issues are your cash inflow and outflow positions:

1. How much CASH EQUITY do you put down (downpayment, closing/escrow costs, improvement costs) to acquire and close escrow on the property and get the property rental ready? You generally want to put down or "invest" as little cash equity as possible. In the current market this generally means 20% to 25% as a downpayment for rental properties. The total cost of the property is important too, but your CASH EQUITY is the most important number. So what you want to determine is "How much CASH EQUITY do I need to acquire the property and make it ready for rental?"

Example:

CASH EQUITY TO BUY PROPERTY			
Property Cost		$100,000	
Mortgage	75%		
Financed		$(75,000)	- Up to 95% - Owner Occupant.
Downpayment		$25,000	
Closing Costs		$5,000	- Escrow, Title Insurance, Etc.
Rehab Costs		$5,000	- Carpets, Paint, Applicances
CASH EQUITY		$35,000	- Cash needed to close escrow

Note: If you buy a property for cash, then your CASH EQUITY would be all the cash purchase price plus closing and rehab costs.

2. How much Annual NET Cash Flow do you earn each year during your ownership? How much is your NET Cash Flow From Sale of the Property. If you are a long term holder, which we advocate, then the cash at sale is less important than the above two items. The reason your cash at sale is less important is because you have to wait so long for these monies – maybe decades if you hold the property for "good". But either way, you want to put down less and have more positive cash flows right from the start – so you will have higher cash on cash returns AND you can pay the bills.

ANNUAL NET CASH FLOWS					
Monthly	Year 1	Year 2	Year 3	Year 4	Year 5
Rental Income	$1,400	$1,430	$1,465	$1,510	$1,565
Expenses	$(1,150)	$(1,170)	$(1,195)	$(1,230)	$(1,250)
Monthly Net CF	$250	$260	$270	$280	$315
Annual NET CF	**$3,000**	**$3,120**	**$3,240**	**$3,360**	**$3,780**

3. Net Cash Flows from Sale

NET CASH FLOWS AT SALE			
Sales Price - Year 5 (3.5% Inc.)		$119,000	
Less:	Sales		
Exp		$(8,000)	
Mortgage Bal		$(69,600)	- Remaining Balance at Sale
Less Taxes		$0	- If Any
NET CF Sale		$41,400	

YOUR TOTAL CASH FLOWS PICTURE ON THIS INVESTMENT, IF YOU SOLD AT THE END OF YEAR 5, WOULD LIKE SOMETHING LIKE THE FOLLOWING CHART.

TOTAL NET CASH FLOWS OVER LIFE OF INVESTMENT
THE "FORECAST" OR "PROFORMA"

	Purchase	Year 1	Year 2	Year 3	Year 4	Year 5
CASH Equity at Purchase	$(35,000)					
Rental Income/Mon.		$1,400	$1,430	$1,465	$1,510	$1,565
Expenses		$(1,150)	$(1,170)	$(1,195)	$(1,230)	$(1,250)
Monthly Net CF		$250	$260	$270	$280	$315
Annual NET CF		**$3,000**	**$3,120**	**$3,240**	**$3,360**	**$3,780**
Sale NET CASH FLOW-Yr 5						$41,400
TOTAL CF	$(35,000)	$3,000	$3,120	$3,240	$3,360	$45,180
CASH ON CASH RETURNS ON $35,000		8.57%	8.91%	9.26%	9.60%	29.09%

How do those returns compare to other investments you might make into stocks, bonds, CD, or other assets? And those returns do not include any appreciation, tax benefits, or pay down of mortgage principal on the loan - which could significantly increase an Investor's returns.

RETURNS GUIDANCE

The 8.57% cash on cash Year 1 return shown above is a VERY Healthy return that one may find on a condominium or townhome. As guidance:

• Single family homes (SFR) should generate 2.0% to 6.0% + cash on cash in Year 1 to be fairly good income producing assets. Returns below those are more prize type assets and where one is hoping for more long term appreciation. We like the healthy positive cash flow investment model over hoping for long term appreciation on prize assets. As you can imagine, cash flow pays the bills while appreciation in value does not. Did we mention about paying the bills enough times. One more time, positive cash flows pay the bills.

• Condominiums should be in the 4.0% to 9.0% returns, and they could go much higher depending on your deal.

• Townhomes typically fall in between SFRs and condominiums.

• Apartment Buildings – It really depends on a lot of factors, however with this spreadsheet you have the tools to pencil out your deal so you can analyze the projected returns. Chapter 15 will help you on apartments with additional guidance.

The important issue is to avoid negative or very low positive cash flow deals.

You will learn to pencil out your own cash flows using the Investment Analysis Spreadsheet that you are going to download to analyze your properties.

LONG TERM RETURNS:

Keep in mind that you are scheduling out your cash flows for one or multiple years and since you are forecasting these numbers, they may not end up being accurate. That is why you need to use the best information you can attain to make the best predictions possible – be conservative. You will see that Real estate analysis really has these vital issues:

REFRESHER – THE THREE VITAL ISSUES IN CASH FLOW ANALYSIS – THAT WE JUST WENT OVER ABOVE!

1. CASH FLOWS - How much CASH EQUITY does it take to acquire the property, what are the Annual NET Cash inflows and outflows during ownership, and how much NET Cash Flow From Sale is generated when the property is sold – the Forecast.

2. INVESTMENT RETURNS - What is the percentage return one will earn on their forecasted Number 1. CASH FLOWS (invested capital) and how does that compare to other types of investments – CDs, bonds, stocks relative to each asset's risk.

3. RISK (PROBABILITY OF SUCCESS) – what is the true probability that one's forecast of the numbers in Number 1. CASH FLOWS… which equates into returns in Number 2. INVESTMENT RETURNS- will really occur….or will one earn much less than anticipated?

You are the one that ultimately takes the risks and earns the rewards for your hard work, so work hard upfront to make your cash flow predictions accurate.

Tip: Just starting out on your long term real estate buying career, read the ARTICLE "Smart Moves to Start your Real Estate Empire".

Article:

Smart Moves to Start Your Real Estate Empire

So you are ready to be a long term investor going into the real estate ownership business. It is a great time to start a long term journey to earning wealth on real estate. This is not just because you have a long term perspective – as real estate equity grows over time – but also because prices are very favorable relative to rents. This translates into some of the best investment returns on real estate in a long time.
There are still significant risks to owning real estate, hassles, losses and stressful issues. Those haven't and will NEVER change, but at least the cash flows on the right properties are relatively healthy.

Just remember – **THERE IS NO EASY MONEY IN REAL ESTATE, EVERY DIME IS HARD EARNED.**

IF YOU DO NOT BELIEVE THIS IS CORRECT, DON'T WORRY YOU WILL LEARN THIS ALONG THE WAY – probably sooner over later!

Luckily, after you study the concepts in the book you will be able to significantly reduce many risks and that should be a big help in your landlord career.

So here are a few tips that can get you rolling in the right direction:

1. Make sure to always be conservative in your estimates of rents and expenses so that when rents collected are lower than one would like and expenses are higher than one would like, you still are able to make your investment returns and cover bills. UNDERPROMISE (even if just to yourself) and OVERDELIVER results!

2. Try really hard to find people who own multiple properties for years and talk to them about the benefits and pains of being a landlord. If you want to be a long term owner, then try to find people who are long term owners – like for decades. They will probably tell you a lot about the stress and issues of owning real estate – but they also will mention they have a healthy stream of retirement income and all the hard work was worthwhile!

3. Real estate is a long term deal, so make sure that is where you want to head.

4. Make sure to do your due diligence following the instructions in this guide and read and learn all you can about real estate ownership from every source you can find.

5. Buy your first several properties as places for you to live as an owner occupant. When you buy to live there, as opposed to being an investment property, you get the best financing terms and can typically put down a small downpayment. Do this three or four times over 4-10 years and you should be in very good financial shape.

6. Living in the property will also allow you to learn the ins and outs of your real estate and make repairs as needed to get it rental ready for long term ownership when you move out and rent it out.

7. Get help from your family if you need for the downpayment. You could either work out an ownership structure with them and provide them a fair rate of return, or they could lend you the money as a second mortgage. Either way make an agreement in writing so everyone - that means you - understands the terms and abides by them. Once you successfully show your relatives you can buy real estate and provide them a fair rate of return on a safe investment, they will lend you more in the future. Be careful about using more than a small percentage of your relative's net worth, you do not want to put them in financial trouble if something goes wrong with the property.

8. Work hard to keep your properties in good shape and work hard to get good tenants and treat them with respect so they stay a long time – Chapter 13.

Those should get your started in the right direction. Take your time, do your Due Diligence, you have decades to get rich on real estate… by learning and taking your time there is a better chance you will make the best decisions and buy the RIGHT properties that will provide you income and wealth in the future.

Final thought: There is great long term wealth in real estate, BUT THERE IS NO EASY MONEY IN REAL ESTATE.

And don't forget that!

End of Article

Note: Chapter 3 and 4 do not include any Federal Income Tax Benefits or Expense – although you should definitely take these into account and we will learn later how to do this in Chapter 6. Nor included on our Investment Analysis Spreadsheet is any appreciation in value – something that is more difficult to estimate but can provide significant increases in your equity value and final cash flows – more on that later.

LETS GET STARTED – SIMPLE SPREADSHEET USERS – THESE ARE VERY SIMPLE and STRAIGHTFORWARD SPREADSHEETS: It's in Chapter 3 on the website when signed in.

• Download the Investment Analysis Spreadsheet ".xls" , then open it up on your computer and save it to a directory.

Then open it up and click "print" and "entire workbook". That will print the two pro-forma pages and two pages of instructions. Read through the instructions as you look at the TAB 1 spreadsheet on your computer. They're really easy and foolproof, so give it a whirl! Even your grandkids can do it!

If you CAN'T SEE the TABS at the bottom of the spreadsheet and a Windows XP user. If you can't see the four tabs at the bottom, look at the little "X" to the top right of the screen that you normally click to close a window. That "X" is to close the MS Excel window, but there is also an "X" to close the actual spreadsheet window. To the left of that "X" in the spreadsheet window is a square and a minus sign. Try clicking the square!

FOR FINDING PROPERTIES AVAILABLE IN YOUR AREA

• For finding properties that are available in the area (or other areas) you want to buy, your real estate agent will supply these listings from the local Multiple Listing Service (MLS), or you can go to www.zillow.com, www.Redfin.com (Chapter 3 – Redfin.com instructions), www.trulia.com, www.google.com www.yahoo.com, or any other real estate listing service you would like.

FOR FINDING RENTAL COMPARABLES

• For finding rental comparables this is a little tougher. Craigslist.org has by far the most information (see Chapter 13 on Renting/Managing property for more Craigslist.org advice) but it takes some time to extract the right information…but www.zillow.com has rental information too. Also Rentometer.com, hotpads.com and FinestExpert.com seem to be good sources. You can use other data sources like your real estate agent, rental listings, or rental magazines. You should also shop, that is drive by and call on signs, other properties. Make sure you are comfortable and use conservative rental projections.

PROPERTY TAXES AND OTHER EXPENSES

Make sure to check with the real estate professional and/or county assessor to see what your property taxes will be if you purchase the property. Rules vary by state and what the prior owner paid may NOT be what you will be paying. So do your homework and make sure. See the article on the website about property taxes.

Other expenses like maintenance, etc. make sure you do some research and be conservative in your estimates, at least $75/month/unit for repairs up to $150/month for bigger houses.

ALSO: Make sure to read Chapter 4 – Rent Vs. Own regardless because it covers the dangers of short term ownership that applies to rental properties too.

COLLEGE STUDENTS

Because lots of students use this guide, let's talk. Having your parents buy a property at your school for you to live in while you are there is probably not a very good idea. First, it will probably end up being short term ownership if you move out of town after school. And as you will read in Chapter 4 that is usually not a good financial move. Second, do you really want to have that responsibility during school when you really should be studying AND having a good time. Leave that responsibility to a few years down the road when you can afford to take the risk and earn the returns on your own property deals. Real estate is hard work….as you know school classes, grades, money, dating, etc. give you enough stress in life on campus…don't add to that during the few brief years you get to enjoy college…life is too short!!!

BUT DO STUDY THIS MANUAL WHILE YOU ARE IN SCHOOL. IT WILL HELP YOU IF YOU WANT TO GO INTO THE REAL ESTATE PROFESSION AND HELP YOU WITH CRITICAL THINKING SKILLS THAT WILL ASSIST YOU IN LIFE. THERE ARE LOTS OF COMMON SENSE ITEMS IN THIS BOOK, SO STAY A RENTER, BUT EARN A GREAT EDUCATION THAT YOU CAN APPLY ONCE YOU GET OUT OF SCHOOL. GOOD LUCK!

Check out my Zillow blog for a couple of articles on that: www.Zillow.com/blog/author/LeonardBaron/

VERY IMPORTANT

OTHER RISKS, TIPS/ITEMS TO CONSIDER:

- Buy properties within a 45 minute drive of where you live. Once you have a major problem and/or have to go through the re-leasing process…and you can actually get to the property quickly, you will understand.
- Houses on Hills….Caution here, normal insurance does not cover landslide or earth movement, nor does Earthquake insurance if it isn't an earthquake. So if rain causes your house to slide and hence be destroyed, you are out of luck. Same with houses on low lands near rivers that could flood. Review insurance options, if any, before you buy. Don't take these issues lightly, really think them through….
- Buy properties in decent shape, not fixers – Read chapter 14 and Beware
- Buy properties you are willing to live in. If you would not live there, skip it. So moderately priced rental properties in working class clean neighborhoods with decent credit quality tenants. Skip the bad areas of town, even if you collect rent the tenant hassles might take up an inordinate amount of your time…
- Positive Cash Flow Properties are ASSETS, Negative Cash Flow Properties are LIABILITIES!
- Don't fall for the old "I'll just pay cash so it will be cash flow positive" line. A bad deal is a bad deal, make sure to pencil out your cash on cash returns. If you buy an all cash deal that only produces a realistic 1.0% return on your hard earned cash equity investment, is that a good deal? You've got a ton a money at risk for very low returns! And year two may only be 1.2%, year three 1.4%... you'll be 10 years in and only 2.5% returns when you could have possibly earned 4% - 10% buying other assets that produce more cash flow, like stocks, bonds, mutual funds, etc.
- Watch for those homes built between 1980 and 1999 with Polybutylene pipes, just make sure you understand the issue. And for condos with PB pipes, you can change out your pipes, but did the neighbors change out theirs? Do some research on the Internet and talk to your home inspector!
- Once you go into escrow, get any seller disclosure documents ASAP. You want to see what they are disclosing before you spend on your home inspection, appraisal, HOA docs, etc.

ProfessorBaron.com

Rental Property Investment Analysis
Single Year Monthly & Annual Cash Flow Analysis

A Smarter Way
to Buy Real Estate

Note: This spreadsheet shows Pre-Tax Cash Flows, You will Learn After Tax Calculations in later Chapters.

BOLD BLUE NUMBERS YOU MODIFY FOR YOUR PROPERTY SPECIFICS

BOX 1 - ACQUISITION INFORMATION ALL INPUT NUMBERS ARE POSITIVE (+)

Purchase Price - Local MLS from Your Agent or www.Redfin.com		$	112,500
Downpayment Amount =	25.00%	$	28,125
Mortgage Amount =	$ 84,375		
Closing Costs - Loan Points/Escrow/Title Fees/Inspection Etc.		$	5,500
Rehabilitation/Make Property Ready Budget - Do Not Underestimate		$	5,000
Total Equity (Downpayment + Closing Costs + Rehab) - **THIS IS YOUR CASH OUT OF POCKET**		$	38,625

BOX 2 - PROPERTY OPERATIONS STATEMENT

Monthly Amounts

Monthly Rent - www.trulia.com, www.craigslist.org or other Source		$	1,225
Vacancy & Collection Loss	3.00%	$	37
Collection Loss Can Be an Issue with Lesser Creditworthy Tenants			
Effective Gross Rent (EGR)		$	1,188

Monthly Operating Expenses

Management Fee Percentage =	(PARTNERS?)	0.00%	$	-
Insurance			$	30
Maintenance/Repairs/Other			$	50
HOA Fees			$	180
Miscellaneous - Anything extra you can think of that may come up			$	25
Property Taxes - You need to Get Tax Info From agent. Could be different from Prior owner amount			$	103
Total Operating Expenses (TOE)			$	388

Net Operating Income (NOI) = EGR minus TOE

	$	800

BOX 3 - MORTGAGE PAYMENT AND CASH FLOWS

Mortgage Payment - Monthly	Interest Rate from Lender =	5.500%	$	479
(Interest Rate Comes From Lender)	Amortization Years =	30		
	(If Interest Only, Input 1000)			
Monthly Cash Flow (COULD BE NEGATIVE)			$	321

Annualized

Annual Cash Flow (COULD BE NEGATIVE)	$	3,854
Cash on Cash (Annual Cash Flow / Total Equity) - COULD BE NEGATIVE		9.98%

BOX 4 - INVESTMENT RETURNS SUMMARY

Year 1 Cash on Cash Return (Compare to Bank CD or Bond) - Except real estate can have much higher risk.		9.98%
Monthly Cash Flow	$	321

DEAL METER says: Positive Cash Flow, Nice!

ProfessorBaron.com
The Due Diligence Site

Rental Property Investment Analysis
Multi-Year & Annual Cash Flow Analysis

A Smarter Way to Buy Real Estate

THIS IS A NICE MODERATELY PRICED CASH FLOW POSITIVE AND VERY GOOD CASH ON CASH RATE OF RETURN PROPERTY, THE KIND YOU WANT TO BUY!

ACQUISITION INFORMATION

Purchase Price - Zillow.com or Local MLS from Your Agent	$112,500
Downpayment Amount Percentage %%%% 25%	$28,125
Mortgage Amount $ 84,375	
Closing Costs - Loan Points/Escrow/Title Fees/Inspection Et	$5,500
Rehabilitation/Make Property Ready Budget	$5,000
Total Equity (Downpayment + Closing Costs)	$38,625

RENT/EXPENSE INCREASE

PROPERTY OPERATIONS STATEMENT 3.00%	Year 1	Year 2	Year 3	Year 4	Year 5	Year 6	Year 7	Year 8	Year 9	Year 10
Monthly Rent - Zillow.com, Craigslist.org, or Other Source 3.00%	$1,225	$1,262	$1,300	$1,339	$1,379	$1,420	$1,463	$1,507	$1,552	$1,598
Vacancy and Collection Loss	$37	$38	$39	$40	$41	$43	$44	$45	$47	$48
Effective Gross Rent	$1,188	$1,224	$1,261	$1,298	$1,337	$1,378	$1,419	$1,461	$1,505	$1,550
Operating Expenses										
Management Fee Percentage = 8.00%	$95	$98	$101	$104	$107	$110	$114	$117	$120	$124
Insurance	$30	$31	$32	$33	$34	$35	$36	$37	$38	$39
Maintenance/Repair/Other	$50	$52	$53	$55	$56	$58	$60	$61	$63	$65
HOA Expense	$180	$185	$191	$197	$203	$209	$215	$221	$228	$235
Miscellaneous/Lawncare/Utilities	$25	$26	$27	$27	$28	$29	$30	$31	$32	$33
Property Taxes Increase %/Year 2.00%	$103	$106	$109	$113	$116	$119	$123	$127	$130	$134
Total Operating Expenses	$483	$498	$512	$528	$544	$560	$577	$594	$612	$630
Net Operating Income (NOI)	$705	$726	$748	$771	$794	$818	$842	$867	$893	$920
MORTGAGE PAYMENT AND CASH FLOWS										
Mortgage Payment - Monthly Interest Rate = 5.50% Amortization Years = 30	$479	$479	$479	$479	$479	$479	$479	$479	$479	$479
Monthly Cash Flow (COULD BE NEGATIVE)	$226	$247	$269	$292	$315	$339	$363	$388	$414	$441
Annual Cash Flow (COULD BE NEGATIVE)	$2,714	$2,968	$3,230	$3,499	$3,776	$4,062	$4,356	$4,660	$4,972	$5,293
Cash on Cash (Annual Cash Flow/Total Equity)	7.03%	7.71%	8.42%	9.16%	9.91%	10.69%	11.49%	12.32%	13.17%	14.05%

This spreadsheet is protected - the passcode "duediligence" will unprotect it.
www.ProfessorBaron.com © LPB Services LLC 12-11

REFUSE TO USE SPREADSHEETS? – WANT TO PENCIL DEALS ON PAPER:

Ok if you've never used spreadsheets, don't worry! Even my handyman Gilbert (he's old school) can hardly use a cell phone, but he can use my spreadsheets. If you can use the Internet and download a file, you can use my spreadsheets. Download it, save it to your computer, then click "print" and "entire workbook". It will print out all 4 pages nice and clean – and the last two pages are instructions on how to use the spreadsheets. Trying asking your grandchildren for help, certainly they will know how and be able to assist! So get into the '90s here, and give it a whirl, it never hurts to try!

Also, doing the analysis by hand means you will have to manually calculate the numbers, which is time consuming and prone to errors. We suggest you give the simple spreadsheets a try, the instructions will tell you exactly which cell to input your numbers and they are really simple. If you can use the Internet, you can manage these spreadsheets. If not, however, you can start off doing by hand and work you way to the spreadsheets down the road:

- If you still want to try them by hand, on the website in Chapter 3 -Download the Investment Analysis Spreadsheet ".pdf", then open it up on your computer and save it to a directory and print it out (or Investment Analysis Spreadsheet Blank Template). You can see that Page 1 is filled in with #'s so use that as a guide for your Page 2 Analysis and the Spreadsheet Instructions are there too. Good luck.

LPB Services LLC © 2010

CHAPTER 4

HOMEBUYER TIPS – RENT VS. OWN

The Rent vs. Own question is an important topic to discuss for those deciding whether or not to buy property. It does NOT always make sense to buy property; it depends on many factors that you need to consider.

YOU ARE NOT THROWING AWAY MONEY RENTING. YOU MAY BE THROWING AWAY MONEY IF YOU RUSH TO BUY A PROPERTY THAT ISN'T THE RIGHT ONE FOR YOU AND THEN YOU WASTE YEARS LIVING IN OR OWNING A PROPERTY THAT DOES NOT FIT THE REASON YOU DESIRE TO OWN REAL ESTATE. OR IF RENTING IS SO MUCH LESS EXPENSIVE THAN OWNING IN THAT PARTICULAR AREA THEN IT MAY BE BETTER TO BE A RENTER AND INVEST YOUR SAVINGS ELSEWHERE. IF MOM AND DAD PRESSURE YOU TO BUY SOMETHING, TELL THEM YOU WILL DO YOUR ANALYSIS ON WHETHER OR NOT IT MAKES FINANCIAL AND LIFE SENSE AND THEN MAKE YOUR OWN DECISION.

NOTE: IF YOU ARE WEALTHY THEN YOU MAY NOT REALLY NEED TO PENCIL OUT YOUR RENT VS. OWN DEAL BECAUSE YOU ARE GOING TO BUY WHAT YOU WANT. BUT YOU SHOULD STILL UNDERSTAND SOME BASIC REAL ESTATE OWNERSHIP ISSUES IN THIS CHAPTER. PARTICULARLY IF THERE ARE LOTS OF COMPARABLE PROPERTIES THAT COULD BE RENTED FOR A MUCH LOWER AMOUNT THAN OWNING AND/OR IF YOU DO NOT BELIEVE YOU WILL OWN THE PROPERTY ALL THAT LONG....IN BOTH CASES YOU MAY WANT TO CONSIDER IF YOU SHOULD STAY A RENTER AND INVEST YOUR HARD EARNED DOLLARS ELSEWHERE.

So do not just buy real estate because someone else says you need to buy to gain equity or tax benefits. In fact, depending on the property and your tax situation, you may be losing equity and there may not be ANY tax benefits to owning property - the tax issue you will learn in Chapter 6.

Personal Residences - Considerations

There are many things to consider in deciding whether or not to buy a personal residence. It IS an investment, not just because you hope to earn some money on it over the long term, but also because you will be taking a large amount of your personal savings to fund the downpayment, closing costs and any repairs needed. You could invest that money elsewhere in much more liquid assets and maybe earn a better rate of return. So, you want to make sure to make a smart financial decision and life decision on owning real estate. Realize, that "investment" could end up a liability to you – hence a money losing investment – if you cannot comfortably afford to pay the mortgage!

One great thing about owning property is that having a mortgage payment due each month will force you to save money – as we are all our own worst enemy when it comes to saving money so forcing us to save money is a good thing. But you need to ensure that you are not substantially negative on a rent vs. own basis – because then you effectively will be forcing yourself to make mortgage payments but you will not actually be saving any money. You will further understand this after reading the chapter.

You also need to make sure you can afford the mortgage. How much can you afford? That does not mean how large of a loan you can qualify for. It means on how big a mortgage can you actually afford the payments and still be comfortable and able to save some other separate money. So, you need to figure out what you are comfortable paying each month for housing expense – that is principal, interest, taxes, insurance, HOA fees, and some reserves for expenses - and be able to pay all your other bills.

Your lender can help you figure out your housing expense - Chapter 7 Mortgage Financing - which will translate into a maximum mortgage amount that the lender underwriting criteria indicate you can afford. With this and your downpayment amount, you will know the price range you can afford. Just make sure, regardless of how much you can qualify for, that you are comfortable with your housing expense taking that amount of your monthly income. Do not buy more than you can afford!

THREE IMPORTANT ITEMS THAT SHOULD SWAY YOU TO STAYING A RENTER FOR THE NEAR TERM

1. STARTER HOMES - Buying a "Starter" property to "Trade Up or Move Up" to a bigger property just a few years down the road is probably not a smart financial plan. The transaction costs, escrow, sales commissions, etc on the buy-in AND on the sell will probably cost you a significant portion of your equity – see chart below. That does not include all the monies you will spend on new carpets, window coverings, landscaping, paint, etc. that will be transferred to the new buyer when you "Move Up". It is unlikely you will recoup those improvement costs in a higher sales price.

You are much better off diligently saving your pennies for a few more years to buy the RIGHT property that fits your needs for the long term. This way the new refrigerator, sidewalk, carpets, tile, etc. will be yours to enjoy for years – instead of being enjoyed by the person who bought your "Starter" home. If you think property prices will increase dramatically in the near term, that might change this analysis. But you had better be a pretty good predictor of the future – and good luck with that!

2. SHORT TERM PLANNED OWNERSHIP - Similarly, it generally does not make sense to buy property overall if you only plan to own it for less than five years – the longer the ownership the better. The same issues come up about transaction costs on both your buying and selling and spending monies to fix up a property that you will not recoup. We see advertisements that talk about how some improvements will give you back 80% to 90% of your value, like new flooring or a new bathroom. Well that means that you are losing 10% to 20% of the money you put into those improvements when you sell the property. Overall, it is really hard to gauge how much you will recoup for improvements to your property, but it will probably be less than you spend on those improvements.

So Military families are the perfect example for this of people who should really think hard before they buy property. There are so many potential issues so if you are only going to be in town for a few years let a landlord take the risk on owning property instead of you! What if you cannot sell it? What if there is a major damage event? Financially, it will probably be less expensive to rent. Don't forget those transaction costs on both ends if you buy and sell.

So Military, stay renters, negotiate a multiyear deal with cancellation options if you need to move. Your life will be less stressful and you most likely will be much better off financially. If you want to own real estate, buy rental property in a city where you have family who can manage or at least keep an eye on it.

As are professional athletes. Their careers average 3.3 years to 5.6 years and they should be buying investment properties that pay cash flow, like apartment buildings, instead of expensive homes that will crunch them financially if their career ends. Or if they are traded to another city's team and then they own a vacant mansion that costs big bucks every month. Of course if they are megastars with tens of millions in the bank…that's a different story.

3. NEW TO TOWN - Don't buy if you just moved into town. Rent a place to live while you take your time to find the RIGHT location to make the largest purchase you will ever make. We know moving is expensive and a pain, but rushing to buy a house that ends up not being what you wanted will be a much bigger pain. You will either be unhappy living there, or it may take a long time to sell the property, AND you probably will lose money that you should be putting into the RIGHT long term property you want to own. So rent for a long enough period, and maybe rent a furnished property and leave your furniture in storage, that allows you to take your time, shop neighborhoods and areas, and pick out the property that fits your needs.

SHORT TERM OWNERSHIP FINANCIAL PICTURE

So this financial would apply to anytime you buy and then sell in a short period of time. You could put the dollar value of any property you are considering buying into this spreadsheet and you will probably find that in general short term ownership is not a smart financial plan.

PROPERTY HOLD - SHORT TERM - 2 YEARS		
Property Cost	$100,000	
Mortgage - 75% Financed	$(75,000)	
CASH FOR CLOSING ESCROW		
Downpayment	$25,000	
Closing Costs	$5,000	- Loan Fees, Escrow
Rehab Costs	$5,000	- You will spend $$!!
CASH EQUITY	**$35,000**	- Cash to close
		escrow
SELLING - AFTER 2 YEARS		
Sales Price	$107,000	(3.5% Inc. /Year)
Sales Expenses 8%	$(8,560)	- Commish, Escrow,
Net Sales Price	$98,440	
Mortgage Balance	$(73,000)	
Cash EQUITY Left	**$25,440**	

SEE, YOU STARTED WITH $35,000 CASH IN YOUR BANK ACCOUNT AND 2 YEARS LATER SELLING YOUR HOUSE YOU HAVE $25,440 LEFT. GREAT JOB, YOU JUST WASTED $9,560 OF YOUR HARD EARNED CASH THAT IS NEVER COMING BACK!

\- MIGHT HAVE BEEN BETTER TO RENT AND SAVE MONEY FOR A LONG TERM PURCHASE!

Note: Unless you believe the property will go up significantly in value, it really does not make sense to buy property for short periods of time - especially with the risk and stress of something going wrong. And often, things do go wrong - leaks, appliance repairs, maintenance, repairs, electric, _____
<= you fill in the blank, etc. If you don't know what other repair items there are on properties, don't worry, you will soon!

The better move is to save your money for years until you have enough of a downpayment to buy the RIGHT property that you are going to own a long time.

BUYING WITH INTENT TO KEEP AS A RENTAL

Alternatively, If you plan to live there a few years and then keep it as a rental for many years, then by all means buy buy buy NOW. Of course do your Chapter 3 Cash Flows analysis to make sure it will be a financially advantageous rental property! This is really the way to go, Read "Smart Moves to Begin Your Real Estate Empire" – Chapter 3. Our attorney says, "Great plan. Buy entry level properties, live there for two years, rent them out and buy another!"

RESTATED:

If you only plan to live in an area a couple or a few years, or only own the property a short while or if you have not done sufficient research to know the local areas, avoid the stress of owning real estate. Rent someone else's property and let them deal with the risks of real estate ownership. What if you move out of town after a couple of years and it takes eight months to get the property sold, or if there is some major problem you need to pay for to fix in a home you do not plan to own very long, or if it sells for much less than you anticipated when you sell it. Live stress free, avoid property ownership unless you know the area and plan to own it for a longer period of time.

RENT VS. OWN - HIGH PROPERTY PRICES, LOW RENTAL RATES – MAYBE STAY A RENTER?

In some areas it just simply is too expensive to own versus the cost to rent suitable living space. This is a much more complex issue and one in which you will have to make some personal judgments on what is the best move for you related to this issue. But let's discuss a few concepts.

Owning real estate can be a long term wealth building process. However, depending on where exactly you want to live, especially if there are lots of similar properties which you consider suitable places to live, you should avoid places where ownership is just too expensive compared to renting. And we really mean areas where there are lots of similar style and type properties that are readily available for sale at any point in time and an owner would be way negative on rent vs. own basis.

We are NOT talking about areas that are expensive but where there is scarcity of available land to increase the supply of real estate. You probably ARE going to be negative there. Negative means that it is less expensive to rent on a monthly basis than to own as per the chart below.

Relating to a personal residence (not investment property) if it is in a prize location, like at the beach or the fancy area of town, and there is NO more land available to build and hence there will not be additional supply coming on the market, even though you are negative on rent vs. own, it may make sense to buy for the long term. At a minimum due to lack of buildable land you won't have increases in supply that could potentially keep prices flat.

As an example, one of the authors lives in an old beach house that was pricey and it would have been much less expensive to rent a comparable property. He bought because he rented nearby for a long time and plans to live in the area for the foreseeable future. So from a life standpoint and long long term financial standpoint it made sense to him to own. If he was not pretty sure he was going to stay in the area, he would have stayed a renter until he made that decision. Plus, near the beach, as far as he can tell "they are not making any no more dirt" so there is a very constricted land supply which constricts the supply of housing and should generally keep prices stable or increasing over time.

Again, this issue is more complicated but let's look at a bad case, not a worst case, but a bad case scenario where you may want to think twice before trading from a renter to a homeowner. This also depends on your wealth level and personal preferences.

In many cities and areas there are revitalized downtowns with luxury condominium units that command high prices to own. And you have already decided that you really want to live in one of these downtown areas because it fits your lifestyle profile – maybe we will term you a "mover and a shaker". Let's take a $500,000 condominium for sale that you might purchase and compare it to a similar condominium that you might alternatively consider renting for $2,300 per month.

```
┌─────────────────────────────────────────────────────────────┐
│                  RENT VS. OWN REVIEW                         │
│              CONDO IN MORE EXPENSIVE AREA                    │
│                                                             │
│  PRICE $500,000 OR RENTAL COST $2,300/MONTH                 │
│                          OWNERSHIP        RENTAL            │
│                                                             │
│  Downpayment 10.0%       $50,000                           │
│  Closing Costs           $10,000                           │
│  Rental Deposit                           $2,300           │
│                                                             │
│  CASHFLOW PICTURE                                          │
│  Mortgage Payment -                       Rent             │
│     $450,000 @ 5.5%/30 YR   $2,565        $2,300           │
│  Property Taxes          $458                             │
│  HOA Fees                $525                             │
│  Insurance               $30                             │
│  Repairs and Upgrades -                                   │
│  $1,200/YR               $100                             │
│  Pretax Costs            $3,678                           │
│                                                             │
│  Tax Savings at 30.0%                                      │
│  (Depends..)             $(756)                           │
│  Net Cost Per Month      $2,922           $2,300           │
│  Add'l Cost of Ownership Per                              │
│  Month                                    $622             │
│  Net Add'l Cost/Year of Owning =          $(7,468)        │
│                                                             │
│  YOU MAY EARN SOME PROPERTY APPRECIATION TO MAKE UP        │
│  THE $7,468 NEGATIVE, BUT YOU MAY NOT. AND COULD BE        │
│  MANY REPAIR BILLS THAT A RENTER WOULD NOT HAVE.          │
└─────────────────────────────────────────────────────────────┘
```

On this chart you can see that ownership is much more expensive than being a renter in this particular scenario ($7,468) more in the first year. Now your mortgage stays constant if you purchased while rents do typically increase, so the $7,468 difference should decrease each year going forward as the cost of "owning" seems to get relatively less expensive over time. However, when you are this far negative it is going to take many many years of way negative cash flows before you breakeven.

So you might have ten years with cumulative negative cash flows of maybe ($50,000) plus before you breakeven on current year rent vs. own analysis. Your hope is that the appreciation of the property value will make up this difference – and it might. However, you need to be cautious about estimating that there will be any appreciation in value to make up that ($50,000) shortfall.

Even if you are wealthy you might just think about whether owning makes sense in this area. You could invest that $60,000 downpayment + closing costs somewhere else like investment property.

RENT VS. OWN SPREADSHEET

Let's move to the finances. Every rent vs. own program we see always comes up with it makes more sense to own. They usually come to this answer by calculating that long term appreciation in value will make up the difference over years of negative cash flows. But if you are too far negative and believe there is a potential that the hoped for appreciation may never come, it might make sense to rent because the appreciation may not make up for the years of negative rent vs. own cash flows.

The attached rent vs. own spreadsheet will allow you to put your pencil to your paper and see what owning will cost vs. renting. If you are close to breakeven and you plan to own long term, it probably makes sense to buy. If you are way positive on renting vs. owning, it probably makes sense to buy as long as you are a long term holder. The property will also probably increase in value over time and owning a home is comfortable and brings stability to our lives.

You can put in some basic numbers into our spreadsheet to get a feel for where your particular targeted property stands. This should help you think and debate if you determine that your deal is really negative on the rent vs. own analysis. If it is far negative, you should rethink whether or not you want to own. Make sure you understand the tax benefits of ownership from Chapter 6 Income Taxes Impact on Cash Flows and this can impact your decision.

Separately, do not forget that owning comes with fixing things like leaky pipes, electrical outlets, maintaining the yard, broken appliances, property tax increases, it decreases your ability to move or change jobs if you need – so just make sure it makes financial and life sense.

IF YOU ARE NOT SURE IT DOES MAKE SENSE, TAKE YOUR TIME, AVOID THE HASSLES AND RENT FOR A FEW MORE YEARS UNTIL YOU ARE SURE!

You can use this attached RentVsOwn Spreadsheet to assist in penciling out your deal.

ProfessorBaron.com

Rent Vs. Own Analysis

A Smarter Way to Buy Real Estate

This analysis is a simple rough estimate cash flow analysis on the costs of renting vs. owning.

Most rent vs. own analysis take into account an increase in value (appreciation) that

makes the "own" seem viable - where on cash flow alone it might not seem very viable.

WATCH THE APPRECIATION ESTIMATES - THEY MAY NOT COME TRUE! WE DON'T CONSIDER ANY APPRECIATION HERE.

Depending on the area of town that you would like to live this will help you understand whether to rent or own.

As noted, we do not consider appreciation, but beware the value could decrease, that is why
we like real estate as a long term investment.

You modify the cells in BLUE

PURCHASE PROPERTY SPECIFICATIONS			OWN	RENT	OVERALL ANALYSIS
Purchase Price/Value of Property		$	150,000		
Downpayment Cash Equity	10.00%	$	15,000		
Mortage Amount	$ 135,000				
Loan Interest Rate	5.50%				
Loan Amortization Years	30				
Closing Costs - Loan Points/Escrow/Title Fees/Inspection Etc.		$	5,500		
Rehabilitation/Make Property Ready Budget		$	5,000		
Total Equity (Downpayment + Closing Costs)		$	25,500		
OWN PROPERTY ANALYSIS					
Mortgage Payment		$	767		
Property Taxes - Need to determine for your particular property!		$	138		
HOA Fees - Homeowners Association		$	250		
Maintenance/Improvements		$	100		
Insurance		$	20		
Mortgage Amortization Principal Paydown (NEGATIVE!)		$	(148)		
Tax Savings (May or May Not Apply Based on Many Factors) There are potential tax savings but it gets a bit more complicated to estimate those amounts. However, it could be SIGNIFICANT - Learn Chapter 6.		$	-		
OWNERSHIP - Total Monthly Ongoing Expenses		$	1,126		
RENTAL - Monthly				$ 1,375	
MONTHLY DIFFERENCE BETWEEN RENTING VS. OWN (Postive here means it is less expensive to own vs. rent)					$ 249
ANNUAL SAVINGS/DIFFERENCE BETWEEN RENTING VS. OWNING					$ 2,985
EQUITY IN PROPERTY Recall that you had to invest approximate to acquire this property					$ 25,500
Return (Savings) on Your Equity if you Buy vs. Rent (Not Including Appreciation)					11.71%

CHAPTER 5

FORECLOSURES, SHORT SALES, REO, MLS

What do all these terms mean? Are there some great deals out there that we are missing out on…. Can we make quick and easy money on real estate?

Myths about Foreclosures and Easy Money

Often we hear on the news or from others, "Foreclosures at a Bargain Price" or there are other incredible buying opportunities. There are good deals out there – however not all "good deals" are the same. And you do not need to do something foolish like trying to buy a property at the county courthouse foreclosure auction to get a good deal. In fact, that kind of risky buying will almost certainly end up landing you a lot of financial pain or worse.

NOTE: LEAVE THAT HIGH RISK REAL ESTATE BEHAVIOR TO THE PROFESSIONALS WHO HAVE SIGNIFICANT EXPERIENCE, TIME, MONEY TO RISK, AND AGAIN SIGNIFICANT EXPERIENCE DOING THESE. If you want to understand why, read article on The $810,000 Home You Can't Live In. And this we have seen a worse situation if you can believe that!

We also hear people talking about the easy money to be made on real estate, or buying with NO money down, some other scheme to make quick profits. Most of those people have probably never owned real estate. or True rewards come with HARD WORK, time and patience!

The great buying opportunities are the houses, condos, townhomes, etc. that are listed in the normal local area multiple listing service (MLS) that is run by the many local Realtor's Association's in the each state. The way you shop this inventory is by interviewing and selecting a real estate professional to represent you in your transaction.

Below we will detail the different types of sales of real estate, what they mean, and why chasing some "great" deal where you have to bid at auction or make fast decisions usually leads to your taking risks that you do not need to and should not take.

We will cover:

- Multiple Listing Service (MLS) Listed Properties
- Foreclosures
- Short Sales
- Bank Auctions of Real Estate Owned (REO)
- For Sale by Owners/Chasing Distressed Property Owners

MLS – Local Multiple Listing Service Listed Properties

The vast majority of residential property sales, probably 99.0%, are sold via your local area's MLS. The only way to shop this inventory is to select a real estate agent affiliated with the local association of realtors and have them provide listings for you to review. So, the local real estate association has 99.0% of all the "listings" of properties available for sale.

Note: The other 1.0% of properties are described further below but they are (1) Foreclosure Sales at the County Courthouse, (2) Bank Auctions of a Small Percentage of Bank Real Estate Owned (REO) and (3) Buying Directly from an Owner (also called For Sale By Owner).

The 99.0% pool of MLS listings include virtually all:

- Bank REO (Real Estate Owned that has been foreclosed upon and now is owned by the bank/lender),
- Short Sales (see description below),
- Normal sales listed by the property owners, typically represented by a real estate professional

Since the MLS has the vast majority of properties available for sale, concentrate here. Why some people waste 99.0% of their time chasing 1.0% of the available properties is a mystery to us. That is similar to repeatedly casting your fishing line into your bathtub…no matter how much time you spend doing this, you probably are not going to catch any fish.

Serious buyers who want to earn long term wealth should stop believing some get rich quick scheme could actually work and they should be spending that 99.0% of their time chasing the 99.0% of real estate inventory that is available for sale in the marketplace – that means listed on the local MLS.

ADDITIONALLY, BUYING THROUGH THE NORMAL MLS PROCESS HAS EVERY ADVANTAGE YOU COULD WANT TO REDUCE YOUR RISK AND INCREASE YOUR RETURNS. IT IS THE SMART WAY TO BUY REAL ESTATE.

Buying property in this manner allows you to contract for the property and have the sole and contractual right to purchase the property (aka lock up a contract). Buying this way will typically give you a 10-17 day STUDY PERIOD to have a home inspector review the property condition, to review any HOA documents and obtain the preliminary title insurance policy binder. You typically put down a one percent (1%) REFUNDABLE earnest money deposit that typically becomes NON-Refundable after the study period has expired. And you get a financing contingency – time to go back to your lender and make sure you can obtain financing to purchase the property.

MAIN BENEFIT (AND THIS IS SIGNIFICANT – REMEMBER – THIS IS THE LARGEST PURCHASE YOU WILL EVER MAKE IN YOUR LIFE) – YOU HAVE TIME TO LOCK IT UP AND TAKE A DEEP BREATH, DO YOUR DUE DILIGENCE, TAKE ANOTHER DEEP BREATH, NEGOTIATE A LITTLE MORE WITH THE SELLER IF NEED……AND BACK OUT IF YOU LIKE at the end of the STUDY PERIOD….OR TAKE ONE LAST DEEP BREATH AND BUY THAT PROPERTY (Close Escrow).

Buying property with time to do your due diligence is the safest way. You have plenty of time to talk to friends, drive the neighborhood, have a home inspection, budget your purchase, review HOA documents, spending all this time/energy/effort/money knowing that if you decide this is the RIGHT home for you, you can move forward and complete your purchase.

And if you don't like what you find, you can negotiate more with the seller over repairs or cancel the contract and get your deposit back. And you will only be out $500 +- dollars at risk - home inspection and appraisal typically.

SPECIAL ISSUE REALTED TO PROPERTIES IN COMMON INTEREST DEVELOPMENTS, PLANNED UNIT DEVELOPMENTS OR HOMEOWNERS ASSOCIATIONS – YOU WILL LEARN THIS IN CHAPTER 8.

One piece of advice. If a condo make sure your study period stays open until you review the HOA documents and finances (Chapter 8). Try, but unlikely you will be able, to review the HOA documents before you have a home inspection done and before you pay for an appraisal. The HOA may be slow to get you those documents, but tell your agent up front that they need to get you these documents before you spend monies. You need to request these the day your deal goes into escrow and call every few days. See the detailed instructions and "HOA Document Request Letter to Escrow" in Chapter 8.

Also, if you are buying from a bank owner – either a short sale or REO, make sure to read their multiple page addendums carefully – especially about inspection periods for the property and HOA documents….they are usually shorter than what you offer in your contract.

AGAIN, BUYING THROUGH THE NORMAL MLS PROCESS HAS EVERY ADVANTAGE YOU COULD WANT TO REDUCE YOUR RISK AND INCREASE YOUR RETURNS. IT IS THE SMART WAY TO BUY REAL ESTATE.

Courthouse Steps/Foreclosure/Trustee Sale

THIS IS THE GENERAL PROCESS IN CALIFORNIA, IT COULD BE DIFFERENT IN YOUR STATE SO MAKE SURE TO FIND OUT HOW IT WORKS THERE. BUT IT SHOULD BE SOMEWHAT SIMILAR.

These are the sales of properties on the County Courthouse steps. ON THESE PROPERTIES YOU HAVE ALMOST NO CHANCE TO DO ANY DUE DILIGENCE. And for that reason we find it foolish to even consider buying here. Not to mention there are a lot of buyers here too, and the more bidders, the higher the prices will go. So getting some great deal at the courthouse steps, while possible, is unlikely to happen in today's marketplace.

Regardless, we want you to understand the process and the SIGNIFICANT RISKS:

FORECLOSURE PROCESS - When a person stops paying on their mortgage the lender (bank or mortgage company or hedge fund or Freddie Mac/Fannie Mae – the entity that owns the mortgage) orders the trustee of the deed of trust, also commonly called a "mortgage" to start the foreclosure process. This is in a non-judicial foreclosure state. In a judicial foreclosure state it is simply a "mortgage" and the bank goes to court first for the right to auction the property.

First they file a notice of default (NOD) and if the homeowner cannot cure the issue via sale, negotiation with lender, loan modification, etc. then the lender orders that the property goes to a foreclosure auction. The auction is published and public information and on a certain date the property is auctioned for sale on the courthouse steps by the trustee - as representative of the bank/lender.

In the current market, the vast majority of the properties offered have loans that are greater than the value of the property – hence NEGATIVE EQUITY (i.e. property worth $300,000 but there is an outstanding mortgage balance of $350,000). In these cases the trustee (on the courthouse steps) states the deed of trust number and property information and the starting bid – the mortgage amount ($350,000 in this case but it could be less if the lender tells the trustee to offer it for less) and sees if there is anyone who wants to bid on it. Usually no one does and the property goes back to the lender as Real Estate Owned. Then, it is typically sold by a real estate agent via the MLS.

Sometimes, the properties sold at the courthouse steps may have some POSITIVE EQUITY in them. For example: Value $400,000 with a mortgage of only $300,000 – but this is very rare in today's market. There are a few groups of small companies in each county who bid on these to try to flip them for a $10,000 to $50,000 profit - but don't forget, sometimes they lose money too! So it is competitive for those few properties. And those groups show up to almost every auction where there is at least one property with some equity as they know beforehand, by calling the trustee or bank, that a certain property is for sale. They have done their comparable analysis and believe that the value of that property is above the mortgage amount. And those groups are experienced buyers who have already had their employees do a full review of the property, title, condition (if possible) and estimate of the value.

At the courthouse steps, the trustee selling the property only speaks in one language – All CASH! (or some money down as an EMD and ALL CASH within 30 days). That makes this tough for individuals. In these foreclosure auctions a buyer needs a cashier check for the entire purchase price to buy a property on the courthouse steps. That is the first barrier to entry, and it is a pretty big one.

Add to that the fact that you probably have not been able to get inside the property with a home inspector, you are not versed in title insurance issues; you probably have not done proper due diligence – LIKE MAYBE YOU ARE BUYING THE SECOND TRUST WHICH IS WORTHLESS INSTEAD OF THE FIRST TRUST – NO KIDDING, IT HAPPENS, and you may have the joy of evicting the current owner and that person may not be happy about the whole situation – aka trashes the house!

And by the way, if you do buy at foreclosure auction…you had better call your insurance agent immediately to get an insurance policy in place – and hopefully the property you have purchased is insurable on commercially reasonable terms. And you had better hope that you can get title insurance for refinancing in the future. And you had better hope there is not a $30,000 mold problem, or cracked foundation, or the seller rips out all the appliances when they leave, or worse!

End result – we do not recommend wasting your time and taking SIGNIFICANT risk trying to buy at the courthouse steps. If you do decide to do this, hopefully you are using someone else's money.

SHORT SALE – What is This? What does it take so long to buy a short sale property? All short sales are listed on the local MLS.

"Short sales" – Short means that the market value of the home is less than the mortgage. So, if the property is sold at market value there will not be enough cash to pay off the entire mortgage (or mortgages) - cash is short of full payoff. This is similar to the NEGATIVE EQUITY noted above for foreclosures.

Individual property owners who know they are "short" who want to sell their property (or they simply cannot pay the mortgage or have already defaulted on the mortgage) call the lender, usually with the help of a real estate agent who is experienced in dealing with the lenders, and try to work out that a property will be a short sale. They need to apply to the lender and provide current income and debt information so the lender can see that they really cannot afford the property.

If the lender deems that an individual owner applying for approval to do a short sale with their upside own property can actually afford the mortgage payments, the lender may deny the short sale. Then the owner can then keep paying the mortgage or many owners in today's market who have significant negative equity are doing something called a "strategic default" and just letting the property go into foreclosure and losing the property. This will significantly hurt their credit score and profile.

If the lender approves a short sale, they will review the purchase offers that the real estate agent has procured from already having listed it on the MLS for sale. The lender will have a property valuation performed, called a BPO, or broker price opinion done to see if the contracted purchase price is in line with market pricing. If the lender determines that the contracted price is market, they will approve the short sale with a letter to the owner and the sale will move forward like a normal sale.

These can take a long time and here is why. When the owner decides to do a short sale, they list it with a real estate agent and take offers on the property. At the same time the owner starts submitting paperwork to the bank to see if the bank will approve a short sale. Probably 30 days on average passes from the time the property is listed until the bank receives the short sale "application" from the owner. Then it takes the bank 60-90 days to review the paperwork. If they approve doing a short sale, it probably takes another 30-60 days to get the Broker Price Opinion done to compare that estimated value to the contract price of the procured offers. If the contract price is in line with the BPO, then it goes to the bank and investor for final approval, which can take another 90-120 days. Voila, six months or more has passed while you the buyer await the bank's decision. Then with everything approved, it usually takes 30-45 days to close escrow.

SHORT SALE SEPARATE IMPORTANT ISSUE FOR BUYERS - Many times the buyer has to come up with additional funds at closing on a short sale because the bank requires a certain amount of net cash to close the deal and the sales price less all expenses leaves insufficient funds for the bank. So you as the buyer have to come up with those additional thousands of dollars if you want to buy the property. There is something you can do to try and reduce or eliminate this issue, so read this ARTICLE – Don't get stuck paying extra on your Short Sale for help with this issue.

Article: Don't Get Stuck Paying Extra on Your Short Sale

Question: We keep hearing that after six to nine months of waiting on a short sale buyers are having to come up with extra money at the closing table to get their short sale purchases completed. Why is this happening?

Answer: When a lender agrees to a short sale, they send a letter to the seller and real estate agents which will includes language in the approval similar to this:
The conditions of approval are as follows:

Sales price - $115,000

Closing costs have been negotiated and agreed upon with the authorized agent.

- Total Closing Costs not to exceed $13,704
- Maximum Commission paid $6,900
- Maximum Allowed to 2nd Trust$2,000
- Maximum for HOA liens $450
- Maximum for Repairs $0
- Maximum Termite Repairs $0
- Max Escrow, title, disclosures ,etc $4,354

Any additional fees that were not approved are the sole responsibility of either the agent, the buyer or the seller to pay at closing.

Net proceeds to the lender to be no less than <u>$101,295</u>.

So the lender requires a concrete amount, the $101,295 in order for the short sale to close. The lender has calculated this amount based off the numbers that the listing agent provided to them. If the listing agent didn't know about unpaid taxes, HOA fees or liens, they will not alert the bank to provision for all those additional funds at closing. Additionally, if the agent made the calculation at the time of contract and it took six extra months to close the short sale, all those additional unpaid funds may be increasing their balances each month. Like an extra 6 months of HOA fees.

Then, when escrow calculates your closing estimate that would include all those additional unpaid amounts that are owed, the net proceeds to the seller/bank ends up being much less than required by the seller.

Guess who gets to make up the difference. You guessed it, YOU! The real estate agents may chip in part of their commissions but absent that you get to make up the difference with cash at the closing table if you still want to move forward and buy the property.

Can you protect yourself so you do not need to come up with extra funds at closing, the answer is usually yes.
Make sure the listing agent checks for unpaid taxes, liens and HOA fees and provides for an additional six months of them when they submit the original net proceeds closing estimate to the lender.

Hopefully the lender will allow all those estimates and use them in their calculation and you the buyer will not have to come up with the extra cash on closing day.

End of Article

Bank Auctions

For properties that have already been foreclosed upon by banks, so the banks own the actual properties, instead of listing all of them on the MLS, some banks allocate a portion of their (REO) inventory for sale at an auction to quickly liquidate those assets. This may be ½ of 1% of annual sales in the local jurisdiction. They have these auctions at local Convention Centers every once in a while and typically sell a lot of properties, that is 100-300 properties. You have probably seen one of these auction houses - REDC company's advertisements on TV (www.REDCauction.com).

Bank or lender auctions can be an fair way to buy real estate, but do not bet on getting any below market deal. There are so many buyers that show up that prices frequently get bid up to the same pricing that you would find on MLS listed properties. There are some positive aspects though of buying this way that allow you to do good due diligence. But will you spend the money AND time required to do your proper due diligence considering you may only have a small chance of being the highest bidder on the property? Are you going to pay a home inspector $350 to look at a property that you only have a small chance of winning during the bidding process.

Conversely, recall that when buying via a Realtor and the MLS, because you contract on a property and have the sole right to buy that property, spending time and money to do your inspections and due diligence is worthwhile. This is because if everything looks good, there is a high probably you will end up owning the property. With auctions, realistically, are you going to do all that work?

Regardless, bank auctions have some good due diligence opportunities and also, you will know right there at the auction whether or not you can buy a property:

OPEN HOUSES - They have open houses so you can go inspect the properties a few weeks before the auction.

HOA DOCUMENTS - They also have some (that is some) of the Homeowners Association (HOA) Documents available for review.

TITLE REVIEW - You have time to have a title representative pull title documents on ownership if you know to do that.

FINANCING - One big plus is that they often have financing available and usually it is fairly priced (decent interest/points pricing). And if you were pre-approved by their "preferred" lender and the deal fails, they say you get your deposit back – the typical $2,500 - $5,000 you must hand over if you win the bidding.

PRIVATE FINANCING (via your own bank/lender) - You can also obtain your own financing – but if it fails, your $5,000 deposit is retained by the seller.

VALUE ESTIMATE - Also, you have time to pencil out the most you are willing to pay for a property and search online (and your realtor should) for comparable market sales to assist in this effort.

CLOSING ESCROW - And they DO want to close escrow as they tell us that 85% of the ones that "sell" at auction do actually close escrow. They have "reserve prices" but apparently the banks approve most of the sales that are at least close to the reserve prices.

TOUGER PART of BANK AUCTIONS, AGAIN:

- $5,000 non-refundable deposit if you win the bidding.
- Do you pay $250-$350 for a home inspector before you buy?
- Can you get the HOA documents and fully review them before auction?
- Can you do the due diligence you need before you put down that $5,000?

MOST IMPORTANT CONSIDERATION - Is all the time, energy, and effort going to get you a property at the price you want to pay – or will you be outbid. There are a lot of bidders on most of the properties so you have to be lucky or pay the highest price to win. If a specific property or complex you like and know well has a property going to the auction – probably makes better sense (and worthwhile – as long as you do your due diligence) to pursue it in that case.

But there are many many more properties in the MLS and pricing is probably close to or just as good on these and you have time to do your due diligence.

Buying Directly from An Owner in Financial Trouble (Sometimes Termed For Sale By Owner)

This is the last issue we will briefly cover. Occasionally we read about some GRQS (Get Rich Quick Scheme) to search out people in trouble on properties and try to buy them out and get some great deal. While possible, it involves a LOT of work chasing lots of people in distress and with very little chance of success. Why spend your time trying to catch that fish in the bathtub when there are very fair deals on properties in the MLS that people or banks already are ready, willing and able to sell. Spend your time finding the property that fits your needs by using a real estate agent and shopping the properties listed on the local Multiple Listing Service and doing your due diligence!

LET'S RESTATE THE FACTS:

1. Smart buyers would never make the largest purchases they are ever going to make in their lives without doing the proper due diligence.
2. In order to do this due diligence you need time to complete the steps.
3. The only way to get that time is to offer on a property and have your offer accepted by a seller with some contingencies and time allowed to complete your due diligence steps.

4. The only place where you can really make and have an offer accepted by a seller is by purchasing via your real estate agent from the pool of available inventory on the local Multiple Listing Service listings.

AGAIN – SMART BUYERS WOULD NEVER MAKE THE LARGEST PURCHASES THEY ARE EVER GOING TO MAKE IN THEIR LIVES WITHOUT DOING THE PROPERTY DUE DILIGENCE. MAKE SURE YOU ARE ONE OF THOSE SMART BUYERS!

LPB Services LLC © 2010

CHAPTER 6

INCOME TAXES IMPACT ON CASH FLOWS

Federal Income Taxes (FIT)

Income taxes can significantly impact your cash flows on a property whether it is a personal residence interest deduction or a rental property passive activity loss. You cannot just assume that you are going to save money on taxes because you buy real estate, because that might not be correct. To find out whether or not you can gain some tax savings from buying real estate, you have to understand how taxes work and review your actual tax situation and picture.

This chapter will take some work to understand, probably six eight hours of your time effort. But it is well worth the time to learn concepts and understand real estate impacts the amount of federal income taxes you pay.

to and the how

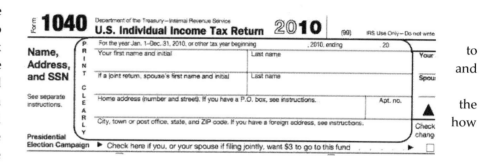

Most people find taxes to be a once per year hassle that they would prefer to avoid. We understand, sympathize and agree with that. However, for helping one calculate their true cash flows picture on real estate, one needs to understand how taxes impact investment returns. Luckily, for the vast majority of people, FIT and how they impact real estate is not really that complicated.

Albert Einstein said:
"The hardest thing in the world to understand is the income tax".

But what he should have said is:
"The hardest thing in the world to understand is the income tax FORMS".

That's right, only our federal government could take something that is simple and straightforward and make every American - except Tax Preparation Professionals who earn a living doing taxes - hate to even think about their taxes.

For we real estate personal residence buyers and investors, by investing a little time to study this chapter, we are going to make FIT easy to understand. And understanding FIT will significantly improve your understanding of cash flows related to real estate ownership.

Note: This chapter is helpful for the vast majority of income tax filers in the US. If you have complicated returns or are self employed, you need help from a Tax Professional to get a clearer handle on your tax picture. But this chapter will further along your understanding of taxes either way so you can ask your Tax Professional the right questions.

Note: Property Taxes - whether State, County or City - are a separate issue. In this chapter we are just discussing Federal Income Taxes – that is what you file on Form 1040 each year. State income taxes, if your state has them, work similar to FIT but we will leave that discussion to you and your tax professional as to your "Marginal Tax Rate" at the state level.

Lastly, the Alternative Minimum Tax (AMT) can significantly alter your after tax investment returns, but they get very complicated and if AMT applies to you that is a conversation for you and your tax professional. Here is more information on the AMT: http://en.wikipedia.org/wiki/Alternative _minimum_tax

Where to Start?

We are going to start with a discussion about the IRS 1040 Form. This is the main form you file for your personal income taxes and allows us to determine the value of tax "write-offs" or "taxable losses" or "tax shields" and how they apply to you based on the marginal tax bracket within which your income falls.

Those write-offs and/or losses can significantly enhance your investment returns, or they can do nothing for you. That depends on a lot of factors and you will understand how that works when you are done with this chapter.

Personal Residence or Rentals/Business Property?

We always have to look at the tax picture as to whether it is a Personal Residence Property and therefore you receive a Personal Itemized Deduction on your IRS Schedule A which ends up on IRS 1040 Form line 40 – or whether it is a Rental Real Estate Loss or Income which ends up on you Schedule E and then to your IRS 1040 Form line 17.

1040 Form

First we will cover the 1040 form and how simple it is to understand for the vast majority of filers. The instructions will detail how this form works. The important thing to understand is that the 1040 form is a reconciliation of what taxes you owe for the past year versus how much money you paid in – a.ka. had withheld from your paychecks - in the past year.

Schedule A – Primary Residence Personal Itemized Deduction for Expenses the IRS allows You to Deduct Against your Normal Salary or Wages Income.

After we tackle the 1040 Form, we will work on Schedule A – Personal Itemized Deductions. We will learn how expenses related to your ownership of your personal residence (i.e. interest expense on your mortgage and property taxes paid to the state) can "shield" or "cram down" or "reduce" your Taxable Income (1040 Form line 43) – which reduces the amount of Tax (1040 Form line 44) you have to pay.

Schedule E – Rental Property Income or Losses on the Financial Operations of the Investment You Have Made.

Once you have mastered how Schedule A Itemized Deductions reduce the FIT Tax (1040 Form line 44) you pay by "shielding" or "cramming down" your Taxable Income, it will be easy to understand how Losses on real estate can also "cram down" your Taxable Income and hence the taxes you pay – subject to some limitations.

The important thing to understand is that by owning real estate you can reduce the FIT you pay, so that cash stays in your bank account instead of being paid to the IRS, and we treat that like a cash inflow because the reason you have that additional "cash flow" is because you acquired real estate.

Lastly, you should never make real estate investment decisions solely due to tax reasons, you need to look at all the factors – cash flows, risk, taxes, etc. – and make your investment decision on all the best information you have available after doing your due diligence.

IRS 1040 Form - Let's get started learning the IRS 1040 Form Package of 11 Pages. Slowly and meticulously work through the instructions while reviewing the noted documents. Take your time. This is not complicated as long as you read carefully and follow the instructions and numbers on the form.

All the learning packages take 20-40 seconds to load ON THE WEBSITE because they are large files.

ALL THREE LEARNING PACKAGES AND MARGINAL TAX RATES MEMORANDUM WILL NEED TO BE PRINTED OFF THE WEBSITE IN CHAPTER 6 AS THEY NEED TO BE SET SIDE BY SIDE FOR REVIEW AND TO LEARN

So go to www.ProfessorBaron.com and please print out the: IRS 1040 Form Learning Package.

IRS Schedule A 1040 Form

Once you understand the IRS 1040 Form, print out the Schedule A Package of 7 Pages. On the site is a short video to get your started - Write-Offs Video. This may not explain everything, but when you are done with this chapter you will know more than Jerry and Kramer do.

ALL THREE LEARNING PACKAGES AND MARGINAL TAX RATES MEMORANDUM WILL NEED TO BE PRINTED OFF THE WEBSITE IN CHAPTER 6 AS THEY NEED TO BE SET SIDE BY SIDE FOR REVIEW AND TO LEARN

Please print out the: Schedule A Form Learning Package.

After you understand the concepts in the Schedule A Form Learning Package like how Itemized Deductions reduce your Taxable Income and hence your taxes, you are in great shape!

MARGINAL TAX RATES

Let's take a break here before we move on to how Taxes Impact our cash flows on Rental Real Estate – Schedule E. Before we move to schedule E we need to learn and understand how MARGINAL TAX RATES work, so that is **how the LAST dollar of income you earn each year is taxed and at what percentage rate.** That rate of tax on your last dollar earned is your "marginal tax rate".

And your actual cash tax savings you receive by using personal residence interest deductions - the $18,000 - and property taxes deductions - the $4,125 - is the amount you are shielding/deducting multiplied by your Marginal Tax Rate. So if your highest marginal tax rate is 25% and you had $18,000 in interest expense deductions against your income, your tax savings would be $18,000 X 25% or $4,500 big ones! Nice!

ALL THREE LEARNING PACKAGES AND MARGINAL TAX RATES MEMORANDUM WILL NEED TO BE PRINTED OFF THE WEBSITE IN CHAPTER 6 AS THEY NEED TO BE SET SIDE BY SIDE FOR REVIEW AND TO LEARN

Click on this Article – <u>How Marginal Tax Rates Work</u> to learn this concept.

You can see the <u>Actual IRS Tax Brackets herein</u>. Click here.

PERSONAL RESIDENCE BUYERS: If you are just buying a personal residence, not an investment property, this is probably enough about taxes for you to learn for now. Except if you are in process of or going to sell your personal residence and of course want to exclude your gain from being taxed. If that is the case, read the Taxable Gains Deferring and Excluding section below.

If you are buying investment property, now comes the most important part of understanding How Taxes Impact your Investment Returns!

IRS Schedule E 1040 Form

You should now have an understanding of how deductions or write-offs reduce your taxable income and hence your taxes. You can also reduce your taxable income with real estate losses, which most properties are going to have for the first few years of ownership. We are about to learn about Passive Activity Income and Losses and how they reduce our taxable income and taxes. This is a little more complicated for novices, but you now know more than most so a little more studying and hard work and you will master the concept.

ALL THREE LEARNING PACKAGES AND MARGINAL TAX RATES MEMORANDUM WILL NEED TO BE PRINTED OFF THE WEBSITE IN CHAPTER 6 AS THEY NEED TO BE SET SIDE BY SIDE FOR REVIEW AND TO LEARN

Please print out the: Schedule E Form Learning Package.

Once you are done with the Schedule E Form Learning Package, it is time to put all the pieces together for doing your rental real estate cash flow analysis on an after tax basis.

The most important item that you should have already learned from this chapter is how Marginal Tax Rates work – because that is the basis for distinguishing your after-tax investment returns against returns on other types of investments and for different investors in different tax situations. If you do not have a solid grasp on Marginal Tax Brackets and how to calculate which one your income falls within and how you use deductions and/or losses to shield income, read and learn the above sections again before you move on to the spreadsheet analysis and workings.

AFTER Tax Calculation Spreadsheet

Now we are going to move to a more complicated spreadsheet. This spreadsheet will allow us to pencil out our After Tax Impacts returns on investing in Rental Real Estate. Instructions are below and again we try to make this straightforward, but you will need to invest some time in this exercise. Some people just use the Chapter 3 basic spreadsheet instead of going this far - and that is perfectly fine. But if you want to get more in depth on calculating your investment returns including your tax impacts, this spreadsheet will be a big help.

The most important issues in going from the Chapter 3 Pre-Tax Analysis to this After Tax Cash Flow (ATCF) analysis is that this incorporates depreciation, marginal tax rates, deductibility of mortgage interest and property tax payments to get to an ATCF investment return that one can earn incorporating those tax impacts. Again, taxes can make a significant difference in your investment returns.

Make sure to always review your spreadsheet for reasonableness once you have input your numbers. It is your responsibility to make sure that when you use someone else's spreadsheet you still review for errors and confirm to yourself that the numbers and calculations are accurate, reasonable and make sense.

Go ahead and download the After-Tax Cash Flows Spreadsheet and the ATCF Spreadsheet Instructions for your use and carefully and slowly run through the instructions and spreadsheet before inputting your own numbers.

CALCULATE BY HAND? It is just too time consuming and prone to errors. We suggest either to stick with the Chapter 3 spreadsheets by hand for your analysis or learn how to use spreadsheets or find someone who can assist you.

Spreadsheet at end of chapter.

USE THE CHAPTER 3 SIMPLE SPREADSHEETS OR THE CHAPTER 6 MORE COMPLEX SPREADSHEETS?

Going forward you can decide whether you want to use the Chapter 3 Pre-Tax or the Chapter 6 – After-Tax spreadsheet, or BOTH for helping you make better investment decisions. Either way, you are light years ahead of most real estate investors just by the simple fact that you are going to pencil out your returns with REASONABLE and CONSERVATIVE estimates of rental revenue and expenses. You are really doing your due diligence and are going to make yourself into a really good long term real estate investor. Nice job!

SALE OF REAL ESTATE FOR TAX PURPOSES

We are going to discuss a few other items herein but for any of these - **YOU NEED TO DISCUSS WITH A CPA, TAX ATTORNEY OR COMPETENT TAX ADVISOR LONG BEFORE YOU ACTUALLY DO ANY TRANSACTIONS OR IT COULD COST YOU A LOT OF MONEY IF YOU DO NOT DO THINGS PROPERLY.**

1031 Exchange for Rental Properties – Deferring your Gain to Avoid Paying Taxes

If you own a rental property and you want to sell that property, you will have to pay taxes on the Capital Gain from the sale of that property. So that is the difference between what you sell the property for and the adjusted basis. Adjusted basis is the price you paid less any Depreciation expense you have taken over the years. Let's say you sell a property for $500,000 and your adjusted basis is $250,000. You have a Capital Gain of $250,000. You will be taxed on that amount.

You can defer (that means not pay) taxes on the sale by doing something called an IRS 1031 Exchange. The general premise is that if you sell the rental property for $500,000 and buy another rental property for at least $500,000 you can defer the gain and not pay taxes on that gain. Somewhere down the road when you decide to sell the property and get out of real estate altogether, you will have a big tax bill from all those deferrals. But that day may never come if you keep doing 1031 Exchanges.

The general rule is that you sell the first property and within 45 days you need to identify the replacement property and close escrow on that identified property within 180 days. But it can be less than 180 days and it gets very tricky, so very quickly. Get some good tax advice long before you plan to try this because it takes some planning. You can find lots more information at IPX Exchange which is one of the nation's largest exchange services providers. Consult a tax advisor.

Two issues – If you do not identify your properties within that 45 days and close upon them in the 180 days - or shorter period depending on when your tax returns are due - the exchange may fail and you will lose your tax deferment. You need to move quickly and should try to have the properties you are ready to buy under contract before you close escrow on the property you are selling – time goes quickly in real estate!

Exchange Company – Use a large national exchange company with sufficient insurance. Some smaller companies in the past years have absconded with exchanger's funds, leaving the exchanger with losses on the funds plus failed exchanges. So do your due diligence on the exchange company and stick with a national provider.

Primary Residence Sale Tax Free Exclusion – IRS Section 121 Exclusion

Your personal residence is also subject to Capital Gains when you sell the property, but the IRS gives us a break. If you have lived in the property as your personal residence for two of the last five years, you can exclude a gain on sale of up to $500,000 ($250,000 for singles) from being subject to taxation. So you sell your residence for $300,000 and you had paid $50,000 decades ago. Normally you would have a $250,000 taxable gain but you can exclude, so not pay any taxes, on that gain. Consult a tax advisor.

FOR ALL TAX ITEMS AND ISSUES, CONSULT A TAX ADVISOR WELL IN ADVANCE OF DOING ANY REAL ESTATE TRANSACTIONS, IT IS MONEY WELL SPENT!

THE AFTER TAX CASH FLOWS SPREADSHEET IS SHOWN NEXT. HOWEVER, YOU NEED TO LOG ONTO THE WEBSITE AND DOWNLOAD ALL THESE:

1040 FORM Learning Package, SCHEDULE A Learning Package, SCHEDULE E Learning Package, MARGINAL TAX RATES MEMORANDUM, AFTER TAX CASH FLOWS SPREADSHEET
AFTER TAX INSTRUCTIONS - - THIS WILL MAKE IT MUCH EASIER TO LEARN. IT IS NOT COMPLICATED, BUT YOU NEED TO TAKE YOUR TIME AND READ THE INSTRCTIONS AS YOU RUN THROUGH THE PACKAGES.

ProfessorBaron.com
For all Your Due Diligence Needs
Rental Property Pre-Tax and After-Tax Analysis
ANNUAL ESTIMATES PRO-FORMA STATEMENT

A Smarter
Way to Buy
Real Estate

Box 1 - Purchase Information		
Units		1
Purchase Price	$	200,000
Closing Costs		4,500
Rehabilitation Costs		3,500
Total Costs	$	208,000

Box 2 - Financing Information			
1st Mortgage (% Price)	75.00%	$	**150,000**
Cash Equity - Downpayment, Closing and Rehab Costs		$	58,000
Interest Rate 1st Mortgage			6.000%
Loan Amortization Years (If Interest Only Input 1000)			30
Annual Mortgage Payment		$	10,897
Annual Interest Year One (See Amortization Worksheet - TAB 2)		$	9,000

Box 3 - PropertyTax Rates, Rev/Exp Increases, Investor Marginal Tax Rate		
Property Taxes Year One (Amount Depends on State Rules)	$	2,200
Property Taxes Inc. per Year - Estimated		1.50%
Rent Increases/Expense Increases - per Year		2.50%
Investor Marginal Tax Rate		25.00%

Box 4 - Rental Unit Information			
MONTHLY & ANNUAL RENTS			
Type ?	# of Units	Rent per MONTH	Total Rent
1BR 1BA	1	$ 1,700	1,700
2BR 1BA	0	$ -	-
2BR 2BA	0	$ -	-
		TOTAL Monthly Rents	$ 1,700
		TOTAL Annual Rents	$ 20,400

Box 5 - Depreciable Basis Calculation		
Depreciable Basis Percentage		80.00%
(Building Value as % of Purchase Price)		
Property Cost	$	200,000
Building Value of Property Cost	$	160,000
Depreciation Years (per IRS code)		27.5
Depreciation Amount per Year	$	5,818

NUMBERS BELOW ARE ANNUAL FIGURES - NOT MONTHLY

Box 6 - Schedule of Cash Flows		Year 1	Year 2	Year 3	Year 4	Year 5	Year 6
Potential Gross Rent	$	20,400	$ 20,910	$ 21,433	$ 21,969	$ 22,518	$ 23,081
Laundry or Other Income		-	-	-	-	-	-
Vacancy & Collection Lo	0.00%	-	-	-	-	-	-
Effective Gross Rent		20,400	20,910	21,433	21,969	22,518	23,081
Expenses:							
Management	0.00%	-	-	-	-	-	-
Insurance		400	410	420	431	442	453
Maintenance/Repairs/Other		1,200	1,230	1,261	1,292	1,325	1,358
HOA Fees (if Any)		3,600	3,690	3,782	3,877	3,974	4,073
Miscellaneous/Lawncare/Utilities		-	-	-	-	-	-
Property Taxes (Check Actual Property Tax Rate/Amounts)		2,200	2,233	2,266	2,300	2,335	2,370
Total Expenses		7,400	7,563	7,730	7,900	8,075	8,253
Net Operating Income	$	13,000	$ 13,347	$ 13,703	$ 14,068	$ 14,443	$ 14,827

Box 7 - OR CALCULATING INCOME TAXES:							
Net Operating Income	$	13,000	$ 13,347	$ 13,703	$ 14,068	$ 14,443	$ 14,827
1st Mortgage Interest (ONLY Interest Portion of Payment)		9,000	8,886	8,765	8,638	8,502	8,358
(See Amortization Worksheet and Instructions)							
Depreciation NON - CASH EXPENSE		5,818	5,818	5,818	5,818	5,818	5,818
Points/Closing Costs Total		-					
Net Pretax (Loss) Income		(1,818)	(1,357)	(881)	(388)	123	651
- 1040 Schedule E							

Box 8 - FOR CASH FLOWS:							
Net Operating Income (Starts again with NOI from Above)	$	13,000	$ 13,347	$ 13,703	$ 14,068	$ 14,443	$ 14,827
1st Mortgage Payment (Principal and Interest Portions)		10,897	10,897	10,897	10,897	10,897	10,897
PRETAX CASH FLOWS	$	2,103	$ 2,450	$ 2,806	$ 3,171	$ 3,546	$ 3,930
Tax Savings/(Owed)	25.00%	455	339	220	97	(31)	(163)
NET AFTER TAX CASH FLOWS	(58,000) $	2,557	$ 2,789	$ 3,026	$ 3,268	$ 3,515	$ 3,767
Cash on Cash Returns **		4.41%	4.81%	5.22%	5.63%	6.06%	6.50%

** This does not include increased equity from 1. appreciation in value or 2. from paying down a portion of your mortgage via each mortgage payment

Source: ProfessorBaron.com - A Smarter Way to Buy Real Estate

CHAPTER 7

MORTGAGE FINANCING FOR PROPERTY

Mortgage financing is another critical part of your real estate acquisition process. Most of the time when people buy property they will borrow money from a bank to fund a portion of their purchase price. This borrowing is commonly known as a mortgage. For example, if you buy a $100,000 townhome the bank might loan you 80% - $80,000, 90% - $90,000 or up to 96.5% - $96,500 of the purchase price. You would then add your own cash from your savings to come up with the total amount of money needed to fund the entire purchase price and closing costs. Your income, credit history, asset base and bank lending criteria will impact the percentage of the purchase price that you can borrow.

The availability of financing and how much you can finance is the first item you need to determine in starting the real estate buying process. And financing has become much more difficult the past few years, but normal loans still available qualified borrowers at very reasonable terms.

We are going to cover the basics on residential financing, how the process works, some tips on better protecting yourself and finding a fair deal on your mortgage. We will also provide many examples of the now highly standardized mortgage documents you will be signing so that you can review and understand them before you are actually going through the process of buying property. Usually you first see these just a few days before you close escrow on your property but you really should understand them beforehand.

This chapter is also written for a typical borrower who can go to a mortgage broker, credit union or bank and has sufficient income, a satisfactory credit score, and enough assets to secure traditional mortgage financing. If you do not have the income level needed to borrow money, have credit issues, or do not have a downpayment, or your parents will not gift you a downpayment, you realistically are probably not going to be able to get normal and reasonable financing to buy property in today's marketplace. If this is the case and you want to own real estate, you should still go to a lender or mortgage broker and find out what you need to do so that in two to four years you hopefully will be credit worthy enough to start buying property.

Note: FHA loans are available and you only need 3.5% down for owner occupied housing. It may make sense to pursue the FHA avenue for a mortgage. Talk to your mortgage lender.

For those of you who want to own real estate and are qualified to obtain financing, this chapter will teach you the basics, how you can better protect yourself, and some tips and techniques to help you better obtain a reasonable deal on a mortgage financing. Overall the complex lending process makes it very difficult to shop for the best rate and terms, however we just want to make sure you understand the process and get a FAIR deal on your loan.

So understanding the process will be your first step and we have other tips and information here that will help you find that reasonable mortgage loan deal!

GENERAL ITEMS

HOW MUCH CAN YOU FINANCE? The first thing you need to do is get to a mortgage professional to determine the amount of money you can borrow to buy real estate and hence the maximum property purchase price you can afford. The lender will evaluate your income, assets, credit score, property type – house, condo, apartments, loan purpose – owner occupied or non-owner occupied investor to determine this amount. This could be a mortgage broker, a bank lending officer, credit union, online lender, or any other home lender. They will then use all your information to estimate your borrowing potential. This will help you determine the amount you can afford so you can shop for properties in neighborhoods that are in your price range.

However, do not forget that regardless of how much a lender says you can borrow, you need to make sure your housing payments are an amount that you can pay each month. So really the question you need to ask is how much can you afford for housing and still comfortably pay your other bills if this is a personal residence. For investment property, the question is will the rent comfortably cover all the expenses – mortgage, property taxes, HOA fees, insurance, maintenance?

SHOPPING LENDERS - You should shop or "get qualified" with more than one lender. So get some referrals from a friend or real estate agent or stop by a local financial institution and fill out an application for a mortgage. The whole lending process for a lending professional is highly complicated and nowadays an unbelievable amount of work for them. It is also easy for a lending agent to really mess up the process and cause you considerable delay and issues. So we suggest you pick an experienced lender, hopefully from referrals, that you believe is competent and you can trust. It will make your life a lot easier as you focus on the other highly important due diligence tasks in your buying process.

Make sure to get a standardized document from the lender called a Good Faith Estimate – GFE Example – click here - of the estimated Rate, Points, and Closing Fees that you will incur on the loan. This will allow you to do a little comparison shopping of rate and terms for your loan. To simplify the parts and understand it better – See article (which is big so may take 30 seconds to download from site) on Dissecting GFE Closing Costs to Comparison Shop – click here. These documents are complex and confusing and we will try to help you dissect them but it is going to take some work on your part. We suggest that you try to get a fair deal by obtaining at least two bids and then pick the lender you believe will be fair and move forward with that lender. Trying to keep two lenders "bidding" all the way to closing, to maybe save a little, is going to take a LOT of energy and effort that may be better spent focusing on completing other due diligence tasks.

Article: Dissecting GFE Closing Costs to Comparison Shop
(You will want to print out the GFE above and the GFE Charges Worksheet from the Website to best learn this information).

Dissecting a Good Faith Estimate

This is another tough and time consuming task in the real estate process. The new federally mandated GFE, new in 2010, is supposed to be more clear for consumers to understand. We believe it is easier to understand then how the space shuttle works, but it really is not easy for consumers to understand. Part of that is simply the overall process is complicated. But we are going to try to help.

Go ahead and print out the 5 page GFE on the website to review as you review this memorandum.

We are going to start by telling you the main risk you have on loans and then we will work from there dissecting the GFE. We are trying to make this relatively straightforward so you get a FAIR deal on your loan.

Again, for purchasing we suggest you interview at least two lenders and get quotes of costs to finance. A lender probably will not give you a GFE until you have a specific property under contract, but they should give you an Initial Fees Worksheet like page 5 in the GFE example in Chapter 7 – Mortgage Financing. The Initial Fees will effectively flow into the GFE they give you once you have a property under contract. In this memorandum we detail how to dissect a GFE. Once you dissect the GFEs you get and review them, make your best choice and move forward with your loan.

Quick Note – Unfortunately the GFE does NOT tell you your monthly total payment will be or the amount of cash you need to close. So ask your lender to sort out these approximate numbers for you off the GFE and other costs not listed on the GFE – like property taxes pro-rations, monthly impound charges, etc.

YOUR MAIN RISK

These risks have also dramatically decreased recently due to tightened regulation, but they can still exist and you do not want to be the one who gets a bum deal.

When you get **qualified for a loan**, the lending professional collects information from you – income, assets, credit score, downpayment – and determines what lending "program" you are qualified for. The best credit risk people get the top program which gives a borrower the lowest interest rate. Really the lowest rate and loan origination points combination – see this in the Chapter on Rate Vs. Points analysis. The lower your credit score, the higher the interest rate you receive, which is reasonable because you are a higher credit risk. Although in general there is not much mortgage financing money available these days for people with lower credit scores, under 620 FICO score.

In the past, you might go into mortgage lender(s) and get qualified. The lender would input your information into their computer program to "rate" you for one of the loan programs. The lender may determine that you qualify for the best rate possible, let's say 5.0% interest rate on a 30 year amortizing loan at 1.0% loan origination point. However, if the lender is someone who is taking advantage of you, he or she looked you in the face and said, "Congratulations, you have qualified for a 30 year amortizing loan at the low rate of 7.0% interest at 1.0% loan origination point". And since you do not know any better, because you were too lazy to go get qualified by a second or third lending professional, you may think that rate is great because you can buy a home.

What we are saying is that an unscrupulous loan officer might attempt to lock you into you a higher interest rate and/or greater fees/loan origination points then you deserve.

This was and still can be the biggest risk you have on doing mortgage financing. The reason a lending agent would do this is because part of their compensation for doing a loan is from two items:

1. Your paying some amount of upfront loan origination or discount points - 1 Point = 1.0% of the loan amount.

2. From a "commission" back from the bank for whom they work. A kind of rebate if you will, called a Yield Spread Premium (disclosed by a mortgage broker) or Service Release Premium (NOT disclosed by a direct

lender or bank). Large national banks, as opposed to private mortgage lenders or brokers, do not use those terms – but they do get the YSPs or SRPs).

There is nothing wrong with these rebates or commissions. In fact if you do a zero points loan or no points loan, the lender gets this rebate from the bank as their primary compensation.

Here is the problem. If you are qualified for the 5.0% loan at 1.0% point, the lender may get back 0.5% or one-half point from the bank as a rebate – again that is fine they basically are charging you a total fee of 1.5% (1.0% loan origination fee plus 0.5% rebate). Nothing wrong with that and that may be fair. However, if you are qualified at 5.0% and 1.0% points, but they tell you and you accept that you are qualified for that 7.0% rate at 1.0% points, and they close the loan with locking you into a 7.0% loan, they are going to get a huge commission back from the bank where they work. And that is not fair if you deserve a lower rate.

Note: As of April 1, 2011, due to new federal laws these rebates are supposed to not be allowed any longer. That might also mean no more "no closing cost" loans will be available. We will all find out together how this rule ends up being applied in the marketplace.

How do you Protect Yourself?

The way you can best protect yourself is to get GFEs from two different lenders to make sure the rate and point combinations are close. There may be several rate and point combinations as noted in this chapter under Rate vs. Points Analysis and picking the best one is a separate issue and task detailed there. But you want to review that both lenders seem in line – not exact, but close. And don't necessarily pick the lowest if they are close, you need to dissect the entire GFE to look at all the costs, charges, points and fees and the rate so you can make the best choice. If one quotes a very high interest rate and one is lower and the costs for both are similar, pick the one with the lower rate and points combination and move forward. Common sense here.

Beware when comparing the GFE of a broker to a direct lender or bank. Since banks do not disclose service release premiums, their quotes can be misleading with artificially low costs. Just dissect and look at overall how much you will pay for the interest rate you get on your loan.

Also, when you are going to get initially qualified, the lender may give you only an Initial Fees Worksheet with an interest rate and points estimate. You are probably just starting the purchasing process. Interest rates change every hour, so the rate and points estimate on the GFE will most likely not be the same a month or months later when you have a property under contract and you are ready to "lock" in your loan rate and terms. When you do lock, make sure the rate and points are still relatively similar to what you originally were given in the GFE. And get that lock rate, terms, points, lock period, in writing or email.

Those rates may have changed slightly, but unless there is a severe interest rate change in the financial markets, they should be similar (within a ¼ point interest rate or so). If they are not close, your lender should be able to explain why they have changed. And really you are pretty much out of options at this point because it will most likely be too late to try to get other quotes – that is why you also try to pick someone from references and you believe you can trust so at the rate lock you are getting a FAIR deal.

GFE Dissecting

Moving forward, your GFE is a summary of all the financial and non-financing terms that may govern your life for the next couple of decades. It is in plain English for the most part and it will be the same as the example in the chapter. So print that example out, get a cup of coffee, and read those three pages so you understand the non-financial terms, like in the "Summary of Your Loan" section. Read the entire document.

The other piece of the lending process is making sure that all the points, fees and costs of borrowing money are in line with the marketplace and other lenders. The way to do this is to analyze your GFE statements that you obtained and break out the parts so you can focus on the important charges where there is the biggest risk of extra fees.

The new GFE, page 2, has sections A and B with 11 numbered categories of charges.

We break the GFE down into three types of charges based on the 11 categories – use our attached worksheet to dissect. This is how you focus on the important costs.

1. COSTS THE SAME REGARDLESS (Worksheet LEFT column) or nothing you can do about the cost. These costs and charges that are pretty much the same regardless and you generally need not worry about because you just have to pay whatever they are. These would be charges like #10. Daily interest charges – these can change dramatically depending on the size of the loan and the day upon which you close escrow, but they are going to be calculated the same regardless of who makes the calculation. You can't get overcharged on these (unless escrow incorrectly calculates it – very very rare) as they are what they are, you pay the pro-rated interest, taxes, insurance, HOA fees amount when you close regardless.

Let's look at an example to illustrate why separating these above **"COSTS THE SAME REGARDLESS"** out from the rest of your costs will help you make better decisions.

Let's say you get a property under contract and you get to GFE bids from two lenders so you can pick one to move forward with on your purchase. Both qualify you and give you a GFE that has TOTAL estimated closing costs - so A + B on the bottom or pages 1 and 2 on your GFE - of $12,205.89 (go ahead and look at the example GFE in the chapter and the numbers will match) and an interest rate of 5.0% on your 30 year amortizing loan. So you just look at the total, you don't break out the costs by section, and you pick one of the lenders because the GFE shows both charge the total same amount. But do they really charge the same amount? You don't know unless you break out the costs. Here's why.

Let's look at #5 Owner's title insurance for $1,175. This amount, when added with all the others, comes up to the $12,205.89 total (A + B on GFE). However, this $1,175 may not even be paid by you, it is usually paid by the seller – so who cares! But upon closer inspection Lender #1 estimates it at the $1,175 and Lender #2 at $500 (this Lender #2 is a fictional illustration for example purposes only). And all the totals still add up to the $12,205.89. So Lender #2 has $675 of additional costs in his quote somewhere – and they may be the costs you actually do have to pay, unlike the #5 item herein that you don't pay. So by not breaking down the costs, you cannot properly analyze the costs.

Note: Why the government requires your lender to put a fee #5 on your estimate statement if it isn't even paid by you is a mystery to us, just ridiculous. But nonetheless, it is required! However, while this is customary in some states it may be different where you are buying property so discuss this with your lender and real estate professional.

And there are also amounts on the GFE that either you simply have to pay because the seller picks them and you have no choice, or they are pro-rations of items like #10 interest that regardless of what it shows on the GFE. The escrow agent, who is neutral to the transaction, calculates these fees per the contract agreement and you just pay whatever they are. There is no negotiation and they would be the same in the transaction regardless. We considered trying to explain how the interest pro-rations work but it is complicated and you need to discuss with you lender. The important issue is that the interest calculation IS WHAT IT IS and as long as the escrow agent calculated it correctly you just pay it.

In summary, you need to split off the costs above, which you use our worksheet to do, and you don't need to focus on those costs because they either are not paid by you, are required by the seller, or are pro-rations that you pay whatever the amount is calculated on the closing date.

More importantly:

2. COSTS YOU CAN GET BIDS UPON (MIDDLE Column)– Focus on the larger costs if you want to try and get bids, like the title policy, escrow costs, or insurance costs. These costs you can shop for or at least question and get the best price, or at least get a comfortable feeling that they are in line with market. This is items like GFE # 11. Homeowner's Insurance, GFE # 6. Required Services that you can shop for like Home Warranty and Transaction coordinators, or GFE # 4. Title Services. This will be time consuming, so you need to think thorough whether or not it is worthwhile to pursue or just accept the proposed charges. The bigger the cost, the more worthwhile it is to review and maybe get a bid. These service providers for escrow and title were probably selected by your real estate agent or the seller's agent, but your agent does not earn monies on these. So ask them questions on why they picked these service providers and if it is worthwhile to get some other quotes. Don't waste your time chasing small dollar amounts. My grandma Weezie always said, "Don't bend over to pick up a penny when a $10 bill is floating by in the wind!"

- The above amounts are also separated on our worksheet when you transfer your GFE expenses to the worksheet, middle column, below.

3. COSTS TO LOOK AT CLOSER BELOW (RIGHT column)- Costs and charges from the broker, lender, or bank that you should request to see in detail on the Initial Fees Worksheet – included with GFE Example – section 800. Herein you want to separate the summation of lines 801-802 from the summation of lines 803–813. The biggest risk again here is that you will be put into a much higher interest rate loan, or higher points, or both than the rate you are qualified to receive. Some lenders may not do these Initial Fees Worksheets, but what you want is a breakdown of the new GFE Section A numbers 1 and 2. Example below:

See example on Website and Print out PDF "GFE Charges Worksheet" on Website

So print out the GFE Charges Worksheet, get qualified and a GFE from a lender (like page 2 GFE example in the chapter) and read the notes with each of the 11 sections.

AGAIN, THIS IS A LOT OF WORK TO DO AS YOU CAN SEE. SO READ AND STUDY AND TRY TO PICK THE LENDER YOU THINK YOU CAN TRUST AND GET YOU A FAIR DEAL. THEN SPEND YOUR TIME ON THE MORE IMPORTANT DUE DILIGENCE TASKS – LIKE EVERYTHING!

A Smarter Way to Buy Real Estate

TRANSFER THE NUMBERS FROM YOUR GFE TO THIS WORKSHEET

THIS IS FOR CALIFORNIA - OTHER STATES MAY BE DIFFERENT SO THIS IS JUST A GUIDE
ASK YOU REALTOR LOTS OF QUESTIONS AND FOR HELP - THE REALTOR IS ON YOUR SIDE!

Category Number	COSTS THE SAME REGARDLESS JUST REVIEW FOR REASONABLENESS AND PAY	YOU CAN BID ON THESE MAKE SURE IT IS WORTH THE TIME AND EFFORT	CLOSER REVIEW NEEDED MAKE SURE YOUR INTEREST RATE IS REASONABLE FOR THE POINTS YOU ARE PAYING
1 Your Origination Charge This is all the section 800 charges from the Dissecting a GFE article. Items 801-802 are your points. that you agreed to pay on the loan, are they reasonable compared to the other bid? Again, you just don't want 7.0% interest at 1.0% point when qualified for 5.0% at 1.0% points. **Total 801-802 plus or minus #2 below:** [ ] **Interest Rate for Paying 801&802 + #2** [ ]			[ ]
2 Your Credit or charge (points) Have your lender explain this. If you are paying extra, add it to 801-802. If you are being credited this amount, subtract it from 801-802. Then compare totals to other GFEs.			[ ]
3 Required Services We Select You have no choice here, so pay whatever they tell you to pay.	[ ]		
4 Title Services and Lender's Title Get a breakdown, you can get quotes for escrow and title policies…just to check pricing but probably not going to be too much and will be some work.		[ ]	
5 Owner's Title Insurance The seller pays for this, not you, so not an issue. Not sure why this is even on buyer's GFE - Big Gov't? This is in CA, may differ in your area, ask lender or agent!	[ ]		
6 Required Services You Shop For		[ ]	
7 Government Recording Charges You pay same regardless, so not an issue.	[ ]		
8 Transfer Taxes Paid by Seller typically in CA. Ask agent or lender.	[ ]		
9 Intial Deposit for Escrow If you are escrowing taxes and insurance this is it and it is the same regardless - so not an issue.	[ ]		
10 Daily Interest Charges Recalculated from original GFE to your exact closing date but recalculation is same regardless so not an issue.	[ ]		
11 Homeowner's Insurance You can, and should get some bids for this. Don't underinsure, but don't overinsure either!		[ ]	

End of Article: Dissecting Your GFE

REFINANCING - If you are refinancing, you have more time and less due diligence tasks, but in a purchase transaction you are going to be swamped with work so go for the fair deal with the lender you are confident can get the loan funded. Be cautious of advertisements for no fee or low fee loans. This just means you are going to have to pay a higher interest rate on your loan. If it sounds too good to be true it probably is! However, no fee or low fee deals may be perfectly fine as long as you properly analyze your options and compare those deals to other lenders' deals. See the Points vs. Rate Comparison information below for more help with this.

PRE-QUALIFICATION LETTERS TO STRENGTHEN YOUR OFFER - As a part of determining your borrowing ability, get Pre-Qualified or Pre-Approved by at least one lender which includes pulling a credit report for you and anyone else who will be buying the property with you. Many times the seller of a property will require that a Pre-Qualification letter (<= click on this to see an example) from your lender be submitted to them stating that you can afford the property that you are offering upon. Even if the seller does not require this letter, including one will make your offer more persuasive and that means a better chance the seller will select your offer over other offers.

So you need to have your lender ready to quickly draft and provide this letter to your agent when you are ready to submit offers on properties. In conjunction with this, keep all your loan documentation ready because on some properties the seller, usually when a bank is involved, will want you to get pre-qualified with THEIR preferred lender in order for them to look at your purchase offer. Ultimately, you can use whomever you wish to provide your mortgage financing, but you need to comply with the seller's requirements if you want your offer considered on their property.

Note: Regarding having all documentation ready as some sellers may want you to qualify with their lenders – get a copy of your credit report from your lender - even though they are not supposed to give you this - to give to the lenders where the seller requires you get qualified with THEIR preferred lender. Some preferred lenders will accept and review a copy provided by you but some will tell you that they need to pull their own original credit report from the credit reporting agencies. If they will accept the copy you provide, that will mean less "inquiries" on your credit report. Credit report inquiries from different lenders for the same type of loan will not impact your credit score if done in a short period of time.

However, if you make offers on properties each month, different lenders pulling credit reports each month can negatively impact your score. If a preferred lender for a specific property wants an original credit report, you or your real estate agent can explain this potential detrimental impact on your score to a preferred lender and that may sway them to accept your copy. The problem is that if you originally had a lender qualify you and your credit score was 720 few months ago and the loan you were qualified for required a minimum 720 score, then you have several inquiries over many months and your score drops to 719, you may not qualify for the original loan any longer. This could mean either a higher interest rate, or more downpayment, or no loan. Just be careful here as it is a difficult financing environment.

NOTE, Do not apply for new credit to buy cars, furniture, sign up for a gym membership, or add debt payments to your credit profile or forget to pay bills – any of them - until AFTER your property and loan close escrow – any of these actions could cause your loan to be rejected at the last minute. Remember, your lender may pull a final credit report at the time your loan funds to look for new debt payments, credit inquiries, or recent derogatory credit remarks.

LENDING PROCESS

This is just the lending portion of your due diligence process. Use the Due Diligence Checklist to make sure all the other due diligence items like home inspection, HOA analysis, title insurance exclusions review are simultaneously being investigated, analyzed, and cleared.

1. Get Qualified so you know what you can afford – make an application so submit your documentation and ask your lender if you can be pre-approved.
2. Go Shopping and make offers on properties.
3. Property Under Contract and In Escrow - Underwriting of loan begins by lender.
4. Pay for Appraisal.
5. Lock Rate and Terms and do Points vs. Rate analysis.
6. Underwriting moves forward - clear all outstanding lender conditions and Bank approves loan.
7. Review Estimated closing statement against your GFE.
8. Sign Loan and Property Documents.
9. Wire in your funds.
10. Bank wires in Its funds.
11. Title Transfers to You – Deed and Deed of Trust (or Mortgage) Recorded at Courthouse and are in the county land records.
12. You can now take possession of your property.

1. GET QUALIFIED – The first step is to get qualified for how much money you can borrow on a mortgage loan. The lender and you will fill out the standardized Uniform Residential Loan Application (<= click on this to see the application). All the banks, lenders, mortgage brokers, etc. use this standardized form because it allows standardization in mortgage origination and underwriting. You need to know the information on this URLA application is what your lender uses to determine your creditworthiness and how much you can borrow to buy properties. The application has ten parts that you fill in and covers the type of mortgage, property information, borrower information, employment information, income and expense information, assets and liabilities, details of the transaction, and declarations by you. Go ahead and familiarize yourself with the document.

In the process of qualifying you for a certain loan amount and loan program, the lender will take the information you provide and verify this information with employment pay stubs, your credit report, tax returns, bank account statements and other documentation. This information is input this into their company's loan automated underwriting program and determine your loan options. Your loan evaluation (underwriting) will depend on your debt to income (DTI) ratio, credit history and "FICO score", your down payment amount, reserves (savings and investments) and other factors.

For example, assume that the underwriting guidelines for your loan require that you satisfy all three requirements as a start:

1. Debt To Income (DTI) maximum of 40.0%,
2. Property Loan to Value (LTV) maximum 80.0% - so downpayment of at least 20.0%, and,
3. FICO Credit score of at least 720.

Note: Your loan program, especially if owner occupant, may allow a smaller downpayment – discuss options and costs with your lender.

DTI - DEBT to INCOME - The lender's criteria may require that the maximum debt payment to gross income before taxes, this is your DTI, that you can have for a certain lending program is 40.0%. So, if you earn $72,000 per year or $6,000 per month, this means that maximum allowable total combined debt payments that you can have are $2,400 per month ($6,000 multiplied by 40.0% = $2,400) to qualify for this program.

And you will have to prove with pay stubs and tax returns that you earn $6,000 per month – no more liar's loans available – sorry Charlie!

So you have $2,400 available monthly capacity to service a new mortgage loan/housing expense – if you have no other debts. However, let's assume you have a $300 monthly car payment as your only other debt payment. So we first take out that $300 from the $2,400 and that leaves you with $2,100 available for housing expense. This $2,100 is the maximum that your monthly housing payment can be and you still be qualified for this loan program. Your housing payment is commonly referred to as your PITI – Principal, Interest, Taxes and Insurance and also includes any HOA fees, private mortgage insurance (PMI) and other monthly assessments on your property.

Let's say you want to buy a $200,000 condominium and you are going to make a downpayment of 20.0% or $40,000 so that you will have a loan of $160,000. Note: When you make at least 20.0% downpayment, no mortgage insurance is required. Will you be qualified to obtain this $160,000 of financing within that $2,100 allowable housing/mortgage expense?

This particular loan will have a payment (PI of the PITI) of $959.28 per month at the market rate of 6.0% interest on a thirty year amortizing loan. Say insurance will run $30 per month, county property taxes are $300 per month ($3,600 per year), and the HOA fee is $350 per month. If we add up all these monthly costs we get $1,639.28 ($959.28 + $30 + $300 + $350) which is well within your $2,100 allowable monthly housing expense. So your overall DTI is 35.0% (Debts of $1,639.28 housing plus $300 car = $1,939.28 divided by your $6,000 income).

This is well within the 40.0% allowable housing expense for this loan program so for this portion of your creditworthiness test, you are approved! This also assumes that your $6,000 per month income is from a steady source of income that will continue for the foreseeable future – like a good solid job where you have worked at least two years. Self employed borrowers and commissioned employees must show two years of stable income on tax returns plus provide a year to date statement of income for their business. But there is more needed to be qualified – read on!

LTV – LOAN TO VALUE – The loan program you select allows a maximum of 80.0% loan to the value of the property you are buying. LTV is determined by the loan amount divided by the lesser of the purchase price or appraised value. So you need to put down the other 20.0% of the purchase price in cash. To prove your creditworthiness for this loan program you must have saved the $40,000 downpayment, plus some closing costs funds, that you will use to make up the difference between what you are paying for the property $200,000 and how much the bank is lending you, $160,000 in this case.

So you need to prove that you have this money and that it is not borrowed from someone else. Depending on the loan program, your parents may be able to "gift" you a portion of this money too and you need to discuss this with your lender. The lender may also require that you have a few months reserves saved so in case you have unanticipated expenses at some point after you close on the property - like medical bills or repairs that decrease the money you have available to pay for housing. Let's say you have $80,000 in your bank account and you can show the lender that money has been there for at least three months, this should suffice and on this portion of the creditworthy test, you are also approved! But there is more, keep reading!

FICO – YOUR CREDIT SCORE – You also need to show the lender that you have a good history of making payments on other types of debts that you have incurred by paying on time, according to the loan terms. These include your car loan, student loan and payments on your credit cards and have always paid back those loans on schedule. Since you only have the car loan payment of $300, and if you have consistently paid on time and on terms of the loan you should be in good shape. Your credit report and credit score will reflect that you have good credit as long as you have paid loans on time, not filed bankruptcy, not been foreclosed upon and have not had lawsuit judgments secured against you. A company called Fair Issac generates the software that calculates your credit score and it is called a FICO score.

If your credit score is low but not by too much, you could pay off some bills or clear incorrect marks on your credit report and have your lender pull and updated credit report that may have a higher score. Talk to your lender regarding the course of action you should take to raise your FICO score. Sometimes it is called a Rapid Rescore and may cost up to $100. Be careful of credit repair companies that overpromise what they can do and charge fees upfront. They may be able to do some good, but there are generally no quick fixes for your credit report. **Do not expect <u>accurate negative credit history items</u> to be removed from your report.**

FICO scores range from 300-850 and an okay score is 660, a good score is 720, and anything over 740 is great. Let's say you have a 768 credit score which is excellent (<u>www.fico.com</u>). Nice job on always paying bills on time and not having too much debt!

So recall the loan program your lender is qualifying you for required those three important items:

1. Debt to Income (DTI) maximum of 40.0%,
2. Loan to Value (LTV) of maximum of 80.0%, and
3. Credit Score (FICO) of at Least 720.

You are qualified on all three of these items – great job, you should be able to buy a property that costs up to $200,000 and probably a little more since your DTI is only 35.0% and the program allows up to 40.0% DTI.

APPRAISAL - The last piece of the puzzle will be ensuring that the collateral, which is the property you buy, is worth at least as much as what you are paying for it. This is because if for some unfortunate reason you stop paying on your mortgage and the bank has to foreclose and take the property, they want to make sure it is worth enough money so that they can recover the money they have lent you for the mortgage – we will cover this below in the APPRAISAL information and in Chapter 17 – Appraisal Property Valuation.

2. WHILE YOU ARE SHOPPING FOR REAL ESTATE – Do not apply for new credit cards or other debt. Do not send your DTI over the allowed maximum by buying cars, furniture, gym memberships, etc. that could reduce your credit score or raise your DTI so that you no longer qualify for your loan. And don't forget to pay any bills like utility bills or cable bills!

Now that you know what amount you can finance, you can go shopping for real estate with your agent and make offers on properties. Keep in touch with your lender to get pre-qualification letters to submit with your offers and so you can get the process moving quickly once you are close to having a property under contract. It takes about 30-45 days to go through the whole loan process once you have a property under contract/in escrow. And you usually only have 45 days to close in the your purchase contract, so you need to respond to lender questions and provide additional information to keep the mortgage loan process moving along. In those 45 days, do not forget that you will also be doing your due diligence on the property condition, HOA, title condition, etc – so you will have plenty to keep you busy.

3. PROPERTY UNDER CONTRACT AND IN ESCROW -TIME TO MOVE FORWARD WITH LOAN – Escrow – Once your offer and contract is agreed upon and signed by all parties, it goes into escrow. Your lender will need a copy of the complete purchase agreement, signed by all parties. An escrow company is a third party company that is NEUTRAL to the transaction. The escrow officer drafts escrow instructions between you, the seller, the real estate agents, the lender, and the escrow company itself that states that escrow is to assist in processing the sales contract – per the sales contract terms.

The escrow contract terms are pretty standardized and state that all parties must comply with both the sales contract terms and escrow contract terms and it covers what happens if any party fails to comply with any of either of the contracts' terms. The overall purpose of escrow is to collect all the monies related to the transaction and disburse all the monies related to the transaction and transfer the property's title from the seller to the buyer AS PER THE SALES CONTRACT TERMS.

Underwriting at Bank in Process – Underwriting is the process of your bank verifying all the information on your application, making sure the loans conforms to its' own lending guidelines and federal banking guidelines. Your lender or mortgage broker will now submit all your information to their underwriting department. They will also request updated employment pay stubs, bank account records and other information and submit them to that department which will carefully review all the information you provide, your credit report, the appraisal report, the title report, and all other pertinent information as they move forward to verify and approve your loan for funding. They may request additional documentation. Be sure to return this information quickly so the process moves forward smoothly and quickly.

4. APPRAISAL – This process is detailed in the Chapter 17 – Appraisal and Property Valuation chapter for your review. Once you have a property under contract your lender will order an appraisal. This will usually cost $300 - $600 and you will pay upfront for this analysis and report. It usually takes 1-2 weeks for the report. An experienced licensed appraiser will review comparable recent sales and listings that are most similar to the property you have under contract. The appraiser will come up with an estimate of value for the property and detail their findings in a report that is submitted to the lender and you. If your contract price is $200,000 and the appraisal comes in at that amount or more, everything is fine and the collateral for the loan, which is the property, is sufficient to qualify for the 80.0% LTV program that you selected.

APPRAISAL COMES IN LOW

If the appraisal comes in low, say $190,000, the bank will still only finance a maximum of 80.0% of the LOWER of the appraised value or contract price. So the maximum they will finance is $152,000 ($190,000 appraisal multiplied by 80.0% maximum LTV). You were planning to put a downpayment of $40,000 and take a $160,000 mortgage loan. Now since the appraisal came in low and the maximum loan you can get is only $152,000, you will need to come up with the $8,000 difference in cash if you want to buy the property.

The other option, which you should try, is to get the seller to agree to reduce the price to the appraised value of $190,000. If it is a bank selling the property, you may have some luck negotiating the price down. Or the seller may be willing to split the difference, say to re-price the property to $195,000. But the bank or a regular seller may just say pay the $200,000 or cancel the deal and you will make the appropriate choice for yourself at that point on whether to move forward or cancel the contract.

Either way, if the appraisal is low, someone needs to give in or several parties need to give in to get the deal done. DON'T EVER WALK AWAY FROM A PROPERTY OVER A FEW THOUSAND DOLLARS, FINDING A GOOD PROPERTY AND CLOSING DEALS IS HARD WORK AND TIME CONSUMING SO GIVE A LITTLE IF YOU HAVE TO!

The appraiser may also make remarks in their report of repairs that are required. You may have to negotiate who will pay for the repairs. The lender may require that the repairs be completed before they will fund your loan. Be careful when paying for repairs BEFORE you own the property. Find out if your lender will instead allow a "holdback" to guarantee the cost of repairs after your close. Note: If you pay for repairs and then the deal fails for some reason – you have a problem and probably will not get the money you spent on repairs back.

5. LOCK RATE AND TERMS – Now is also the time to lock in your guaranteed interest rate and terms for your loan. When you qualified for your GFE, the lender estimated an interest rate and loan terms. But interest rates change many times a day and you typically do not lock in a rate until your property is under contract.

MAKE SURE TO GET YOUR AGREED UPON RATE, POINTS, AND TERMS IN AN EMAIL OR WRITING SO THAT YOU HAVE A RECORD OF THAT.

Thirty year fixed interest rate amortizing loan. While there are many loan options like fixed rate long term loans and adjustable rate loans, we suggest a long term 30 year fixed amortization loan. This is the standard and most prevalent loan available in the US. <u>Click here to understand how Amortization works</u>. Each time you finance or refinance you pay thousands of dollars in fees and costs in addition to all the time it takes to apply, get documents together, meet with lender, etc. If you do a 30 year fixed interest rate amortizing loan you are done with financing until your loan is paid off.

This also depends on the current interest rates available, but 30 year loans are typically reasonably priced - "price" equals the interest rate and points combination you pay. And, if you do a 30 year loan you will never have to qualify again or pay additional financing costs. One similar option - If you can afford the much higher payments one other option may be a 15 year amortizing loan, so discuss that with your lender. However, the loan program you select depends on your situation, holding period expectations, and market conditions. Be sure your loan officer helps you evaluate your situation.

SEE MORE ON LOAN OPTIONS BELOW

Rate vs. Point Analysis –When you are ready to lock in your rate your lender will provide you with the current market interest rates for your loan program and can usually give you some options on the rate vs. upfront loan origination fees/points for your long term financing. A "point" is one percent (1.0%) of the original mortgage loan balance.

The available rate and point combinations for a 30 year amortizing loan may be something like the following:

Points	Rate
1	5.000%
1/2	5.125%
0	5.250%

– Let's say the lender tells you 5.250% interest rate at 0 points. If you want a lower rate, like 5.000%, you ask how many upfront points do you need to pay to get that rate. Not all lenders have options, but many do. So as per above, the lender says that it costs 1 upfront point for the lower 5.000% rate. So you are paying 1 point, or 1.0% of the loan amount, to save .25% on your annual interest rate. Is that a good deal?

Let's throw some numbers out here. On a $100,000 loan you would pay 1.0% or $1,000 to lower your annual mortgage interest rate .25% which equates to savings of about $250 per year ($100,000 loan multiplied by .25% lower interest rate). So for your investment of $1,000 you are getting paid back, or stated another way saving, $250 per year. That means you will get your $1,000 investment back in four years – so a four year Payback Period. After those four years when you have now been fully paid back, you still save about $250 per year going forward for many more years on the loan. But a four year payback period, as long as you will own the property for many more than four years, sounds like a fair deal to us.

The Point vs. Rate options differ depending on the current marketplace, so sometimes your rate may only drop .125% for paying 1 point upfront. So that would be an eight year payback...and that is a long time. Sometimes the option may be to drop your rate .375% for paying 1 point, so that is a three year payback and a great deal.

So ask the lender to give you some Rate vs. Point Options and figure out how many years it will take to recoup any extra points you pay upfront to reduce the annual interest rate on your loan. To do a really good analysis you would need to figure out what your after-tax cost of paying the points and after-tax interest savings would be, but that gets pretty complicated and we do not feel worth the effort. We suggest do the simple payback period analysis and make the decision that is best for you – the shorter the payback period the better.

Depending on the lender there may be other ways to lower your rate. Maybe put down a bigger downpayment like 20% instead of 10%, or agreeing to a prepayment penalty, or impounding/escrowing property taxes and insurance premiums, or keeping a checking account at the bank and having your loan payments paid automatically out of the checking account. Ask the lender if there is any other way to lower your rate – other than paying additional loan points/origination fees.

6.   UNDERWRITING MOVES FORWARD AND LOAN APPROVED BY BANK –   Once the bank underwriting department has verified all your information on your loan application, the property appraisal and condition information, insurance information, and that your loan conforms with the bank rules and program in which you are going to borrow, they will typically approve your loan subject to final closing conditions. Those conditions are generally updated bank statements or other supporting documentation and other issues. Sometimes they are tough to satisfy like having a signed lease for the premises before they will fund a loan for a rental property or having the termite work completed prior to closing. Either way, you need to get those conditions satisfied so the bank will fund your loan.

Sometimes your lending bank may be a little negotiable on some of the terms, so if they are really hard to satisfy...don't hesitate to ask them to review and consider modifying the closing condition or accepting a slightly different satisfaction.

7. SIGN LOAN DOCUMENTS WITH NOTARY – As those conditions are being satisfied just a few days before your loan closes, your loan documents are prepared and ready for your review and signature by the escrow company notary. There are probably 50-80 pages of loan documents, disclosures, applications, releases that you need to review and sign as a part of your loan. Most are very standardized these days and conform with rules from Freddie Mac and Fannie Mae, but you still need to read and understand them. Two of the most important documents are ones that combined we commonly term the mortgage. It is actually a Deed of Trust and a Promissory Note in about one-half the states. In some states it is simply called a "mortgage".

REMEMBER, you become obligated to the terms and conditions of your loan when you sign your loan documents and your loan is funded. This is your last chance to be sure your loan is what you expected. So make sure your loan is what you expected.

The <u>Deed of Trust</u>, click for Example, is the document you sign where you promise your mortgage lender that you will do certain items to protect the property and pay your mortgage during the time until you pay off your mortgage. Items like making your payments on time as required in the promissory note, keeping proper insurance on the property, keeping the property in good condition, you give rights to the lender to foreclose if you fail to pay your loan and the lender has the right to collect legal fees against you in this case. Read through it to see what you will be promising the company that lends you the money. It is also recorded at the county courthouse to give notice to all other parties that there is a loan on the property and if it is the "first trust deed" that means it is first in line to be repaid when the property is sold. Any normal bank mortgage loan is going to be a first trust deed.

The Promissory Note, click for example, or Mortgage Note shows the amount of the loan, the date of the loan, the payment amount, when payment is due, if there is a prepayment penalty, when payment is late, fees for defaults, where to give notice, etc. This is your promise to repay your loan and the terms upon which you agree to repay that loan. This is your contract. Review it carefully BEFORE you sign it.

The Estimated or Preliminary Closing Statement or HUD-1 Final Closing Statement– Escrow will prepare a preliminary closing statement showing estimates of where all the money you borrow and invest will go. It will include incoming monies from the bank loan, your earnest money deposit, seller credits, tax assessments, insurance, transfer taxes, your downpayment, and outgoing monies for escrow, title, notary, lender fees, etc. You want to review and compare this estimate to your original GFE to make sure they are close and that no large additional charges are on your estimated closing statement.

The total amount could be very different from the original GFE due to interest and property taxes based on the date and day of the month you close on your property. Those items are explained in the Dissecting GFE Closing Costs to Comparison Shop article from above. You want to focus your attention on the costs that you can control. Once you close escrow the estimated closing statement will be updated to a the HUD-1 Final Closing Statement, a federal government required disclosure that again will never match perfectly to the GFE or your Estimated Preliminary Settlement Statement. Just review it to ensure that it is close and no fees or costs are way out of line with the original estimates. Some costs can change – other cannot change, discuss with your lender.

The Truth in Lending Disclosure Statement – This is a standardized statement required under federal law to give you a comparison of the cost of obtaining a loan. It would help you analyze loan options if you obtained one from each lender when you were initially qualified by them for a loan. If you did receive them, it makes it easy to compare loan options based on the total costs of the loan. However, many items change like rate and points options, and interest rates from the time you initially qualify to the time your lock in your loan rate and terms. So this may be useful, but more than likely dissecting your closing costs and focusing on the important controllable costs is going to be your better bet to get a fair deal on your loan.

You will sign all these documents and the escrow officer, notary or attorney will leave you a copy of them to review or you may review them as you sign them. Either way, you want to just understand what you are signing and if you do not understand something then ask questions and make sure you are comfortable with the documents BEFORE you sign them.

8. REVIEW YOUR ESTIMATED CLOSING STATEMENT AGAINST YOUR ORIGINAL GFE – Now is the time to pull out your original GFE and review it against the Estimated or Preliminary Closing Statement for any discrepancies or issues you see. It will not match exactly and you need to look at your Dissected GFE Analysis so items like Interest and Property Taxes do not skew your analysis. But you are looking for large dollar items – that are not favorable to you – that do not seem correct. Question the escrow agent if you think there is an issue.

9. WIRE IN YOUR MONEY – The Estimated Closing Statement and the escrow officer will let you know how much money you need to fund in order for the deal to close. The amount of these funds will be a

combination of your downpayment and closing costs and you will either wire them into to escrow, per escrow's instructions, or bring a cashiers check just a few days before closing is to occur. Escrow usually will add or pad some additional monies to cover any extra costs and after the HUD-1 is finalized the escrow company will refund the difference to you. Once your funds are in escrow it is time to close out escrow and transfer title.

10. BANK FUNDS MORTGAGE LOAN – The bank will also fund the mortgage loan amount at this point and there should be enough money in escrow to cover the purchase price and all costs based off of the escrow agent's calculation. Sometimes there are final issues and items, do not stress out. The escrow officer will alert you to them items and just do your best to provide whatever information or documentation is needed.

In general, real estate closings typically take several days longer to close than anticipated – DO NOT GET STRESSED OUT – just relax and assume it will take a few extra days.

11. TITLE TRANSFERS TO YOU – When all monies are in escrow and all escrow agreement and contract agreement items are cleared properly, escrow will release the Deed to be recorded in the county courthouse recorder's office. An individual hired by the title company will go to the recorder's office to check for any new liens up to that moment. They will record the new deed documents giving you ownership and the deed of trust giving the bank a security interest in your property. Then escrow will disperse all monies to the parties per the agreement and voila……

You own the Property!

In a few days you will receive the HUD-1 Final Closing Statement and a refund check for any unused funds. You may want to compare this again to your Estimated Closing Statement as a final check.

Make sure you get a copy of the Title Insurance Policy (Chapter 11) because title issues may not arise for years and you need this document. It may not come in the mail for a couple of months, but don't forget to follow up and get a final copy. Title issues are very very very rare, but they are usually big dollar amount issues and you need your written proof that you have coverage just in case! Make sure the final Schedule "B" matches the Preliminary Title Policy Schedule "B" that you were given weeks beforehand and you reviewed per Chapter 11 – Title Insurance instructions.

LETS COVER A FEW MORE ISSUES RELATED TO MORTGAGE FINANCING, LENDERS, TYPES OF LOANS

Where to get a mortgage loan?

There are many options on where to get a mortgage loan. You can go into the local branch of a bank, credit union, or mortgage brokerage company. You can get a referral from a friend or your real estate agent. You can call from a commercial on TV or find a mortgage bank or broker on the Internet. The industry is highly regulated so luckily a lot of the loan documents are standardized which helps you better analyze what a lender has to offer based on the interest rate, the loan origination and discount points, loan terms and fees. However, you have to take the time to learn how to analyze the offers so that you can make the right decision – and that is what takes time.

In general, you will not get a better deal by going to a major bank over a mortgage broker. Brokers borrow money from wholesale lenders, mark up the cost to you so they can earn a commission or salary, and lend to you at that marked up cost. Bank loan officers typically do the same thing, except they are borrowing from their own bank's wholesale lending division and marking up the cost to you. There are some TV advertisements for direct lenders who say they save you money because their people are on salary not commission, but guess what, they are generally doing just about the same process.

To protect yourself, as previously discussed, you need to get qualified by at least two lenders and obtain GFE statements from each and compare the terms and fees of a proposed loan to see which one is the better deal. In order to do this, you need to understand that <u>Dissecting GFE Closing Costs to Comparison Shop</u> article AND take the time to analyze the offerings each lender puts on your table.

In general the lending process is time consuming and confusing, so you want to make sure you are doing some analysis to get a fair deal and we suggest pick the lender you think can do the best job for you and move forward on finding a good property.

An educated and fair loan officer WILL be a value-ad service to you. The loan officer can help you evaluate your financing options and guide you through the process from prequalification to the close of your purchase.

Better Understanding Loans – Lender underwriting models will take your application information and assign you to a loan "basket" based on your credit worthiness. So maybe the:

SAMPLE UNDERWRITING MODELS SAMPLE LOAN "BASKETS"			
Pricing Tier	**Typical Borrower**	**Rate**	**Points**
Top Credit Profile	Low DTI, Lots of Assets, Great Credit	5.00%	1.0
Fair Credit Profile	Sufficient DTI, Some Assets, Fair Credit	6.00%	1.0
Low Credit Profile	High DTI, Few Assets, Low Credit Score	No Loan For You Now **	
** Work with a Lender to Formulate a plan to improve borrowing potential.			

AGAIN, what you want to watch out for is if you are qualified for the excellent credit profile 5.00% loan above but since you do not know any better – because you did not get additional quotes from other lenders – that you get the 6.00% loan. The lender and bank make more money on this loan if they "sell" you into a higher interest rate loan – at the same number of loan origination points – than you are qualified for based on your credit profile.

That is, all things being equal you should be able to secure a loan at a certain number of loan origination points at about the same interest rate from every lender. If a lender can only offer you an interest rate on a loan that is much higher than other lenders offer you then they are probably earning some additional monies and of course you want to pick the lender who can offer you the lower rate at the same loan origination points number and amount.

By working with a reputable lender and doing some analysis you have the greatest chance of receiving a fairly priced loan.

Types of Loans

There are a few types of loans but many different terms for residential properties up to four units (Commercial residential loans of five units and above are different and covered in Chapter 15 – Small Apartment Buildings).

Loans may have fixed interest rates, intermediate interest rates (for the initial 3, 5, 7, or 10 years) or periodic adjustable interest rates. Some loans permit interest only payments while others require rapid repayment (e.g. a 15-year term). The "best" loan for you depends on your current financial situation and your ownership strategy.

Primary Residence Loans or Owner Occupied Loans

This is a loan where you are going to live in the property. This can be up to a four unit building as long as it is your primary residence. You sign a document stating that you intend to occupy the property for at least twelve months after closing. Lenders have learned that primary residence type loans have the lowest default rate of any loans and due to this fact they usually have the lowest interest rates of any type of loans. So your loan as an owner occupant with your great credit may be 5.0% at 1 point compared to maybe 5.75% as an investment property.

So one good bet on starting your real estate empire is to buy properties that you will live in for at least one year with a primary residence owner occupied loan, you get the best interest rate and can put down a smaller downpayment, and then after a year move out and make it into a rental unit. The loan terms do not change when you move out as you keep that great financing for the life of the loan. Misleading the lender about your occupancy status intention is a serious offense so make sure you are forthcoming.

Banks have different programs for how much of a downpayment you need to fund when purchasing a personal residence. You will need to discuss these options with your lender to see what program works best for you based on how much you have in savings to use as your downpayment. If you put down at least 20.0% of the purchase price, hence borrowing 80.0% (or 80.0% LTV), you will generally get the lowest interest rate on your loan. With 20.0% down you will also not have to pay for something called private mortgage insurance or PMI.

PMI is an insurance that benefits the lender in case you default on your loan. So if you stop making your mortgage payments and cannot cure your default, the PMI insurance company will cover a portion of the lender's loss in a foreclosure. This does not relieve you of making those payments, you will be foreclosed upon eventually if you fail to pay back your loan on the terms that you and the bank agreed upon in your promissory note. This will also ruin your credit report and FICO score. PMI runs about $60 per month per $100,000 in borrowing. So if you have a $200,000 loan, the PMI will be about $120 per month. Years down the road when you have paid off some of the mortgage loan through the regular amortization of the loan, and/or you have built some equity because prices have increased, or you have made additional principal payments to pay down the loan and your LTV drops to 80.0%, you can work with your mortgage lender to cancel the PMI. See Article on cancelling PMI.

Federal Housing Administration (FHA) insured loans can allow qualified owner occupied borrowers to put down as little as 3.5% in cash and borrow 96.5% of the money in a mortgage loan. So LTV would be 96.5%. However, with FHA loans you need to pay an upfront mortgage insurance fee of several thousand dollars and ongoing PMI until you get down to only 78.0% of the original loan amount. So these programs benefit people with less savings, but the cost is the insurance that you have to pay for to insure your loan.

Veteran's Affairs (VA) guaranteed loans can allow qualified veterans to buy an owner occupied home with zero downpayment and no closing costs. The seller must agree to pay the closing costs and the VA charges an "Upfront Funding Fee" that is added to the loan amount. There is no monthly mortgage insurance.

Investment Property or Non Owner Occupied Loans

These are loans on properties that you are going to rent out to tenants from when you take ownership. Your interest rate and points combination will also be somewhat dependent on your personal income, downpayment amount and credit score. So you need to go to a lender and get qualified to see what program you fit into and what will be your interest rate. However, your downpayment amount is typically going to be 25.0% on these loans in the current marketplace. This is why buying a property for rental purposes but living in it for the first year and then moving out is such a good idea. Again, you can put down a much smaller downpayment on a personal residence, therefore conserving your cash to buy your second property down the road.

Rental properties may also allow you to use some of the income the property will generate to be included as part of your DTI ratio numbers. The bank will verify the rental income amount by having the appraiser do a rental market comparables study that will cost approximately $100-$150. If the property already has a tenant, they may take that rental amount from the written lease you provide to them. For the income issue, the bank will use 75.0% of the estimated rental income the property can generate and subtract out the property taxes, insurance and HOA fees and that net amount can be included to increase your overall income and hopefully decrease your DTI percentage – which should make you better qualified. If this calculation produces a net loss, the difference is treated like a payment that will increase your DTI ratio.

Loan Terms

The standard loan today is the 30 year amortizing fixed interest rate loan – See <u>Amortization Article</u>. We've heard about all the exotic and interest only loans of the past few years and most of those programs are not available in the market place any longer. With a 30 year fixed rate loan the lender takes the amount of money you are borrowing, like $200,000, and using the interest rate on the loan that you have selected based on your credit profile, calculates a mortgage payment that will pay the interest and principal each month for 30 years to repay (amortize) the loan. See <u>Amortization Article</u> for more on this.

The nice thing about these loans is that your loan payments are constant for good at the same starting rate – so even though your personal income or rental income increases, you mortgage stays the same. So years down the road it will seem like a pretty small payment as inflation increases your income. Note: Your payments may adjust to reflect changes in your property taxes or hazard insurance premiums if those amounts are "escrowed" or "impounded" as a part of your loan.

Article: Loan Amortization

Most mortgage loans today are 30 year amortizing loans. What this means is that a computer takes your Original loan balance amount, your agreed upon loan Interest Rate, and 30 years - really 360 months - and calculates your monthly constant Mortgage Payment. The total Mortgage Payment is always a constant total amount per month for the entire term of the loan – it does not change. This Mortgage Payment amount is comprised of principal and interest and if that constant payment is paid each month for the next 30 years it will result in your loan being fully paid off. Yeah!

PAYMENT STAYS CONSTANT, BUT THE PRINCIPAL AND INTEREST PORTIONS OF PAYMENT CHANGE WITH EACH PAYMENT

Let's say your mortgage payment is calculated as $100 per month. That is the amount you will pay each month for the next 360 months – 30 years. In the first month the Interest Portion may be calculated as $90 and since the total Mortgage Payment is $100, we know the Principal Portion is the rest, or $10 of the $100 Mortgage Payment. In the second month the Interest will decrease slightly and might be $89 and Principal will increase to the difference of $11. Third month, $88 and $12. Fourth $87 and $13. Every month on an amortizing mortgage the Interest Portion will decrease while the Principal Portion will increase – but combined will always add up to the total fixed constant payment of $100 in this case.

THREE VARIABLES TO AMORTIZATION

There are three variable components to amortization. Original Loan Balance, Interest Rate, Years of Amortization. To make this simple to understand, here is an example of a 10 year amortizing loan with one annual payment per year so you can see the process:

Loan Balance: $100,000, Interest Rate 5.0%, Amortization Years 10

Note: Mortgage loans are typically 30 year and monthly amortizing, but to make it simple to understand we are using a 10 year annual amortizing loan – so one payment per year amortized over a 10 year period.

The chart on the last page illustrates Amortization. Look at the chart as you read this explanation. You might want to print page 3 so you can review while reading below.

YEAR ONE OF A 10 YEAR AMORTIZING LOAN - Example

At the start of year one we begin with the original Beginning Balance of $100,000. The computer calculates the Mortgage Payment of $12,950, which is combined principal and interest, based off our three variables from above and this amortizing payment is fixed for the entire ten year term of the loan. See the Mortgage Payment Column how it is $12,950 each year downward.

HOW MUCH OF THE $12,950 IS PRINCIPAL AND HOW MUCH IS INTEREST - First we calculate the Interest Portion of the Mortgage Payment by multiplying the Beginning Balance of $100,000 by the 5.0% Interest Rate to get the $5,000 Interest Portion as shown on the chart (5.0% X $100,000 = $5,000). So of the $12,950 Mortgage Payment we know that $5,000 is the Interest Portion and the remaining amount is the Principal Portion or $7,950 – on chart. What is important to remember is the current payment Interest Portion is always the current year Beginning Balance multiplied by the Interest Rate.

ENDING BALANCE YEAR ONE – To get the year one Ending Balance, we take the $100,000 Beginning Balance and subtract the Principal Portion - $7,950 – of the Mortgage Payment and the difference is the Ending Balance of $92,050.

BEGINNING BALANCE YEAR TWO – The Beginning Balance, since it is the next day, is essentially the same amount as the Ending Balance form the prior period, or $92,050 – see column year two. With a typical monthly mortgage it would be the end of the prior month and the first day of the next month instead of "yearly amortizing" that we are illustrating herein.

AMORTIZATION CONTINUES - So the process starts again - we have our year two Beginning Balance of $92,050. Now our Interest and Principal Portions will change. Our Interest Portion is the year two Beginning Balance of $92,050 – see chart - multiplied by our fixed 5.0% Interest Rate to get $4,602 – see that amount in Year 2 Interest Portion Column. Then we subtract that from the $12,950 constant payment to get our year two Principal Portion of the Mortgage payment which is $8,348 ($12,950 - $4,602). Our Ending Balance is the year two Beginning Balance of $92,050 less the $8,348 Principal Portion which calculates to $83,702 – see chart. This $83,702 is also the Beginning Balance of year three and the process starts all over again.

MORTGAGE AMORTIZED – PAID OFF – IN TEN YEARS - Since we calculated this $100,000 loan to be amortized over ten years at 5.0%, you can see this process on the chart that flows through for all ten years and voila, at the end of year ten, the mortgage Ending Balance is $0 – your loan is paid off!

PRINCIPAL AND INTEREST CHANGE EACH YEAR - You can also see on the chart how the Interest Portion of your Mortgage Payment decreases each period because your current year Beginning Loan Balance is decreasing and that simple calculation of the Beginning Balance multiplied by the Interest Rate gives you a smaller Interest Portion each new period. Of course that means your Principal Portion pay down is bigger which is good because you are paying off your loan faster – Great job!

FEDERAL INCOME TAXES - The last knowledge item is that when you do your taxes, which you will learn in Chapter 6, only the Interest Portion of your Mortgage Payment is tax deductible, not the Principal portion. Keep that in mind and you will understand that later.

End of Article: Amortization

ProfessorBaron.com
Simple Amortization Schedule

Original Loan Balance (PV)	$100,000	Excel function - Payment
Interest Rate - Fixed	5.00%	= PMT (Rate,Nper,PV)
Amortization Years (Nper)	10	

Year	Beginning Balance	Mortgage Payment	Interest Portion	Principal Portion	Ending Balance
	Yr. 1 = Original Loan Amount, Then Prior Year Ending Balances	Calculated by Computer - 3 Variables	Current Year Beginning Balance X Interest Rate	Mortgage Payment less Current Year Interest Portion	Beginning Balance less Current Year Principal Portion
1	$100,000	$12,950	$5,000	$7,950	$92,050
2	$92,050	$12,950	$4,602	$8,348	$83,702
3	$83,702	$12,950	$4,185	$8,765	$74,936
4	$74,936	$12,950	$3,747	$9,204	$65,733
5	$65,733	$12,950	$3,287	$9,664	$56,069
6	$56,069	$12,950	$2,803	$10,147	$45,922
7	$45,922	$12,950	$2,296	$10,654	$35,267
8	$35,267	$12,950	$1,763	$11,187	$24,080
9	$24,080	$12,950	$1,204	$11,746	$12,334
10	$12,334	$12,950	$617	$12,334	$0

There are also 15 year amortizing fixed interest rate loans and they may be a good option. The interest rate will be a little lower but the payment will be much higher so the real question is do you want to have such high payments? Have your lender calculate what the payment would be and you can make the decision.

There are also Adjustable Rate Mortgages (ARMs) where the interest rate may be fixed for 1, 3, 5, 7, or 10 years and at the end of that period it adjusts to a market rate. These loans typically have a lower interest rate than the 30 year loan because the
bank lending you the money is taking less risk because they are not allowing you to lock in a long term fixed interest rate. These ARMs also typically amortize over 30 years but payments could change based on market interest rates.

There are some other terms available on loans and you need to discuss those with your lender. Like a loan where your payment is only the interest on the loan and it is not amortizing, so your payments are a little lower. Lenders introduce new programs from time to time and eliminate others, so be sure your loan professional keeps up with the mortgage market changes.

RECOMMENDATION

We suggest doing a 30 year fixed rate amortizing loan right now due to the low rates in the marketplace. If you do this long term loan you may never have to refinance and pay all the costs of refinancing and go through all the hassle and stress again.

Secondary Mortgage Market and Portfolio Lenders

Almost all loans originated today by a bank or mortgage lender are then sold to another very large financial institution who holds the loans long term – reselling them is called the Secondary Mortgage Market. This does not impact your loan or your decision making process at all. These large institutions do have certain loan criteria and sometimes you may be denied a loan based on the fact that you do not conform to their guidelines. It happens the most often once you have loans on greater than four individual properties. In these cases, there are a few companies called Portfolio Lenders who may do the loans. The rates and points are generally higher and most of the loans are 5 or 7 year loans. It may make sense to do these loans, but you need to think though the combination of rates and points, the term of the loan, and other issues to decide if it makes sense for your situation.

Conforming Loans and Jumbo Loans

The loan amount is also an issue and will impact your borrowing rate and availability of a mortgage. In most parts of the US, if the loan is over $417,000 for a one unit property it goes from a "Conventional" loan to a "Jumbo" loan with a higher interest rate. Some high priced areas like San Francisco may have higher amounts that are still conforming. Duplex/Triplex/Fourplex properties also have higher conforming limits. You will need to discuss this with your lender to get a feel for what qualifies as Conforming and what would be the higher interest rate if your loan is a Jumbo. Jumbos may also require higher downpayments even if they   are   Personal   Residences.   Loan   limits   information   here: https://www.efanniemae.com/sf/refmaterials/loanlimits/

WHY IT IS HARD TO SHOP MORTGAGES & HOW YOU CAN GET A FAIR DEAL

There are many moving parts in figuring out how much it will cost you in total closing fees and you are usually crunched for time. That is why it is hard to shop for mortgage on a purchase...it is a little easier when you are refinancing. To get a FAIR deal interview and get two estimates from lenders and compare them with the knowledge you have learned in this chapter. So Dissect your GFE!

COMPARING YOUR GFE TO ESTIMATED CLOSING DOCUMENTS

When you are close to closing and get the estimated closing costs worksheet from Escrow, compare those terms and closing costs to your GFE to resolve any items and you should re-compare your GFE or estimated closing costs worksheet to your Final HUD 1 statement that you will receive after you close.

FINAL THOUGHTS

It is a lot of work to do all these tasks, but that is why you should try work with a lender who is experienced, with good references and whom you feel you can trust. There are plenty of them out there, so do a little work finding one, review your GFE estimates, and work with them to get your loan and transaction closed!

CHAPTER 8

HOMEOWNERS ASSOCIATION ANALYSIS

HOA ANALYSIS IS AN EXERCISE IN DISASTER AVOIDANCE. FEW HOAs ARE IN "GREAT" OR EVEN "HEALTHY" FINANCIAL AND OPERATIONAL SHAPE, most are in "satisfactory" shape at best. There is reason to be concerned on even these satisfactory shape HOAs and you will have to make some decisions on your own about the risk you are willing to take. But herein we just want you to have the tools and knowledge to avoid clear and present upcoming financial DISASTERS.

This could mean cancelling your purchase, maybe at the last minute (maybe after you've already spent $500 - $1,000 or more) because you may not receive the HOA documents to review until the last minute and you determine the HOA has some major issue(s) that causes you to cancel your purchase.

HOT TIP OF THE CHAPTER:
One thing you might consider, after you fully read this chapter to understand the issues with HOAs, is to find out the property management companies in town that manage HOAs. I hear being an HOA property manager is a pretty lonely living and a clinical psychologist I know told me that those managers are always looking for someone just to "be a friend and to listen" to what they have to say! So as a future real estate buyer you should realize that those managers are the ones who know where all the bodies are buried! What I mean by this is that an HOA manager who manages lots of properties is going to be able to tell you which ones are in good financial, operational, and legal shape with boards of directors that function well. So that manager is the individual whose brain you want to pick for information – assuming there are a few morsels left to pick after the HOA boards and community members beat up on them each month!

Now you may not know this, but April 1ˢᵗ each year is **"National Take an HOA Property Manager Out to Lunch Day!!!"** And a recent national faux survey by PropertyManagerHOA.com found that 90% of Property Managers really love going out to lunch when someone else is paying the bill! And that survey also found that the number jumped to 99.99% when the word "lobster" or "prime rib" was on the restaurant's menu. In fact, 100% of those respondents said they would never refuse an offer of lunch, regardless of the day of the year, from anyone who offered to take them out to Red Lobster, Cheesecake Factory, Outback Steakhouse or any restaurant that has valet parking and the word lobster, fish, steak, crab, ribs, seafood or prime rib in their name.

And there is one more thing, and this is a little known secret in the HOA property management industry – If you quietly whisper to your lunch guest, "Order anything you want on the menu, I'm paying," they'll have the loosest lips in town with respect to spilling the beans on all the HOAs in the area!!!! So practice that phrase well, again, "Order anything you want on the menu, I'm paying, even the Lobster Burger"!

ALL JOKING ASIDE – Think about their knowledge level and experience....it's well worth your time to take them out! So do it!

The last item at the bottom of this chapter is the HOA Due Diligence Checklist that you will use to keep track of your progress on analyzing the HOA to better protect yourself in your purchase.

There are lots of examples and forms in this chapter which can be downloaded and viewed at www.ProfessorBaron.com.

WE APOLOGIZE BUT THIS IS NOT AN EASY NOR A STRAIGHTFORWARD TASK, IT IS DOWNRIGHT COMPLICATED. BUT IT IS VITAL TO YOUR FINANCIAL FUTURE TO READ, LEARN AND UNDERSTAND THE ISSUES.

WE ALSO CANNOT STRESS ENOUGH THAT YOU NEED TO LEARN THESE ISSUES AND ITEMS WELL IN ADVANCE OF MAKING OFFERS ON PROPERTIES. THIS CHAPTER SHOULD TAKE A NORMAL PERSON A COUPLE OF WEEKS TO LEARN, UNDERSTAND AND DIGEST AND IF YOU DO NOT COMPREHEND THE ISSUES AND KNOW HOW TO ANALYZE THEM BEFORE ESCROW OPENS ON THE PROPERTY YOU HAVE UNDER CONTRACT - IT WILL BE TOO LATE TO DO A GREAT JOB PROTECTING YOURSELF.

NOTE: WE ARE TRYING TO MAKE THESE TASKS EASIER TO UNDERSTAND SO THAT YOU DON'T THROW YOUR HANDS UP IN FRUSTRATION AND DECIDE TO SKIP THESE EXTREMELY IMPORTANT TASKS – BUT THEY ARE SOMEWHAT COMPLEX AND YOU NEED TO TAKE YOUR TIME TO UNDERSTAND.

Here is an interesting article from Kelly Bennett at Voice of San Diego that you may want to peruse to get a better feel for the issues see article on website: <u>When Fixing Up the Lobby Becomes a Luxury</u>. Beware that even if unit owners, like you, are in fine financial shape Risk Number 1 below or other risks could be issues. Running through all the due diligence steps and tasks will help you gain a better understanding of your overall risks.

HERE ARE YOUR RISKS:

1. Unfunded or Seriously Underfunded Reserve and Replacement Accounts – In this case there are long term repairs and replacements that will be needed (roofs, private streets, mechanical equipment) in the future but the HOA has not saved anywhere near enough money to pay for these.

2. Litigation – HOA in litigation or Potential Litigation or Lawsuits may occur – so the HOA could spend a lot of money filing or fighting litigation and most lenders will not lend money on a project that is in litigation. This also means that you may have trouble selling your unit until the litigation is ended – which could be years – and possibly beyond that date.

3. Water and Mold Issues – Potential large dollar uninsured repairs that were not anticipated – so potential regular or emergency special assessments for large amounts.

4. Too Many Rental Units in the Project – You many have trouble obtaining financing or it may be more expensive (aka higher interest rate) and the project may not be as well taken care of and harder to sell the unit due to all the rentals in the community.

5. New Project Few Owners – Less than a majority percentage of the units are sold and the developer is in financial trouble. So who will be paying the HOA fees on the unsold units to cover the property expenses to keep the lights on, elevators working, maintenance is what you need to determine.

6. Insurance – Not being properly insured for the inherent risks you potentially incur on the Interior part of the unit you own. Cash buyers beware! See Chapter 10 – Property Insurance.

7. Is the building on a ground lease? Or does the HOA own the pool, parking lots, clubhouse, streets? We know you will think…you've got to be kidding…but we are not. In extremely rare instances the HOA may be leasing common areas because the original developer made them separate and kept ownership. If you ask, the HOA should disclose this to you if they do not own any common areas or have long term leases on large value items - and you need to get more information. If this is the case, read the <u>ARTICLE HOA Doesn't Own the Common Areas</u>.

8. One owner controls multiple Units – If the original developer or a subsequent owner has control over more than 10.0% of the units this may be an issue with financing and other issues. Read ARTICLE – <u>HOA Owner with 10.0% Control or More</u>.

You can perform due diligence to analyze the overall condition of the HOA and help you better make decisions on whether or not large increases in HOA dues or special assessments or other problems may be occurring or may be in the near future. This information will help you assess whether or not you want to be an owner in that particular community and hence the association. This due diligence will take some significant time, but your hard earned money is at risk.

Background about Issue

Definition – Common Interest Development (CID) – This is commonly known as a Homeowners Association or HOA. For this chapter, we use the term HOA to describe a CID entity – they are the same thing.

When you buy a property in a Homeowner's Association that governs a condominium, townhome, co-op or similar community you are not just buying your unit, you are making an investment into that larger HOA entity. HOA's can also govern Single Family Home communities, Master Planned Communities and other common ownership developments. HOA fees are usually the clue, but not always. And similar to how you pay for utilities, repairs, and updates for your unit, so does the HOA for the entire community. However, unlike your unit, repairs to the HOA can run into the hundreds of thousands or millions of dollars depending on the type of property.

As an owner in the HOA you pay monthly fees to cover the Homeowner's Association annual expenses, repairs, and replacements. A portion of your HOA fees go to paying HOA current year operating expenses and a portion are set aside in reserve or replacement accounts for long term capital repair/improvement items. The operating expenses may be utility bills, maintenance of common areas, landscaping contracts, elevator contracts, property management fees and other yearly expenses. The long term capital repairs and replacements are items like roofs, private roads and streets, painting, mechanical systems – which can be very expensive – and other items.

There is financial risk, and other risk, related to your ownership in the HOA. The review and analysis of the condition of the homeowners association in any HOA type of community (condominium association, townhome association, co-ops, Master Planned Communities or PUDs, etc.) is becoming one of the most important issues to understand in buying real estate in a community governed by an HOA. The reason for this is that while HOA fees are collected to pay for operating expenses and capital repairs to properties, due to a number of factors over the years, the HOA Boards of Directors are learning that many times there has not been enough money collected in the current year and/or over the years to pay all the costs associated with running many of these communities.

So what happens when there is not enough money for capital repairs/improvements? The Board of Directors either increases HOA fees or owners are required to make special assessment payments to the HOA so that HOA can pay the bills. Either way, those increased fees or special assessments come out of your pocket because you are one of the owners.

The association members may be able to vote to block increases, but that means there will not be enough money to make needed repairs. And when items are not repaired, the problem and costs usually increase quickly. This usually ends up costing everyone more.

AGAIN: DO NOT WAIT UNTIL YOU ARE IN ESCROW TO STUDY AND LEARN THIS CHAPTER. IF YOU ARE MOST LIKELY GOING TO BUY IN AN HOA RUN COMMUNITY, LEARN THE CONCEPTS IN THIS CHAPTER LONG BEFORE OFFERING ON PROPERTIES. THIS IS SO THAT YOU CAN KEEP YOUR EYES OPEN FOR POTENTIAL ISSUES AND ASK THE IMPORTANT QUESTIONS OF YOUR REAL ESTATE AGENT, THE SELLING REAL ESTATE AGENT, THE OWNER, AND TO GET THE PROCESS MOVING TO OBTAIN THE DOCUMENTS YOU NEED TO REVIEW AS SOON AS YOU HAVE A SIGNED CONTRACT FOR PURCHASE.

We implore you to protect yourself, at the end of the day it is your money at risk, not ours. And if you fail to protect yourself, and your money disappears into a black hole of HOA dues and special assessments, you will wish you had done the hard work upfront to avoid buying into that HOA community.

Once you learn all the concepts, you will be using the HOA Due Diligence Checklist to keep track of the process. It is at the bottom of this chapter.

THIS IS NOT AN EASY TASK FOR MANY REASONS, but the goal is to help you avoid a community where the HOA is virtually out of money but has many capital repair/improvements that need to be repaired or replaced. Let's term this significantly unfunded or underfunded to pay for repairs and/or capital improvements like roofs and private streets. That is your biggest risk – either significant increases in HOA fees or one-time assessments – like $5,000 or $10,000 per unit. Other significant risks may also present, and you need to understand and evaluate those too.

Let's look at the significant challenges you will have to overcome in doing this analysis:

Issue 1. Getting the needed documents to do your analysis. Click here for advice and a list of the items that you need – <u>HOA Due Diligence Documents (Or HOA Due Diligence Documents Spreadsheet)</u>. When a seller accepts/signs your purchase offer, they are giving you the right to see documents related to the Financial, Legal and Operational matters of the Homeowners Association. When your contract goes into "escrow" the escrow agent orders the Homeowner's Association documents.

This package is commonly called the "Annual Budget Package". That package probably includes a LOT, but not all, of the documents you need to review and analyze. So use the included HOA Due Diligence Documents list to request other documents you need.

HOA Due Diligence Documents

A Smarter Way to Buy Real Estate

ProfessorBaron.com

Buying Real Estate is the largest and riskiest purchase you will ever make in life.
Experienced buyers do their homework to protect themselves from the inherent risks.
You can also protect yourself, you just need to know what to do and how to do it.

**Download the latest version of the checklist at www.ProfessorBaron.com
to study these concepts and use once you have a ratified purchase**

HOA Documents to Review - PREPARED LETTER FOR ESCROW IS NEXT DOCUMENT IN CHAPTER.

As soon as your contract to purchase goes into "escrow" have your real estate agent forward the "HOA Document Letter Request to Escrow" to the escrow agent. You need to pressure both real estate agents and the escrow agent to get the Homeowner's Associat

NOTE: Do NOT give this list to the seller until they have ACCEPTED/signed your purchase offer. If you forward this list upfront, they may select another person's purchase offer instead of yours if they believe your demands are too onerous or that you may

NOTE: YOU MAY HAVE TO PAY FOR THESE UPFRONT - PER THE AGREEMENT IN YOUR PURCHASE CONTRACT.

ALSO, THIS IS GOING TO BE AN EXHAUSTING LIST FOR ESCROW TO GET FOR YOU, BUT YOU NEED TO PUSH HARD FOR AS MANY OF
DOCUMENTS AS THEY CAN GET FOR YOU THAT ARE AVAILABLE. ESCROW WILL NOT BE HAPPY ABOUT THIS, BUT IT IS YOUR MONEY
AND FINANCIAL FUTURE ON THE LINE, NOT THEIRS NOR THE REAL ESTATE AGENTS'.
YOU WILL PROBABLY HAVE TO GET ON THE PHONE WITH THE HOA MANAGEMENT COMPANY TOO, SO JUST DO IT.

1 Current Year Budget - Detailing how the HOA Fee was calculated, estimated revenues and expenses for the year, hopefully compared to the prior year's actual numbers, and showing how much is being allocated to the long term repair and replacement accounts.

2 Current Year to Date Financial Statements - so you can see how the HOA is doing in the current year.
Income Statements and possibly the Balance Sheet (or HOA current cash holdings) are available.

3 Annual Financial Statements - Prior two years - Income Statement, Balance Sheet, Statement of Cash Flows
These should be AUDITED statements for larger HOAs.

4 HOA Board of Directors Meeting Minutes, Notes and Documents for the past 24 Months
Community Newsletters, Any Special Notices

5 Reserve Study - Prepared in the past Few Years and may have some updated information.

6 Annual Funding and Disclosure Statement - For California - see State Disclosure Requirements here:
http://www.reservestudy.com/dynamic.php

7 Covenants, Conditions and Restrictions (CC&Rs) and Bylaws

8 Demand Statement for Individual Unit - Shows how much HOA fee if any is outstanding on unit, Violations or Litigation
Percent Owner Occupied and maybe Percent of HOA fees that are Delinquent in community

9 Insurance Policies and Binders - Master Policy, Liability, Earthquake, Others

10 ALL other State Required or Mandated Disclosures

11 Ground Lease or Any commons areas, pools, roads, clubhouses, or equipment that are NOT owned by the HOA and/or leased from third parties? Nature of and Amount & Term of Leases:

12 HOA Still controlled by developer or any owners who own greater than 10.0% of the units?

You may not get all these documents. Your task is to learn the due diligence steps in this chapter and determine what risks, if any, are present in this community.

Then make your decision on those identified risks and if you are willing to accept those risks.

LETTER TO REQUEST DOCUMENTS FROM ESCROW – We have prepared a letter for you to use to request documents.

Click here <u>HOA Document Letter Request to Escrow</u> (or in spreadsheet Form here: <u>HOAEscrowDocumentRequest.xls)</u> and fill in the blanks and send to escrow once your contract is signed by the seller. You may not get all these documents and/or the HOA or management company may not even have them, they may not ever have had them prepared before, nor will they now for a new buyer, so you may be out of luck (not having documents is more common for smaller communities).

Homeowners Association Document Request for Escrow Officer

Date of Request: _____

Date HOA Doc
Review Contingency _____
Expires

TO: Escrow Agent/Company _____

Phone/Fax Numbers/Email _____

Escrow Number and Date Open _____

Dear _____, in conjuction with the above escrow and property sale, the buyer hereby requests the following documents be ordered expediently from the HOA Management Company or Board of Directors.

Additionally, please forward this list to the RESPONSIBLE PARTY at the HOA and determine if any of these documents will NOT be provided to the buyer and the reason they are not available.

<u>**THANK YOU AND WE APPRECIATE YOUR ASSISTANCE IN THIS MATTER.**</u>

HOA Community Name/Address _____

Buyer Phone/Fax Numbers/Email _____

Date Documents
Received _____

Selling Agent and Contact Info _____

Buyer's Agent and Contact Info _____

<u>RESPONSIBLE PARTY - DOCUMENTS/INFORMATION AVAILABLE? Please check Yes or No.</u>
<u>   If NO, please NOTE what is NOT available, or where that information can be located, or why it is not available.</u>

YES   NO

1 [ ][ ]   Current Year Budget - Detailing how the HOA Fee was calculated, estimated revenues and expenses for the year, comparison to the prior year's actual numbers, and showing how much is being allocated to the long term repair and replacement accounts.
             NOTES:

2 [ ][ ]   Current Year to Date Financial Statements - How the HOA is doing in the current year.
             Income Statements and the Balance Sheet (or HOA current cash holdings).
             NOTES:

3 [ ][ ]   Annual Financial Statements - Prior two years - Income Statement, Balance Sheet, Statement of Cash Flows
             AUDITED where available.
             NOTES:

4 [ ][ ]   HOA Board of Directors Meeting Minutes, Notes and Documents for the past 24 Months
             Community Newsletters, Any Special Notices
             NOTES:

5 [ ][ ]   Reserve Study - Most Recent prepared in the past Few Years and most recent update.
             NOTES:

6 [ ][ ]   Annual Funding and Disclosure Statement(s) per State Law
             NOTES:

7 ☐☐ Covenants, Conditions and Restrictions (CC&Rs) and Bylaws
NOTES:

8 ☐☐ Demand Statement for Individual Unit - Showing current HOA fee, if any is outstanding on unit, Violations, Litigation,
Percent Owner Occupied and Percent of HOA fees that are Delinquent in community
NOTES:

9 ☐☐ Insurance Policies and Binders - Master Policy, Liability, Earthquake, any Others
NOTES:

10 ☐☐ ALL other State Required or Mandated Disclosures
NOTES:

11 ☐☐ Any commons areas, pools, roads, clubhouses, or equipment that are NOT owned by the HOA and/or leased from third parties?
Nature of and Amount & Term of Leases:

12 ☐☐ HOA Still controlled by developer or any owners who own greater than 10.0% of the units?

Buying Real Estate is the largest and riskiest purchase you will ever make in life.
Experienced buyers do their homework to protect themselves from the inherent risks.
You can also protect yourself, you just need to know what to do and how to do it.

You just need to do your best to get whatever documents you can and analyze them and make your best decision. Either way, this request is going to be unappreciated by your escrow agent and an exhausting task for the agent to get you all these documents. This task may include your personally calling the HOA Management Company or Board Members directly to request and discuss this information. If you need additional information, make the calls yourself to move this process along – do not rely wholly on the escrow agent. It is not going to be easy, but only these documents (or their information in some other form) will allow you to do the most complete review and due diligence on this largest purchase of your life.

In addition, most banks and some sellers are making the buyer responsible for paying for these documents - per your negotiated contract, so you may have to pay $175 to $450 upfront to the HOA management company to start the process of obtaining the documents. That money is gone gone gone if you back out on the purchase of the deal fails for any reason. They may also want additional monies if you want 24 months of Board Meeting Notes instead of 12 Months they provide. It is not a very functional or fluid process. But we can sum it up again….**Welcome to Real Estate!**

It can take up to several weeks to get these documents from the HOA management company even if the escrow agent diligently orders them the day escrow is opened. During this time, you the buyer are doing your home inspection and paying for that, paying for an appraisal by the bank to determine financing, and in some cases paying for the HOA documents that you need as noted above. So while you are moving along in the process and excited about your new property, AND spending money, one of the most important issues that could cause you significant financial and other pain down the road remains unresolved while you wait for those documents.

- FIRST - MAKE SURE YOUR CONTRACT CONTINGENCY TO REVIEW THESE DOCUMENTS STAYS OPEN UNTIL YOU RECEIVE THEM AND HAVE ADEQUATE TIME TO REVIEW THEM. Some bank addendums to contracts will say that you have ten days (or whatever the addendum states) to complete your review and if you do not object – that contingency is deemed removed. So your real estate agent needs to prepare an addendum to extend this contingency item and have the seller agree to that condition. So that contingency extension should stay open until you have ALL the HOA documents you requested AND enough time to adequately review them (probably 5-7 days is reasonable).

- Also, rarely does the package of documents you receive from the HOA management company, via Escrow, include ALL the documents you need to do a proper analysis. So then you have to request additional information and documents which take additional time to receive. Get on the phone with them, be nice but demand what you need. Go pick them up at the management company office if you need and that is possible.

- Let's say you receive the documents seven days before you are scheduled to close escrow. You have already spent $1,000 on appraisal, inspection, etc., you have shown the property to your friends and family, you have given notice to your landlord that you are moving, and you have scheduled the movers. If you then review the HOA documents and it is clear the HOA is in very bad financial shape, are you really going to back out of the purchase at that point?

— **THE ANSWER IS THAT YOU NEED TO GET THESE DOCUMENTS AS SOON AS POSSIBLE.** The minute your contract goes into escrow, have your agent call and email your list of required documents to the escrow agent. Stress that those documents are vital to your decision about whether or not to go through with the purchase. Then get on the phone yourself with the escrow agent and be nice, but firm, that you need those documents ordered in the next 24 hours. You also need the escrow agent to forward your list of required documents to the HOA management company (or Board of Directors if self-managed or whomever produces them) and confirm whether or not they will be providing each of the documents.

Give the escrow agent two days and then follow up with them. Be nice and appreciative of their assisting you in this effort, but again stress the importance of these documents to your decision making process. The HOA/Management Company may not provide or be able to provide all the documents – so find out why. But if you understand the issues related to HOAs after studying this chapter, then hopefully the documents you DO get will give you the information you need to make the right decision. Just getting these quickly will be frustrating, but keep the pressure on to get the documents you need.

One Beware – If you are not going to take the significant time to understand how to review the documents and actually take the time to review them, then don't waste your time trying to get all the documents. We recommend you do the hard work up front to get them and analyze them - so herein you will need to commit to yourself to complete the process. And since we know you want to protect your financial future, make that promise to yourself now.

Issue 2. – Analyzing these documents, fully understanding the condition of the HOA, and making your decision on whether to move forward or not with your purchase. Herein we will list the documents and a brief explanation of what they are and why you need to review them. Further below we will get into the details.

– **RESERVE STUDY/RESERVE FUNDING and ASSESSMENT AND RESERVE FUNDING AND DISCLOSURE STATEMENT** from BOARD OF DIRECTORS Vital Statistics like (CA 1365.2.5 Disclosure) – This document will give you information about long term repairs that are needed to the HOA, when repair or replacement is needed, how much money should be saved as of today for those repairs, AND MOST IMPORTANT – How much is ACTUALLY saved compared to what SHOULD BE SAVED. These are needed to further assess the financial condition of the HOA, the amount of money saved to pay for long term capital replacements and repairs, and other financial or operational issues.

– **FINANCIAL STATEMENTS** – The Budget which details how HOA fees are determined, The most recent Year to Date Income Statement and Balance Sheet. The Prior two years Income Statements, Balance Sheets and Statements of Cash Flows. These are needed so you can assess the financial picture of the HOA and if there is enough money being collected and was collected in the past to cover current year operating expenses and long term capital repairs.

– **BOARD of DIRECTORS MEETING MINUTES and RECORDS** – For past 24 months. These are records of meetings of the HOA Board and their discussions. These are needed to see if there have been discussions about issues with the community, like litigation, major repair items, contracts, unit owner violations, or other vital issues.

– **CONDO UNIT DEMAND STATEMENT** – This shows additional information about your unit and the condominium association. It typically confirms HOA fees, any unpaid fees your unit currently owes, unit violations, litigation issues, etc.

– **CC&Rs** (Covenants, Conditions and Restrictions) and **BYLAWS** – These documents will tell you everything about the rights and restrictions of the community and the unit you will own. These are needed so that you understand exactly what you are buying and the rules within which you will be agreeing to live related to ownership of your unit.

– **HOA INSURANCE COVERAGE and POLICY** – These documents show the type of insurance that the HOA carries. These are needed to determine the type of insurance you need related to ownership of your unit. You also need to get a quote from your insurance agent as some areas like coastal areas have very high insurance rates and you need to review and compare how that impacts your investment returns or the cost of owning a personal residence.

– **OWNER OCCUPIED PERCENTAGE and UNITS DELINQUENT on HOA   FEES** – You need to know these statistics to determine if financing is available, at what cost, and if is primarily a rental community or if it has significant owner occupied units.

– **CLUE REPORT** – To check for prior insurance issues on the unit or other units in the community which could be a clue to trouble ahead for the unit.

OVERWHELMED YET? Unfortunately we are just getting started. You will be overwhelmed by the time you are done analyzing the documents. But you have to hang in there and take the extensive time to understand this due diligence.

You will be significantly reducing your risk by understanding the guidance in this chapter and completing as many due diligence steps as you can to the best of your ability.

Again, you may not be able to get all of these documents, but larger professionally managed communities should have these available depending on the state in which the community is located. If you cannot get them all you will need to review what you can get and from the guidance in this chapter hopefully be able to make an educated decision on the condition of the HOA in which you will be an owner.

HOW HOA FEES ARE CALCULATED:

Let's take a look how HOA fees work which will better help us understand why we need to get a full financial picture before we buy. See budget on page 109.

The Board of Directors (BOD) reviews and approves a budget before the start of the year that sets what the monthly HOA fees are to be paid by each unit. These monthly fees generally are used for two purposes, to pay for the current year HOA OPERATING EXPENSES like landscaping, utilities, water, management fees, elevator contracts, etc. AND to set aside monies for long term CAPTIAL REPLACEMENT ITEMS like roofs, private streets, painting, elevator upgrades, etc.

PART I – OPERATING EXPENSES - Let's say the BOD reviews the past year financials and sees that in the prior year it cost $230,000 to operate the community (so just the current year operating expenses). They all agree, based on estimated costs prepared by the management company, that they need to collect a little more or $240,000 for the upcoming year to pay all the operating expenses. Click Here to see a HOA Fees Budget. (or herein: HOA Fees Budget Spreadsheet) And print it out now and we will run through the expenses which guide the Board in setting the monthly HOA fees. So read below and look at the budget you just printed when we direct you to **LOOK AT BUDGET.**

So the Operating Expense piece of the HOA fee is $200 per unit per month.

Operating Expenses for Year	$240,000
Monthly Operating Expenses	$20,000
Per Unit Monthly Fees – 100 Units	$200

Now **LOOK AT BUDGET** you printed and in getting to this $200/unit/month the first thing the BOD did was use last year's actual costs to help them project how much costs will be in the upcoming year. On the budget, to the right of OPERATING EXPENSES they filled in all their projected numbers and they estimate the $20,000 per month will be the cost to operate the community – See "Total Operating Expenses" line Item of $20,000 or $200 per Unit per Month.

PART II – Reserves for CAPITAL IMPROVEMENTS – The other part of the fee is the amount that is to be put away for long term replacements to the community. We will understand better how this works when we describe the Reserve Studies below, but for now let's just assume:

Capital Improvement Reserves Required
(Current Year $ for HOA Reserve Funds Account) $120,000
Monthly Required Reserves $ 10,000
Per Unit Monthly Required Reserves $ 100

So you can see that the LONG TERM CAPITAL RESERVES per unit is $100 per month. This may not be enough to get your HOA "FULLY FUNDED" for long term repairs (explained below), but it is the amount that the BOD decided upon for this year to put some additional monies away toward their FULLY FUNDED goal. Increasing fees to get to FULLY FUNDED might put some or many homeowners into financial distress – and the BOD wants to avoid that because some people might make the decision to stop paying their HOA fees if it is too much.

LOOK AT BUDGET – So under "Reserves" you can see the $10,000 or $100 per unit per month that the Board has approved. On the budget at Reserves it is noted that the $10,000 per month, for the whole community, will get the community to 50% "Funded" over a few years going forward and that if the community wanted to get to 75% Funded, it would have to put $13,000 per month into reserves. But the Board, on behalf of the owners, made the decision to hold the line at $10,000 per month because $13,000 per month would be more than residents could really afford to pay in these tough economic times. This reserves amount is the real variable here. The more that is put away for long term repairs on a regular schedule, the less the chance of special assessments down the road to make up a shortfall for needed capital repairs. It is a balancing act and decision by the Board between how much residents can and want to pay monthly versus the risk of not having enough funds for HOA owned repairs to roofs, roads, mechanical equipment, etc.

PART III – The total amount that needs to be collected from owners we now know is $30,000 per month – which is budgeted and approved by the Board of Directors - or $300 per unit per month ($200 for OPERATING and $100 for LONG TERM CAPITAL REPLACEMENTS).

LOOK AT BUDGET – And that is the amount of "Regular Assessments" under Income section of the budget that unit owners will pay $300 per unit per month. There may be some Interest Income from the cash held in reserves or laundry or water reimbursement income that might reduce this monthly HOA fee per unit, but one way or another there needs to be enough money to pay operating expenses and put away for long term repairs.

THEREFORE - In a perfect world all owners would pay $300 per month and that would cover all the operating expenses and put away the $120,000 for long term repairs which would increase that Reserve/Replacements Fund. We all know that we do not live in a perfect world - and in the current financial climate many people are not paying their HOA dues. So the question is how much cash will ACTUALLY be collected overall in the next year, and is that even enough to pay the current year operating expenses and put away monies for reserves? Sometimes the Board doesn't budget anywhere near enough to pay operating costs AND put money away for long term repairs. This could be due to expenses being much higher than anticipated, HOA fees not being collected due to financial issues, or the board just did not do a good job with the budget.

Either way, if there isn't even enough money collected in the current year to pay even the operating expenses, the HOA may have to "dip" into money already saved in the long term reserve accounts to pay current year operating expenses. That may be okay on a short term basis like a couple of years and as long as it is not too much, but it depletes the Reserve/Replacements Fund so that has to be made up somewhere down the road (more on this related to Reserve Studies/Reserve Funding). But you need to know whether or not this is happening because if it has happened for the past many years it may go on for many more years and continuously deplete the long term reserves – and that could be a problem.

Back to HOA Fees Calculation – So that budget and the above information should give you a good idea on how HOA fees are calculated, reviewed, determined and approved by the Board.

ProfessorBaron.com
Real Estate Investment and Due Diligence 101
A Smarter Way to Buy Real Estate

Budget for This Coming Year
Estimated Amounts Based off Prior Year's Actual Results
For the Year Ending December 31, 2010

		ESTIMATED BUDGET 2010 MONTHLY	Notes:
Number of Units = 100			
Income - Cash Inflows			
INCOME	Regular Assessments	$ 30,000	This is actually the last number calculated after all other numbers get filled in below. Read chapter for details!
	(100 Units X $300 per Unit X 12 Months)		
	So, $300 per unit per month.		
	Total Income	$ 30,000	
			Notes: Compared to Prior Year No Note = Same as Prior Year
Operating Expenses - Cash Outflows			
OPERATING EXPENSES	Gas & Electric	$ 550	Increase 3% from Prior Year
	Water & Sewer	$ 5,300	Increase 10%
	Sub-Meter Reading	$ 1,215	Decrease less readings 5%
	Landscape Maintenance	$ 3,800	
	Landscape Supplies/Repairs	$ 410	
	Tree Service	$ 300	Defer work to following year
	Pool Service	$ 355	
	Pool Repair/Supplies	$ 120	
	Rubbish Services	$ 2,500	Decrease - Bid to new vendor
	General Maintenance/Repairs	$ 800	Up per Reevaluate Actuals
	Administrative Supplies	$ 600	
	Audit/Tax Preparation	$ 83	
	Legal/Collections	$ 400	Up 10%
	Reserve Study	$ 34	
	Management and Accounting	$ 3,000	
	Property Insurance	$ 445	Up 5% per Insurance Co.
	Permits	$ 23	
	Corporate Taxes	$ 65	
	Total Operating Expenses	$ 20,000	= $200/Unit/Month
RESERVES	Long Term Repairs and Replacements (Funding per Month)	$ 10,000	- $100/Unit/Month - Per Reseve Study Expert Advises to get to 50% funded. - Expert said need $13,000/month to get 75% funded, but residents cannot afford that much this year so the Board approved $10k/Month.
	Total Expenses (Op Exp + Long Term Reserves)	$ 30,000	
	Excess Revenues over Expenses	$ -	SHOULD NET TO ZERO - BREAKEVEN

RESERVE STUDY/RESERVE FUNDING and ANNUAL FUNDING AND DISCLOSURE STATEMENT.

HOW MUCH IS ALREADY PUT AWAY FOR LONG TERM RESERVES/REPLACEMENTS IS ONE OF THE MOST VITAL FINANCIAL QUESTION WE NEED TO ANSWER IN DOING OUR DUE DILIGENCE. The way we figure this out is by determining what "Percent Funded" are the long term repairs and capital replacements.

The purpose of a reserve study is to determine if the HOA has put away enough money to cover long term repairs and replacements. So a company like Association Reserves would go to a property and inventory all of the Capital or Long Term repair/improvements related to an HOA's assets, roofs, streets, mechanical equipment. They would look at the current state of the assets and estimate a remaining useful life for those assets and the cost to replace each asset at the point, many years out, when they believe it would be at the end of its' useful life.

PERCENT FUNDED ISSUE

A simple example will best illustrate this concept - let's talk about the roof and assume it is the year 2010. Again, we note "simple" but it is not – just take your time and read every word on the document.

GO TO THE WEBSITE AND PRINT OUT THIS <u>SIMPLE RESERVE STUDY EXAMPLE</u> (or herein: <u>Simple Reserve Study Example Spreadsheet</u>) TO REVIEW. On page 111.

In this document, we would look at the roof and determine that it is 5 years old (new in 2005) and will last another 5 years (until 2015). Let's assume it is 2010 or halfway through the useful life of the roof. So 5 years from today it will cost $500,000 to replace based on inflation adjusted estimates of roofing costs at that time.

The HOA hopefully has been saving money for the past five years (part of the RESERVES and CAPITAL REPAIR/IMPROVEMENTS BUDGET and FUND) and since it is at one-half its' useful life and will cost $500,000 to replace, we should have $250,000 saved today on our way to reaching the $500,000 goal in five years to pay for a new roof. Since our schedule dictates that we should have $250,000 saved, if we do have $250,000 saved, we are 100% funded for this one item – that is FULLY FUNDED. If we only had $125,000 saved (just for the roof item) and we are supposed to have the $250,000 saved then we are 50.0% funded ($125,000 of $250,000 = 50.0%). If we are less than FULLY 100% FUNDED we are going to have to make up the difference over the next five years. To meet that goal, just for this one item, we will have to either increase HOA fees or at the five year point (year 2015) have a special assessment to pay for the   roof.

Either way, if you own in this community, you will be the one paying higher HOA fees or Special Assessments with the other owners to save enough money to make the needed repairs to the HOA capital replacement items when they need to be replaced.

So in a reserve study, it isn't just the roof, it is ALL the HOA owned components. So we would put together a schedule of all the items, their useful lives, their estimated costs to repair/replace and how much money should be saved at this point. We would also need to know how much more needs to be saved each year so there is enough money in the Reserve Fund to pay for repairs as they come due.

As noted in the simple Reserves Study example you can see that whether or not the HOA is fully funded – or at least healthily funded – depends on many different factors that have occurred over the years since the HOA and community was created. If the Percent Funded is low, that will need to be made up over time via either increased HOA fees or special assessments. Hopefully the Board of Directors is taking steps to close the shortfall, but raising HOA fees is tough in this tough economic climate.

The average HOA, depending on the type of property, is probably 30.0% to 50.0% funded. Some are in better shape, some much much worse.

So you need to answer the question to yourself, "What percent funded (how much money does the HOA have saved compared to what it should have saved) is the HOA to be able to make repairs and replacements to capital items when those items need to be repaired or replaced?"

UNFUNDED DOLLAR AMOUNT in TOTAL and PER UNIT ISSUE

The second issue to look at here is the total UNFUNDED DOLLAR AMOUNT per unit. So in the past example, let's say the HOA only had $125,000 saved at the five year mark of the $250,000 they should have saved. They are $125,000 short – TOTAL UNFUNDED DOLLAR AMOUNT of being fully funded – if the roof was their only asset. If there are 100 units in the community, that is only $1,250 per unit underfunded ($125,000 shortage divided by 100 units) and that is not too much. You could expect over the next five years that you will have higher HOA fees to make up this shortfall or at the point when the repair is needed owners would have a one-time special assessment to chip in to cover that $1,250 unfunded amount per unit.

However, what if the UNFUNDED DOLLAR AMOUNT in TOTAL is $1,000,000 and there are 100 units in the community, that is $10,000 per unit – and that is something that should be more concerning to a potential buyer. Or what if the UNFUNDED DOLLAR AMOUNT in TOTAL is $2,500,000 in a big building with only 100 units, that is $25,000 UNFUNDED AMOUNT per Unit – and that should really concern a potential buyer in that Community or Building because at some point, each owner is going to have to make up that difference when the Board of Directors decides it is time to make the needed repairs and/or replacements.

Recall that NO community only has a roof, so the reserve study adds up all the components, useful lives, costs to fix at how many years out, and comes up with a TOTAL Percent Funded for the entire community.

Your job is to review the PERCENT FUNDED for long term repairs and replacements and the UNFUNDED DOLLAR AMOUNT per Unit so you can determine if you should avoid buying into that community because they just may not have saved enough money in the past years to come anywhere near close to having enough money to pay for all the expected capital items repairs and replacements over the next bunch of years.

Percentage Funded and Risk of Special Assessments:

- We believe that a community that is 0.0% to 30.0% funded has a 1 in 3 or 33.0% risk of a special assessment on each unit in the property.
- We believe that a community that is 30.0% to 70.0% funded has a 1 in 10 or 10.0% risk of a special assessment on each unit in the property.
- We believe that a community that is 70.0% + funded has 1 in 100 or 1.0% risk of a special assessment on each unit in the property.

How much that special assessment might be is uniquely related to each specific HOA and the PERCENT FUNDED and UNFUNDED DOLLAR AMOUNT per UNIT – and to figure that out you need to review the latest reserve study.

COMPARE RESERVE STUDY DATE TO CURRENT CASH RESERVES HELD BY THE HOA - You also need to look at the date the latest reserve study was done, or the most recent update, and see how much cash (Bank CDs or other Liquid Investments) was on hand as of that date in the HOA Reserves Fund according to the Reserve Study – because that is the number they used for calculating both the Reserve Funding Percentage and the Unfunded or Deficit Dollar Amount per Unit. If the study was done three years ago and there was $500,000 noted in the Reserve Study you need to compare that to the latest HOA financial statements to see if that $500,000 is still in the Reserve Fund (or if it should have grown by now and to how much in total).

It may be depleted because the HOA made capital repairs that were on schedule and in that case that is fine (i.e. they paid for a new roof, repair roads, etc.). But if there is a much lower amount of cash on hand than noted in that Reserve Study and the money was not used for scheduled capital replacement items, you need to ask the Board or Management company what was that money used for? Was it emergency repairs? Was it used to cover shortages in normal HOA operating expenses? Was it used to fight or file litigation?

Depending on the use, now the percent funded may be lower than the reserve study notes and the fund may be depleted and not available to repair or replace capital improvement items. Why is there less money in the Reserve Fund than there should be and what problems coming down the road does that create for you as a potential owner? And maybe you should really consider whether or not you want to be an owner in this community???

SOME HOAs MAY NOT HAVE RESERVE STUDIES OR IT MAY NOT BE REQUIRED IN THAT STATE - In some states and/or some HOAs, they may not have had reserve studies done or maybe not one done in many many years. In that case, you are really buying into a community with a lot of financial risk that you have very little ability to quantify. In this case, it is truly buyer beware. What can you do? You need to gain an understanding of what the HOA actually owns and is responsible for the maintenance of and repair of each year and over time. If not many items and not a large dollar amount is the responsibility of the HOA, that would be good. If there are large dollar items that the HOA owns and has to maintain, and the HOA has no Independent Reserve Study and/or does not know what future repair and replacements costs will be, that is a potential problem.

Additionally, realize that the estimates for the costs to replace long term capital items are just estimates based on many assumptions. Those estimates from the past we now know have typically been much lower than actual realized costs that are experienced when repairs are actually made – so beware. Even if the HOA is in decent financial shape per the reserve study, it should always be trying to increase the percent funded to reach the 100% funded goal because of the unknown repair and replacement costs and issues in the future.

Here is a complete Reserve Study Template that should hopefully be somewhat like the study done for your targeted community – however there are many different formats for these reports and few standardized documents which makes this analysis tough.

In the above Reserve Study there is this Reserve Balance Table that is really the most important item a buyer would want to review. Hopefully the reserve study for your targeted community has a schedule similar to this schedule which shows where the HOA is related to the Percentage Funded, where the HOA is related to being FULLY FUNDED and hopefully a path for it to make up any shortfall.

There are also state mandated disclosures and the California disclosure is pretty straight forward as we next explain.

RESERVE FUNDING AND DISCLOSURE Summary – CALIFORNIA REQUIRES and "Assessment and Reserve Funding Disclosure Summary" per law for every HOA. Different states have different rules and regulations, and unfortunately more often than not the rules do not require reserve studies, funding, much disclosure or other useful information for buyers into a community. But again, you take the risk of increased HOA fees, special assessments, or deteriorating property conditions if needed work is NOT completed and hence the value of the unit you are buying may decrease due to repairs not being completed.

You can see the disclosure rules and laws for different states here: <u>Reserve Study Laws</u> at www.ReserveStudy.com.

Understanding the California Form will give you further information on what you need to analyze, regardless of the state within which your targeted property is located.

Click here to see the California <u>Assessment and Reserve Funding Disclosure Summary</u>. The entire document has vital information but we would advise you to carefully review number 6 which shows that this HOA is only 29.6% funded, which generally is very low. However, a close review shows that UNFUNDED DOLLAR AMOUNT per UNIT (noted as "Reserve Deficit) is only $1,161.69 – per unit – so that is your risk. That would not scare us because the HOA can become FULLY 100% FUNDED if every owner writes a check for just $1,161.69 or the owners could make this pretty small deficit per unit amount up over time. On the other hand if it showed that the reserve deficit was $14,000 per unit that would scare us.

www.reservestudy.com - for Example

TO SUM UP THE ISSUES AND RISKS RELATED TO RESERVE STUDIES AND RESERVE FUNDING.

In doing your due diligence, you need to assess what percent funded the HOA is and how much any unfunded (or underfunded) amount is per unit. If they are healthily funded like 50.0% plus, the financial risk of higher HOA fees or special assessments is lower – not zero, just lower. But if that 50.0% comes out to $20,000 per unit in underfunding, you need to think about the risk that you may need to come up with those funds at some point in the future.

GUIDANCE – Again, HOA Financial analysis is a exercise in disaster avoidance. If the HOA Percent Funded is very low like 25.0% and the unfunded amount per unit is high, like $12,000, you need to assume that in addition to your regular HOA payments you may need to come up with that $12,000 at some point. This could be either higher HOA fees along the way or a one-time assessment in the future years. Be very cautious about older high rise condominium associations that are significantly underfunded on a Percent Funded and on a Underfunded per Unit basis as payments you make to the HOA will most likely increase in one of the two forms in the future. And with older buildings, it always seems all costs, operational and capital and replacement costs, end up being much greater than originally anticipated!

FINANCIAL STATEMENTS OF THE HOA

The financial statements of the HOA are the next piece of the pie that will help you determine the financial health of the Association. The risk here relates directly to whether or not there is enough money being collected by the HOA to pay for the current year operating expenses and the long term capital repair/improvements - the Percent Funded from above. You want to look at the financial statements to see if the HOA dues that are actually collected during the year are enough to pay for current year operating expenses and put some money away into the Capital Reserves. If the Percent Funded from above is high (healthy HOA), then a year or two of bad financials, which most HOAs are experiencing these days, is not that big of a deal.

However, if the Percent Funded is low and the Unfunded Amount per Unit is high, and the HOA had a bad last year and this year is also looking bad, that is cause for concern. So a "really bad financial year" can be defined as the HOA dues actually collected are not enough to even pay the current year operating expenses, this might mean that the HOA would dip into the Long Term Capital Reserves Fund and take money to help pay the current year Operating Expenses. So instead of putting away additional monies for Long Term Items, the HOA is actually depleting those reserves – which they, or better stated YOU as an owner, will have to make up in the future.

Realize/Recall that one way or another expenses need to be paid for or the project might get run down and then owners lose value in their units as buyers decide not to buy into that HOA community.

The good news is that Audited Financial Statements which should be available for any large HOA community (smaller communities may or may not have them and they may not be audited, so you have to make your best guess on whether or not they seem reliable) are pretty standardized according to US Accounting Rules. Reviewing the prior year too is a smart move to see if there is any trend like continued borrowing from the reserve funds to fund current year operations. There are three statements that you should receive for the latest complete Fiscal Year of the HOA Operations, go ahead and print them out – Click here to see Financial Statements (or herein: Financial Statements Spreadsheets).

Go to ProfessorBaron.com to print out these documents:

1. Income Statement;
2. Balance Sheet;
3. Statement of Cash Flows.

Let's first look at the most current year 12 month Income Statement (And we are trying to make this as simple and straightforward as possible). Recall before the start of the year the HOA approved a budget that would provide for funds to pay for current year operating expenses and to put away some monies into the reserve funds. They took the total amount needed and divided it by the number of units and months to set the monthly HOA fees that an owner pays.

That was at the start of the year, now it is year end and we can see how they did. These financial statement figures do not match the prior above BUDGET, they are just for illustration purposes.

Income and Profit Statement

Box 1 on the Right shows that they collected $377,832 in total income which $270,154 was allocated for Operating expenses and $107,178 was to be put away for Long Term Reserves. Hopefully that is close to the amount that was budgeted at the beginning of the year so the HOA stays on financial track.

Box 2 shows "Bad Debt Expense" and this is the amount of Regular Assessments that the Board believes it will NOT collect due to many reasons, foreclosures, etc. It is good that they budget that amount and in this case it is 5.55% ($20,970/$337,332) and that is not too bad. Uncollectible HOA dues could be a lot more in these tough financial times.

Box 3 shows the overall Income less expenses. The Operating Fund side should break even, but you can see they had more expenses then revenue, in fact ($54,243) more in expenses than revenues. That is not a good thing because they did not budget and/or collect enough monies to pay all the operating expenses. The good thing is they did collect enough money to still put away $90,161 towards long term reserves for future capital repair/improvements.

Box 4 however shows the result of not having enough income to cover all the expenses, you can see how the HOA effectively lost the ($54,243). So what did the Board decide, it decided to dip into its' Reserve/Replacement Fund to the tune of $53,832 to pay operating expenses. So the amount that would be put away towards long term repairs is going to be less due to this dipping. They really only put away $36,329 (the $90,161 less the ($53,832)) for the year into Long Term Reserves. They will have to replace/make up that borrowed ($53,832) over the future years. But at least they saved some additional monies in the current year.

How does this happen? The HOA may just have not budgeted very well due to inexperience or other factors, or costs may have been much more expensive than anticipated, or people in financial trouble or units in foreclosure were not paying their HOA dues. Unfortunately costs related to long term repairs are still increasing and at some point more money will need to be collected to cover all the shortfalls. If you buy into this community, that will be YOU paying more into the HOA fund. How much more depends on how the HOA does financially. And the Board simply raising HOA fees may not work, that may cause more people to not pay and simply default or walk away from their units. Once things start to go really bad, especially older communities with lots of foreclosures and lots of items that need to be repaired or replaced, it usually gets worse. So if the situation appears dire, you may want to avoid buying into this community.

We just saw their current year operational statements where combined between the Operating Fund and Replacement fund they paid all the bills and put away $36,329 for the year. So the real question is how does this equate, if at all, into increasing their CASH is in the Long Term Reserves Accounts at year end.
Balance Sheet

You can see in Box 5, page 2, that there is $144,586 of cash in the Long Term Reserves Fund as of the end of the year. So again, you would want to know what percent funded does this equate related to the long term funded and reserve study for replacing capital asset items owned by the HOA.

Again, if the reserve study shows a high Percentage Funded then a couple/few bad years like in our example probably will be made up over the following decade as the economy recovers and people start and/or new owners start paying their HOA dues. But you need to be cautious of HOAs that are in poor shape financially. As noted before, one factor that might lower your risk is the Unfunded Dollar Amount per Unit is low. For some communities, like one or two level townhome communities or PUDs, the items that need repairs/replacements may only be roofs, private streets, painting etc. And if the Percent Funded is very low – which should be a concern – but the total unfunded amount per unit is only a few thousand dollars, then your risk may just be those few thousand dollars per unit. On the opposite extreme, if the Percent Funded is low and it is a very old high rise building that needs millions in repairs (hence tens of thousands of dollars per unit is Unfunded) then most likely you will be chipping in extra money in the next years.

TO SUM UP THE ISSUES AND RISKS RELATED TO THE CURRENT FINANCIAL STATEMENTS.

The current financial statements will show you how good a job the Board and Management Company are doing on collecting HOA dues AND paying current year bills AND most importantly putting away additional monies to cover long term repairs and replacements. A few less than stellar years may be okay if the HOA is healthily funded on a Percent Funded Basis or if the Unfunded Dollar Amount per Unit is low. But if the financials are bad, the Percent Funded is low and the Unfunded Dollar Amount per unit is high, you need to really consider whether or not this project is the right one for you.

BOARD of DIRECTORS MEETING MINUTES or other RECORDS

The Board of Directors of the HOA is in charge of managing the functions of the HOA. They have meetings (monthly, bi-monthly or quarterly) to discuss items and issues and make decisions on spending your HOA dues, budgets, hiring a management company, etc. Typically Minutes or Records of what is discussed and decisions made at these meetings are retained and available for review by current owners and a prospective buyer.

These records are what you need to review to determine if there have been any discussions about lawsuits or litigation related to the community, any major repairs or replacements, water or mold issues, specific unit HOA rule violations, unpaid dues, and every other item of business of the HOA. You need to review and read these items to learn of problems, lawsuits, and issues that could impact your ownership of your unit. For example, there may be discussions of construction defects or water issues in the Minutes. Either of these issues could be very large dollar expenses and they may not be provisioned for in the HOA dues or Long Term Reserves. In a case like this, you need to request more information from the Board and determine the potential expense to the community and take that into account in making your decision.

Beware because litigation usually will cause a bank to reject providing mortgage financing for a unit in a community. Even if you can and do purchase, like with all cash, if you decide to sell it may become an issue and effectively reduce the value or sales price of your unit. Water and mold issues can cause the same problem, not only can they cost hundreds of thousands of dollars to repair in a good sized complex, but they can scare away future buyers and hence less demand for the units which can cause values to decrease. Mold issues are typically uninsured, so the HOA ends up paying all the repair bills – that means YOU end up paying your pro-rata portion of all the repair bills.

EXECUTIVE SESSIONS also need to be considered – These would be rare in most communities, but beware. Some items may also not be disclosed if they are discussed in an HOA BOD meeting "executive session" which is private. Good luck on getting this information. You might want to question if there were any executive sessions or private discussions between board members related **TO YOUR UNIT** that you may purchase but would not be noted in the BOD minutes.

You may also want to request to know if there have been any executive sessions or private discussions that are "material" to the operations, financials, or legal issues related **TO THE COMMUNITY** as a whole. Like a potential lawsuit or other material issue. When we say you might want to ask, who you might ask is tougher to define. It might be the management company or it might be the Board of Directors. It is going to be a challenge getting this information and it might or might not contain material information that you need to know to make a better decision on your purchase. We do not have additional advice here, but if you suspect there may be some problem(s), issue(s), item(s) or other material fact upon which you believe you need to gain a better understanding – ASK. If you cannot get answers, beware.

THEREFORE, request and read the Minutes and any Other Records you can get, they may be the only record of HOA non-financial issues and are important to review.

COVENANTS, CONDITIONS and RESTRICTIONS (CC&Rs) and BYLAWS

The CC&Rs and Bylaws dictate the rules and regulations that you are agreeing to live by if you purchase into this community. They can govern pets allowed, number of rental units allowed in the building, cars and parking issues, keeping your patio, deck or other areas clean, what improvements you can make to your unit, and many other issues. This could be a 50 to 200 page document with much of it in legalese. So schedule a few hours of your time to sit down and read through these documents.

Typically they cover items and issues that are to the mutual benefit of all owners, but some might have specific issues like the number of units in the association that can be rental units. If you are buying the unit as a rental unit and there are already the allowed number of units, you may not be able to rent your unit. So you need to review these documents and any and all additions and addendums to the CC&Rs and BYLAWS and make sure you are comfortable with the rules, laws and guidelines within which you will be governed.

CONDO UNIT DEMAND STATEMENT – See page 121

When you go into escrow on your unit, another document related to the purchase of your exact unit is called the Unit Demand Statement (or something similar to that name) <u>DEMAND STATEMENT EXAMPLE</u>. This document provides additional information about your specific unit, like an HOA violation by the prior owner, any unpaid HOA dues or special assessments. It also notes whether or not there is any current or pending litigation. It also should note the amount of owner occupants vs. the rented units (non-owner occupied). So again, review this one or two page document for any information that is important to your purchase.

ProfessorBaron.com
Demand Statement - Condominium Unit
A Smarter Way to Check Out Your HOA

Demand Statement for Pacific Condominiums Homeowners Association

Requestor:	Escrow Corporation of Pacific Beach
Contact:	Bob Jones
Address	900 Garnet Avenue
	San Diego CA 92109
Phone #:	858-555-1212
Fax #	858-555-1212
Contact Email:	BobJones@escrowcorp.com

Subject Property

Seller:	Kent Dorfman		Buyer:	John Blutarsky
Seller:				
Contact Email:	KDorfman@FaberCollege.edu		Contact Email:	Bluto@FaberCollege.edu
Subject Address	123 Delta Tau Street		Trans #:	568934T3
Unit #:	124A			
City:	Faber City		Date Ordered: 12/4/2006 Closing Date 1/8/2007	
State/Zip:	Pennsylvania 22204		Buyer Phone: 858-867-5309	

ProfessorBaron Property Management Company provides the following Information on the above Unit

Unit Assessment Information

Total Regular Asssessments: $225.00	HOA Assessment Paid: Monthly
Assessments are are Paid Through: 12/01/10	Assessment Next Due Date: 01/01/11
Owners Current Balance As of: $0	Owner Occupancy: 63.0%

Regular Assessments are Due the 1st of the Month and are delinquent 15 days after the regular due date. The penalty charged on each delinquent assessment payment is $10.00.

Is the Association involved in Current or Pending Litigation: No

Are there any HOA Violations on this Unit? No   Description of Any Violation:

Are there any Special Assessments: No

Description of Special Assessment, Date Due, Amount:

ProfesorBaron.com HOA Data Provider Corporation

HOA INSURANCE COVERAGE and POLICY

This is an insurance policy that is procured and paid for by the HOA. It may protect common areas from liability, like someone suing if they fall on the property and get hurt. It may protect the physical structure of the unit, like from a fire. It may protect from an owner above your unit having a flood that damages your unit. IT ALSO MAY NOT PROTECT ANY OF THESE.

THIS IS PARTICULARLY IMPORTANT IF YOU ARE BUYING WITH CASH. IF YOU ARE FINANCING THE UNIT, BANKS GENERALLY WILL REQUIRE CERTAIN INSURANCE COVERAGE. This is because they have learned over time that there is high risk in not having the proper insurance in place. So they require proper insurance as a check and balance and help you the owner get the right insurance. BUT IF YOU ARE PAYING CASH YOU DO NOT HAVE A BANK LOOKING OUT FOR YOU AND YOU HAD BETTER MAKE SURE YOU KNOW WHAT IS COVERED AND WHAT IS NOT COVERED and get additional insurance to cover risk issues.

Obtain these copies of all the HOA insurance policies and get together with your insurance agent to determine what is covered and what personal coverage you need related to your unit and liability. The Chapter 10 Property and Liability Insurance chapter will assist you in purchasing the right coverage for your investment.

Other Insurance Coverage - HOAs may or may not have earthquake coverage, flood coverage, or other types of coverage. They may or may not be needed depending on the Board of Directors and your assessment of the risk, or they may be too expensive and that is why the HOA does not carry a certain coverage. There is some risk here and discuss with your agent the coverage options and then you can make the insurance decision of cost vs. risk of loss. It may not be an easy decision, but you will have to determine what works for you. Just as an example, if the HOA and you do not have earthquake insurance and your unit is destroyed by earthquake, you will still owe the mortgage even if the unit is destroyed and you may be completely out of luck. Again, you need to really think about the coverage vs. risk of loss and what makes sense for you. There is no easy answer.

Last insurance issue, in some places insurance for condos, or any property for that matter, could be very expensive. This would be coastal hurricane areas or where there is erosion. You may not be able to get regular insurance, you may need to buy it through the US Flood Insurance Program. Make sure you get a quote for insurance very early in the process as you do not want to think insurance will be $500 per year to find out late in the process that it is $4,500 per year.

CLUE REPORT. Also, have your insurance agent run a CLUE OR CUE report to see if there have been any past insurance claims on your unit or the building. If there have been lots of instances of damage to units for whatever reason, you want to know that so you can adjust your financial projection to reflect paying deductibles or potentially uninsured issues.

OWNER OCCUPIED VS. RENTAL UNITS and UNITS that are DELINQUENT paying HOA FEES

Another very important issue with HOAs is the number of owner occupied units vs. the number of investor owned rental units. A typical community might have 65% owner occupant and 35% investor units. This is important because a lot of banks require at least 60% owner occupied to be willing to lend mortgage money to a person to buy the unit. Some banks will charge a higher interest rate but do these loans. This is due to the fact that the banks have learned over time that communities with a large number of renters have higher default rates on loans.

It is believed that in general renters do not take as good care of common areas as owners and cause more issues in communities thus potentially decreasing the values of the property. Even if you are buying with cash, you should take this into account because it will reduce the number of potential buyers down the road for your unit if the percentages stay low.

Delinquent on HOA Fees. This is another statistic you should review because you could have some trouble getting financing if too many units are delinquent on HOA fees. For your analysis, we suggest trying to determine whether or not this is a short term issue caused by current financial crisis or a longer term issue caused by other issues and problems with the community that may be tough to turn around. In the long term case, it might be smart to avoid buying into that project. You will probably need to ask the management company for this information.

NEW PROJECT, TOO FEW OWNERS

So a new building is coming on the market and you want to buy one of the units. The developer has created a budget to pay for operating expenses and put away monies for long term reserves and divided it by the number of units so you know you HOA fees from the start. The developer must chip the same amount of HOA fees for each and every unit that he still owns. Let's say there are 100 units in the building and you buy one of twenty that are sold and then the market slows. The developer must continue to pay on the other 80 units until they are sold to other people like you.

Let's say due to the local economic conditions, the developer all of a sudden gets into financial trouble and stops paying his portion of HOA fees on the 80 units he owns. Some state real estate departments make a developer pay a bond, let's call it insurance, in case he runs out of money so that the HOA fees on the 80 units he owns continue to be paid. But maybe he didn't pay his current bonding/insurance premium due to bankruptcy and all of a sudden the management company and hence the HOA is only collecting fees on twenty percent of the units. And this isn't nearly enough to pay for lights, water elevators, etc. to keep the building operating. Guess what, you and the other owners may have to figure out how to pay all the bills, and it isn't going to be easy or inexpensive.

Therefore, if you are buying into a new building you had better make sure you know where the money to pay HOA fees is going to come from on the developer owned units. That means getting in writing assurances from the developer that clearly prove to you what will happen if the developer files bankruptcy? Are the HOA fees bonded/insured, how long are they bonded/insured for – 1 year? 2 years? Life of the project until it is sold out? Is there a maximum limit that a bonding/insurance company will pay in case the developer fails?

What are the state rules on bonding for HOA fees on developer owned units? And you had better have the developer provide written documentation that the bonding/insurance premium is PAID in full and for how long? And you should follow up and get written documentation from the Bonding/Insurance company that the policy is in effect. This is going to be a LOT of work, but it will be a lot harder if you have to figure out how a small number of unit owners have to come up with enough cash to pay for operating a large building.

ONE OWNER OWNS GREATER THAN 10% OF UNITS. This is a risk because in case that owner stops paying HOA fees on all his or her units, this may send the HOA into financial distress. The more units that one individual owns, the greater the risk if he or she stops paying.

NEW BUILDING – Last issue, for new buildings it is very tough to budget the HOA fees. Especially if that developer has not built that type of building in that local area before. And, developers, who create the budgets, have an incentive to budget low and maybe unrealistic numbers so buyers think, WOW, low HOA fees! So you buy into that complex and after the first year HOA fees go up a lot and Reserves are below the required amounts. Guess who will get to make up the difference going forward??? That's right, YOU as the owner. So in new buildings, if the HOA fees seem to be good to be true, they may very well be....just beware…

GOOGLE IT Lindsey, Google it! One smart reader "Lindsey G" Googled a prospective purchase at "**112 Ocean Drive, 11701**" and decided that might not be the right house for her. Give that address a whirl if you so dare! So, Google the association name, address, possibly with the words lawsuit, litigation, mold, construction defects – you never know what you might find!

THE DUE DILIGENCE CHECKLIST CAN BE DOWNLOADED AT WWW.PROFESSORBARON.COM

Use this **HOA DUE DILIGENCE Checklist** to keep on track. Good luck!

Or in spreadsheet form here: HOA Due Diligence Checklist.xls.

HOA Due Diligence
Property

ProfessorBaron.com

Buying Real Estate is the largest and riskiest purchase you will ever make in life.
Experienced buyers do their homework to protect themselves from the inherent risks.
You can also protect yourself, you just need to know what to do and how to do it.

Download the latest version of the checklist at www.ProfessorBaron.com
to study these concepts and use once you have a signed purchase

Property Address: _____   HOA NAME _____

HOA Management Company _____

HOA Contact Information _____

HOA Document Review Contingency Expiration Date _____

OVERALL NOTE - Few HOAs are in great shape in these difficult financial times. What you want to avoid is buying property in an
   HOA community that has significant multiple issues that could cause you to have to "chip in" a lot of additional monies over
   they next bunch of years so the HOA can stay afloat and keep the property maintained.

YOU MIGHT ASK - "ISN'T THERE AN EASIER WAY TO DO THIS?" UNFORTUNATELY, THE ANSWER IS NO.
DUE DILIGENCE IS HARD WORK AND TAKES TIME. EITHER YOU ARE GOING TO SPEND THE TIME TO LEARN THE ISSUES AND WORK TO AVOID
DANGER, OR YOU ARE GOING TO TAKE THE RISK OF MONETARY LOSS.

IT IS YOUR MONEY AT RISK AND IT IS BUYER BEWARE!

DUE DILIGENCE TASKS

Check them Off As you Go or Note your Findings

_____ Did I study the HOA Due Diligence Chapter and ALL its' information way in advance of offering on HOA governed properties?

_____ Did I forward the "HOA Document Letter Request" to escrow the day escrow opened?
   - Note, do not give this list to the seller before they sign your contract, they might select a different offer if they believe your
      document request is onerous. Also - it goes to the escrow agent, not the seller.
_____ Am I keeping the light pressure on escrow, the seller's agent and my agent to obtain the needed documents ASAP?
   NOTE: You may have to pay upfront the cost to obtain these documents if bank owned or short sale. Depends on Contracted Terms.

_____ Am I keeping track of my HOA document contingency expiration date and having my real estate agent prepare an addendum to
      keep this contingency open until I have ALL the documents I need and several days to review those documents to my satifaction?

_____ Do I understand how the HOA Budgeting works with a portion of fees going to Operating Expenses and a portion to Reserves?

_____ Reserve Study - Is the HOA putting enough monies away for long term repairs and replacements?

Percent Funded = _____

Unfunded Amount Per Unit (Deficit/unit) = _____

_____ Did I compare the DATE of the Reserve Study to the latest financial statements to ensure the Reserves Cash balance in the study was still in line with the most recent financial statement cash balance for the Reserves Account?

- If there is a lot less money in reserves, did I determine why and is it reasonable - like they made scheduled capital items replacements and repairs to the property. Or something that could indicate trouble, like emergency water issue repairs?

     Major Risk Here - Reserves Percent Funded Low, Deficit Per Unit High = Future HOA Fee Increases or Special Assessments.
     Mitigating Factor - If the HOA does not own/have to maintain large dollar value assets - most do have large value assets though.
     Mitigating Factor - Board has decided to increase fees and/or has a plan in place to increase reserves.

_____ FINANCIAL STATEMENTS - Did I review the most recent financial statements to determine if the HOA was breaking even on Income/Revenues minus Expenses?

If they were short and took money from Reserves to pay current year operating expenses, was it a lot? Did it happen in the prior year? Is the Board taking corrective action to raise HOA fees? Was there some unforseen reason they were short of funds for Operations - what is the reason? Is it going to continue or is it a short term (1-2 years) issue?

_____ Which way, financially, is the HOA heading? Lots of foreclosures and vacant units could mean trouble- hence higher fees.
Watch the Bad Debt Expense line items on the Income Statement - a high amount as a percentage of Regular HOA Due Assessments means they did not collect a lot of money - which could mean trouble.

_____ BOD Meeting Minutes - Did I review the HOA Board of Directors Meeting Minutes for the past 24 months to look for any major issues like water issues, construction defects or other litigation, Unit Violations, HOA fee delinquency issues?
Any other special HOA notices or documentation issues by the HOA that needs to be reviewed?

_____ Conditions, Covenants and Restrictions (CC&Rs) and Bylaws. Did I slowly and carefully review the CC&Rs and Bylawys of the community so I know the rules that I will have to abide by if I decide to purchase a unit here?

_____ Unit Demand Statement - Did I reviview the demand statement to confirm HOA fees, any unit violations, litigation, etc issues? Or any outstanding HOA liens on the unit?

_____ Insurance Policies and Binders - Master Policy, Liability, Earthquake, Others - Do I know what is covered and what is not covered by the HOA Policy? Do I know if there were any CLUE Report issues with the Unit? Do I know what coverage I need to obtain and the cost of that coverage for my financial projection? Discuss all insurance options with your insurance agent.

_____ Owner Occupant vs. Non-Owner Occupant - Do I know the percentage of Owner Occupants and the issues related to this per the HOA Chapter. If many renters, have I discuss this with my mortgage lender and the issues this creates?
Am I sure units in this building can be financed?

_____ New Building? - Am I familiar with the developer owned unit HOA fee assessment issue and doing my homework?
Am I sure units in this building can be financed?

_____ Ground Lease? Equipment or Common Areas Leased from Third Party? One Owner great than 10% Ownership?
Read Chapter Memos.

_____ Google the community name and address. You never know what you may find!

IF THERE ARE UNRESOLVED ISSUES YOU FIND RELATED TO THE FINANCIAL OR OPERATIONAL CONDITION OF THE HOA THEN YOU NEED TO DO MORE ANALYSIS UNTI YOU ARE SATISFIED TO MOVE FORWARD. BETTER TO BACK OUT NOW OVER BUYING INTO A PROJECT WITH TOO MANY ISSUES OR TOO MANY UNKNOWN ISSUES!

OTHER NOTES, ISSUES, CONCERNS?

_____

_____

_____

_____

CHAPTER 9

HOME INSPECTION/FIX UP COSTS

Doing a home inspection once the seller has agreed to and signed your purchase offer is typical of all real estate purchase contracts. It is one of the contingencies that allows you to have a competent inspector do a thorough review of the property to test appliances, water, electric, mechanical equipment (heater and A/C) and do a general review of the condition of the property. They typically prepare a written report to summarize their findings. Having an experienced person do the inspection is one of the most highly recommended due diligence tasks that a buyer should do when purchasing a property. The cost, depending on the size of the property, is typically $200 to $500 dollars and takes 1- 3 hours.

During the inspection the inspector will usually convey information to your real estate agent about items that need repair. Then the agent will request, in writing, that the seller fix the items or credit you some monies at closing to cover the costs of those repairs – even for properties that are sold AS IS sometimes the seller will kick in some monies to get the deal done. The seller can review the request and fix items, credit monies, or say no to doing either of those. At that point you can move forward with your purchase or cancel the purchase and get your earnest money deposit returned.

Exterior Surface and Components

Many times this inspection is only the second or third time you the buyer have entered the property. Sometimes a buyer does not even show up to the inspection and lets the real estate agent handle the whole process. And many times, the buyer is more

Exterior Walls: Stucco, Wood siding Gaps or holes not properly sealed at several areas. This can lead to moisture penetration and damage. This can also be used as a conduit for insects to enter the house. Recommend caulking these areas. Minor stucco damage was noted. Patch and repair was noted in one or more areas.

interested in determining whether or not their couch will fit in the living room or what color they want to paint the kitchen than determining all the issues that need to be repaired or replaced with the property.

No showing up for an inspection, or relying on your real estate agent for this task, or not paying 100% attention to the inspector's work and asking questions is NOT A SMART MOVE. Would you buy a used car without test driving it? This is the most expensive purchase you will ever make. Home repairs are very expensive and one needs to have their eyes wide open going into their purchase.

The inspector's report typically details whether something in the house needs to be repaired or not. The inspector also looks for major problem issues they see with the property.

THIS IS NOT GOOD ENOUGH. THIS IS NOT GOOD DUE DILIGENCE. THIS LEAVES YOU THE BUYER WITH SIGNIFICANT RISK ISSUES AND POTENTIAL COSTS THAT YOU NEED TO AND CAN ADDRESS BEFORE YOU BUY THE PROPERTY. IF YOU FAIL TO TAKE THE TIME TO DO THIS, AND YOU END UP SPENDING A LOT MORE MONEY ON REPAIRS AND/OR REPLACEMENTS ONCE YOU TAKE TITLE TO THE PROPERTY – YOU WILL UNDERSTAND WHY IT IS VITAL AND WOULD HAVE BEEN A SMART MOVE TO SPEND A LOT OF TIME ON THIS DUE DILIGENCE TASK.

You need to protect yourself and that means spending significant time understanding the condition of the property and the costs to repair or replace items that may be past their useful lives or that you are most likely going to update in the near future. Our attached Home Inspection Checklist will be a big help!

Let's look at why you need to do your due diligence here.

As an example, the inspector's report may detail that the air conditioning unit is serviceable and works. But what if the A/C unit is 15 years old and it is way past it's useful life. He may note that, but are you adding up all the costs of items that you will need to repair in the next few years? The inspector's report is not going to note that you will be spending $3,500 in the next few years to replace that unit. But do you think that would be good information to know? What if it is the house furnace too, and the kitchen cabinets, and the water heater, and the bathtub or the paint job, or the paint color? Would that be good information to know? Rarely do buyers spend the time to really get a feel for all the work that needs to be done in a property they are going to buy. But let's be a little smarter here and at least gain an understanding of the actual condition of the property and all the property's fixtures and systems.

NOTE: Every property needs work and you could find enough issues with almost any property to reject it and you would never end up buying real estate. We do not want that, but we are simply trying to assist you in making sure that the total cost of everything that needs repair or replacement today or in the near future is not TOO MUCH.

Do Your Own Inspection First

The best way to do this is to take the **Home Inspection Checklist** and have your real estate agent schedule for you to go to the property for a couple of hours when the owner is not present. This is so you can take your time without an outside pressure or interference from the seller. If you can get another set of eyes there with you, and preferably someone who has done some renovation or updates to their house and has some knowledge of costs, that is best. Spend some time going through the checklist at the property and make notes about what items you will repair or replace at the property. You do not need to be a home inspector to make the following determinations:

- What areas need to be repainted or do I plan to repaint because I do not like the color?
- What flooring do I need to change due to its' condition or because I want to change it?
- Kitchen – Cabinets? Countertops? Refrigerator? Dishwasher? – Will I replace any of these?
- Bathroom – Vanity, Sink, Bathtub, Toilet – Will I replace any of these?
- Windows and Doors – Will I replace any of these?

Study the checklist well before you go and do your inspection! Then, take measurements of the approximate square footage for items like flooring or wall and ceiling painting or vanity size or the number of kitchen cabinets or square footage of the countertop so you can use these to get estimates of costs. Take some pictures of items like kitchen cabinets or bath vanities so when you are talking to the home repair store person you can recall what information you need to discuss. And take lots of notes so you can remember items and issues you foresee.

And do not go to the store and price out the least expensive items and think that is all it will cost. After you close escrow and you are actually doing the renovation you will not make the same decisions. You will think, "that other vanity is more but so much nicer let's buy that one instead" or "I know we were going to buy the $18 per square yard carpet but the $32 per square yard is so much better, with the Stain Guard and upgraded padding, let's just get the better stuff". So try to be realistic about what you are going to buy. And do not forget sales taxes and delivery costs!

You should do this inspection of your own days before you are scheduled for the professional home inspection so that you can get some costs and further discuss issues with the expert – your home inspector. Recall that from the day your contract is signed (or approved by the bank in a short sale) you typically have

10-17 days to remove the home inspection contingency. So you need to get inside the property quickly to do your own inspection, so you can get to Home Depot or Lowes in the next few days to get cost estimates, then have your home inspection done, then firm up the cost estimates, then try to negotiate a little more with the seller as needed all within that timeframe.

As you can imagine, time goes quickly so you need to be ready to move in an expedient manner.

Now when your professional home inspector comes, you will be much more prepared to ask questions and the home inspector will greatly appreciate your having some knowledge and asking good questions. Obviously you need to be at the inspection, talk to and ask lots of questions, and continue using our checklist to run through and catalog any additional items that need attention. Once you have these cataloged, you should take the significant time it takes to obtain cost estimates to fix and repair or replace those items. It may end up being a lot of money and you may move forward regardless of the seller's response to your repair requests, but wouldn't you prefer to know what you are getting yourself into?

Again, all houses need work and repairs and it usually costs more than one believes, but by taking the time to understand what is needed related to repairs and costs for the biggest purchase you are ever going to make is just being smart. You may come up with $25,000 worth of items that will need repair or replacement in the not too far off future – and that may make you cancel the deal, but either way at least you know the situation.

So you need to do your due diligence here. You can do this, but you need to commit your time, energy and effort to do a complete and thorough job.

So we have created a **Home Inspection Checklist** that you should use during your home inspection. There may be other items that are not on the list but you need to quiz the home inspector on what other issues and costs he foresees related to the property – HE IS THE EXPERT!

TWO ADVICE ISSUES HEREIN

First, make sure your home inspector knows that you expect him or her to do the inspection "WITH YOU", not "FOR YOU" so that he agrees and understands what is expected. An inspector will probably not be used to this request, but you are paying for this and you need to get his or her advice on the issues. Honestly, buy them lunch or pay them some extra money if you need so they really go through everything in detail with you. Make sure the inspector knows beforehand that you have a healthy checklist of items that you want to cover during the inspection and you expect good advice and a thorough explanation of the full condition of the house and all it's fixtures, mechanical systems, structure, appliances, water, electrical, etc. – EVERYTHING. Bring additional people with you if you can, preferably someone with experience in rehabilitating homes, to ask pertinent questions.

Second, make sure to be cautious about comments and advice from anyone else who is not a licensed contractor or who does not have significant and recent experience doing property rehabilitations. Few people, possibly including your home inspector, know costs to rehab or replace fixtures, carpets, flooring, etc. If anyone comments that something couldn't cost all that much – be careful. Everything costs that much and probably more! YOU ARE THE ONE THAT NEEDS TO SPEND YOUR TIME AT THE HOME DEPOT, LOWES, OR WITH A CONTRACTOR TO PRICE OUT THE COSTS TO FIX, REPAIR OR REPLACE ANY ITEMS THAT WILL CONVEY TO YOU AND MAY NEED TO BE TAKEN CARE OF IN THE NEAR FUTURE.

EXAMPLE HOME INSPECTION – See on website.

Here is a sample of a high quality home inspection that clearly indicates the issues this inspector found at the property. Home Inspection Example.

CHECKLIST FOR YOUR HOME INSPECTION

We have created the attached home inspection checklist to help you during your inspection. Again, ask the inspector lots of questions, this is your chance to do your due diligence and protect yourself.

Tips:

- Buy 10.0% off coupons for Lowes and Home Depot on Ebay (the 20.0% off ones are fake). Each store usually will take the competitor's coupons.
- AskTheBuilder.com you want to understand how a contractor does work, like install a kitchen faucet, toilet or tile – Find it on www.Youtube.com and we like www.AskTheBuilder.com too and www.HowStuffWorks.com .
- RepairClinic.com is great for buying parts of appliances if you want to try and fix it yourself.
- Read Chapter 14 Flipping, Fixer Uppers – Bewares - before you consider taking on either of these strategies. And…BEWARE.
- Notice of Non-Responsibility – Spending a Lot on a Rehab – Want to Avoid Liens if the General Contractor doesn't pay the Sub-Contractors – Click here for Notice Of Non-Responsibility information.
- Consider changing out all the water valves and flexible feeder lines, plus washing machine rubber houses. Many times they are decades old and it is time to have them changed out to reduce your risk of floods.
- Handymen do not carry insurance and your insurance may not cover them, so be careful on what you are having them do. Also, make sure to negotiate fixed prices, if possible, for all the work you will have them do before they commence the work.

HOME INSPECTION CHECKLIST

Print all the tabs of this spreadsheet – 12 pages

Home Inspection Checklist

HOME INSPECTION CHECKLIST IS IN THE APPENDIX AT END OF BOOK

WE ONLY INCLUDED A FEW PAGES OF THE HOME INSPECTION CHECKLIST IN THE APPENDIX, PLEASE PRINT THE ENTIRE CHECKLIST AT PROFESSORBARON.COM

CHAPTER 10

PROPERTY AND LIABILITY INSURANCE

Property and Liability Insurance coverage is one of those issues that most real estate owners do not believe is all that important to fully understand - until their house catches on fire, floods, or a tree falls on the roof and they learn the hard way that their policy does not cover all the costs to rebuild. Most people, especially first time buyers, have little idea what the insurance policy they pay for does or if they have the right coverage and deductibles. This is because property insurance is relatively complicated - but we are going to make it easier to understand for you. After you learn the basics herein you will be able to sit down with your agent and ask the right questions to ensure you have the coverage you believe is adequate.

Overall, Property and Liability Insurance protects you from many of the risks and hazards of owning a home or investment property. Your main goal in carrying insurance is to be reimbursed for large dollar losses on properties that you would have had to pay for out of your pocket if you did not have the insurance coverage in place. These are items like if a fire burned down your home, or if someone fell on your property and was badly hurt and there were big medical bills to pay. Other covered "perils" would be broken water pipes, a tree falling through your roof, or if you were sued by a neighbor for your dog biting their child.

COVERAGE TYPE	INSURANCE COMPANY LIMITS OF LIABILITY	
Building Property/Dwelling	$ 178,000	
Separate Structures	$ 35,000	
Personal Property	$ 133,500	
Loss of Use/Additional Living Expenses	$ 48,500	
Family/Personal Liability Protection	$ 300,000	occurrence
Guest Medical for Others Protection	$ 1,000	person
Extended Replacement Coverage	$ 44,500	
Building Code Upgrade Coverage	10.00%	
DEDUCTIBLE ON LOSS	$ 2,500	

Proper coverage property insurance is really important because it protects you from devastating losses and disruptions to your life and livelihood. Luckily for you, lenders today will not loan money to buy homes without proof of home insurance – and they are doing you a big favor here. The first introduction to home insurance for a new homebuyer is during the close of escrow on a property. This is a very exciting time for a buyer, and reviewing an insurance policy does not usually top the list of priorities. Your property is a major investment for you. Whether you are a new homebuyer or have owned a property for years, it's important to spend a little time to review your insurance options and understand what you are buying.

During the past several years we have witnessed some major fires and natural disasters in California, floods in the Southeast, disasters in the Northeast that affected thousands of homeowners with claims on their home insurance policies. The purpose of this chapter is to provide some basics tips to help you evaluate your insurance policy. This chapter does not contain everything you need to know and it is always best to consult with your agent and your home insurance contract for complete details.

Let's begin by reviewing a few common homeowner questions that will get you to start thinking about the important coverage issues you will learn in this chapter:

Question #1: Does my home insurance policy cover almost anything happening to my home, such as maintenance issues, termites, construction defects, and more?

Typically, no. The general purpose of home insurance is to protect you from those perils that are out of your control such as a fire, rain storm, wind storm, theft, tree falling on your roof, or a pipe bursting. Home insurance covers your home structure, from the top of the slab, to the walls, and roof to the interior of the home up to the policy limits. As homeowners we have control over maintaining our home such as repairing a leaking roof, painting our home or repairing a leaking faucet – so those are yours to maintain. There is not much we can do about a fire sweeping through our neighborhood other than electronically storing data and photos about our property and having adequate insurance to protect us from the worst case scenario.

FYI - A home policy excludes coverage for earth movement, earthquake and natural disaster flood. Insurance Carriers do offer extra policies for these specific needs and you will have to decide what coverage is adequate for your comfort level.

Question #2: The insurance company agent wrote a policy for my home so it must be the right coverage for me? After all he or she is the expert not me!

Insurance agents gather some specifics about your home such as square footage and year built to estimate the minimum dwelling limit an insurance company will insure your property for. Then a conversation is needed between the insurance company and the homeowner to determine if the computer calculation is enough coverage for your unique need. For example, if a kitchen just had a $100,000 remodel, your policy coverage limit may need to be increased by that $100,000. The computer system has no way of knowing about the kitchen remodel.

IT IS YOUR RESPONSIBILITY TO DISCUSS THE COVERAGE YOU NEED WITH YOUR AGENT AND ENSURE THAT YOUR COVERAGE IS ADEQUATE TO REIMBURSE YOU FOR THE COSTS OF REBUILDING IN CASE OF A LOSS. IF THERE IS ANYTHING NON-TYPICAL ABOUT YOUR PROPERTY LIKE AN EXPENSIVE SOUND ROOM BUILD OUT OR ARTWORK OR ANTIQUES, YOU NEED TO TALK TO YOUR AGENT ABOUT THESE TO ENSURE THEY ARE INSURED IN CASE THEY ARE DESTROYED OR STOLEN.

Question #3: It's in my garage, or in my home, or on my property so it must be covered?

It may not be covered. It's important to call out some specific examples that were discussed during the California wildfires. Anything motorized such as a car, a boat, a motor home, dirt bike, etc needs its own insurance policy to be covered in a fire, such as an auto policy with comprehensive coverage for your car (for the peril of fire).

There are also limits on specific personal property items such as jewelry, watches, rugs, furs, guns, coins and more. As an example, theft of jewelry has a limit of coverage because these items are easily stolen. It's also difficult for an insurance company to know how to determine premium for jewelry since every homeowner has a unique need both large and small. Therefore, insurance companies set a limit of coverage on jewelry from theft and you can increase the coverage based on your unique need. So if you have some possessions of special value it's a good idea to review them separately with your agent.

Another helpful tip is home insurance views your business life and your personal life as separate issues. If you run a business out of your home and have samples, or supplies, you business items/inventory need a business insurance policy to be protected. Or let's say you hire a non-licensed contractor for a remodel on your home, this is considered a business relationship not covered by your home insurance policy.

A home policy primarily covers your home structure (walls, roof, interior of structure), it is not a landscaping policy and does not cover leaking sprinklers.

Question #4: What if I get sued from my dog biting someone or sued for something else, am I covered?

Typically yes. The liability coverage portion of your policy covers if you get sued. It does not cover business lawsuits, drunk driving, or issues where you were negligent or did not take due care to avoid damages. Dog bites, slips and falls, etc. are typically covered however some policies exclude certain dog breeds that the insurance companies have learned are aggressive – so ask your agent.

To make sure you understand the basics, here are the policy types information we will cover:

- Primary Residence Policy for a Single Family Residences.
- Landlord Policy for an owner who rents out a Single Family Home.
- Condominium/Townhome/Co-op Interior Policy – Primary Residence and Landlord Policies
- Renter's Insurance Policy
- Umbrella Liability Policy
- Earthquake Insurance Policy
- Flood Insurance Policy
- Other policies, helpful tips and useful information

Make sure to read all the coverage types and issues in this first "PRIMARY RESIDENCE" section because many other coverages below simply note: Same as Coverage above in the Primary Residence (PR) coverage section.

PRIMARY RESIDENCE POLICY FOR SINGLE FAMILY RESIDENCES: This coverage is for the single family home you live in on a full-time basis.

Note: if you have 2 primary homes, one would be considered your primary home and one would be secondary. Its important to review with your agent to insure each property properly.

Print this <u>Insurance Policy Example</u> to review as you read below.

ProfessorBaron.com
Insurance Company
A Smarter Way to Insure Real Estate

Insurance Policy Example

Policy Number: 94-66594-652
Policy Type: Property Hazard and Liability Insurance
Policy Period Date: From: 05-20-2010 to 05-20-2011 at 12:01 A.M. PST

Named Insured and Property Address:

Leonard P. Baron
1835 73rd Ave NE
Medina, WA 98039

Property Specifics: Single Family Detached Home
1,800 SF Wood Frame and Stucco Home Built 1959 - One Story Average Constuction Materials
Composition Roof, Copper Plumbing, Cement Slab Foundation, Drywall/Sheetrock Interior Walls
Bedrooms: 3, Bathrooms: 2.5, Average Grade Kitchen, Smoke Alarms, Flooring: 40% Ceramic, 60% Carpets

COVERAGES: We insure for the coverages and limits as specified below.

DEDUCTIBLES: Your deductibles on losses are as specified Below.

COVERAGE TYPE	INSURANCE COMPANY LIMITS OF LIABILITY	
Building Property/Dwelling	$ 178,000	
Separate Structures	$ 35,000	
Personal Property	$ 133,500	
Loss of Use/Additional Living Expenses	$ 48,500	
Family/Personal Liability Protection	$ 300,000	each occurrence
Guest Medical for Others Protection	$ 1,000	each person
Extended Replacement Coverage	$ 44,500	
Building Code Upgrade Coverage	10.00%	
DEDUCTIBLE ON LOSS	$ 2,500	

This policy does not cover earth movement including earthquake or flood damage.

Discounts: Auto/Home, Non-Smoker, Experience Rating, Smoke Alarm, Multi Policy Discount

Policy Premium - Annual: Due 05-20-2010 $ 275.32

Agent: Bob Smith
Phone: 800-555-1212
Agent Number: 85-6523

ProfesorBaron.com Insurance Corporation

Section I — Property Coverages

Coverage A – Dwelling

The physical structure of the home, roof, walls, floors, windows, doors, etc. This coverage insures the cost of rebuilding or repairing the dwelling structure for a covered loss, NOT the land. Your total purchase price or value of the property includes both the value of the land and building. In some high cost areas, land (your lot) can be a significant portion of the total value of the property so you do not want to buy $500,000 worth of coverage for a property where the cost to rebuild the structure is only $200,000. You will be paying much higher premiums than you need to adequately protect yourself. You need to determine with your insurance agent how much it would cost to rebuild your current home if a fire burned it to the ground. Most agents have estimates for the cost per square foot to rebuild a home.

The very best tip of this entire chapter: In California it is about $150-$200 per square foot to build a non-luxury home with a square footage up to about 3000 sq ft. So if your home is 1,500 square feet, the cost to rebuild may be $225,000 to $300,000 depending on if your home has higher quality materials like granite kitchen countertops or expensive hardwood flooring. You need to work with your insurance agent to estimate the cost to rebuild in your local area and then you pick the maximum amount of coverage you want. The higher the amount of coverage, like if you picked the $300,000 instead of the $225,000, the higher the annual premiums you will pay for insurance. Costs to rebuild do differ based on the local area within which you live and the quality of your home so again work with your agent on the appropriate coverage.

A tip to keep your policy current on an annual basis: At every policy renewal take your dwelling coverage divided by your square footage and ask yourself, is this enough in the current year, did we make any changes, purchases or upgrades? Adjust the policy accordingly.

BUT GET THE RIGHT AMOUNT OF COVERAGE OR A LITTLE MORE – IF YOU DID HAVE A TOTAL LOSS IT PROBABLY WOULD COST MORE THAN YOU THINK SO FOR THE LITTLE EXTRA PREMIIUM EACH YEAR IT IS BETTER TO HAVE MORE COVERAGE. INCREASE YOUR DEDUCTIBLE, DETAILED BELOW, TO LOWER YOUR PREMIUMS.

Coverage B – Other Structures

Unattached Garages, Sheds, etc. – This coverage is for structures that are separate from the main building and can include barns, hot tubs, pools, gazebos, detached solar or other structures. So discuss these structures with your agent to make sure you are adequately covered in case they are damaged. It is your responsibility to alert the agent to the fact that these separate structures exist and you need coverage for them as a typical home policy will provide 10% of your dwelling coverage for "other structures" and the insurance company does not know if you have a greater need unless they are notified. Additionally, if you have anything newly built on the property like an expensive deck, they only way your agent is going to know is if you tell them, so make sure to get adequate coverage for all those separate structures.

Coverage C – Personal Property

Your home policy calculates an estimated dollar limit of coverage (typically 50-75% of coverage A) for your loose personal property. Make sure this limit is adequate to cover all your items such as Tables, Chairs, Couches, Clothing, TVs, Beds – Do you have any expensive hobbies that might take a good portion of your limit of coverage? It is smart to take pictures and inventory a majority of items inside your house and store the data electronically out of the home. This is especially true if there are more expensive items that you own. This coverage does NOT cover expensive jewelry, and you may require additional coverage to properly protect artwork or special high value items. If you have these items, you need to disclose and discuss them with your agent.

Coverage D – Loss of Use/Additional Living Expenses

This really is a wonderful coverage. If your house burns down or suffers damage due to a covered peril which causes you to need to rent another house, this coverage helps you cover the cost of the additional rent and living expenses up to the policy limit. The insurance company will generally estimate based on your existing property how much it will cost to rent a comparable property and how long it will take to repair or replace your property up to the covered limit.

Coverage E – "Personal Liability" or "Family Liability Protection

Family Liability is lawsuit protection for you and resident relatives from others suing you, where you are found negligent in your personal life (not a business situation). If you get sued the insurance company will pay to defend you if the suit is a COVERED issue and pay the legal bills and any settlement or judgment against you up to your maximum covered loss amount that you selected. Most people do not even know that their homeowner's policy gives them some protection if someone files a lawsuit against them. Common coverage limits range from $100,000 to $1,000,000. A typical amount is $300,000 but you can do more or less based on your need. If your net worth is $300,000 or less then $300,000 is probably enough coverage – but if your net worth is higher you probably want to purchase more. The cost to increase this coverage to the maximum limit is minimal.

If you net worth exceeds the $300,000 coverage limit, you should consider a Personal Umbrella Policy to give you a higher coverage limit. They are inexpensive, typically just a few hundred dollars per year for $1,000,000 of extra liability coverage over and above your homeowners liability coverage limit– read more below on Personal Umbrella Policies.

F – "Liability – Medical Payments to Others" or "Guest Medical Protection"
This coverage is for a guest who incurs a minor injury on your property such as slipping on stairs and breaking a wrist with a visit to urgent care. Negligence does not need to be proven to pay on this claim up to the limit on your policy. Typical limits are $1000-$5000.

Extensions of Coverage

Extended Replacement Cost Coverage A-many carriers will provide a certain percentage of coverage above your dwelling limit in the event of a total covered loss. So if your dwelling is covered for $300,000 and your policy has extended coverage of 150%, then the maximum insurance will pay is $450,000 ($300,000 x 150%). This is a cushion of coverage and can be used if your dwelling limit is not enough to rebuild your structure. This coverage cannot be used to upgrade your home and only what is needed to rebuild will be allowed, so if it takes $400,000 to rebuild, you would be paid $400,000 not the full $450,000. Your carrier may provide this coverage as needed or it may be reimbursed to you after you incur the initial expense. Typical coverage amounts are 120-150% above your dwelling limit.

Contents Replacement Cost Coverage C – make sure your property is insured for "replacement cost" of your items. You can save a little by insuring your property on an actual cash value basis which means the insurance company will depreciate each item for how long you have owned it. The savings on premium is minimal for actual cash value coverage and replacement cost coverage is recommended.

Building Ordinance or Law –this is an automatic coverage on most personal residence policies, but double check that you have building code coverage regardless. Typically your carrier will provide 10% of your dwelling limit for building code coverage. Building codes are constantly changing and this coverage provides help if you need to repair your home from a covered loss and extra money is needed to bring the repair up to the current building code. Make sure you have this coverage.

DEDUCTIBLES

If you do have a covered loss, let's say a fire destroys your entire kitchen, you have to pay a portion of the loss. That portion is called your deductible. So if the loss is agreed upon by you and the insurance company as $25,000 and your deductible is $1,000, the insurance carrier will only pay you $24,000 because you have to pay the first portion of the loss – the $1,000 deductible. You typically have some options on your deductible, $500, $1,000, $2,500, $5,000.

The higher the deductible you select, the lower your annual premiums – so that is your trade off decision. However the important thing to know is that if you do a higher deductible like $7,500 and you have a $5,000 loss, like your garage door and windows are damaged, you pay the entire amount for that single loss since it isn't over your deductible. So you need to factor that in to your thoughts about what deductible is comfortable for you.

GENERALLY, PROPERTY INSURANCE COVERS THESE PERILS:

Fire or Lightning, Windstorm or Hail, Explosion, Riot or Civil Commotion, Aircraft, Vehicles, Smoke, Vandalism/Malicious Mischief, Falling objects, Weight of Ice or Snow, Increase/decrease in electrical current, Rupture of a steam or hot water heating system, Water or steam that escapes from plumbing system, freezing of plumbing, Theft, damage to covered personal property caused by breakage of glass

GENERALLY, PROPERTY INSURANCE DOES NOT COVER THESE PERILS:

Flood, Water that Backs up Through Sewer, Overflow from Sump Pump, Water Below the Ground Surface, Earth Movement, Building Codes, Failure to Take Reasonable Steps in a Loss, Intentional Criminal Acts, Nuclear Action, War, Collapse, Soil Conditions, Vapors, Wear and Tear, Mechanical Breakdown, Growth of Trees, Rust or Mold, Toxic Anything, Smog, Settling or Cracking, Insects-Rodents, Seizure by Government Authority, Vacant Building Issues, Seepage, Theft while under Construction, Theft while Home is Vacant, Faulty Construction

LANDLORD POLICY FOR A SINGLE FAMILY HOME: This policy is for a single family home that you rent out to others

The proper form of insurance is designed to protect you for each specific need. It is true that an insurance company may see a rental property as a greater risk, as a tenant may not give the same care and attention to a property as the primary owner. This can mean a little higher premiums. The premiums are calculated based on the risk for an insurance company and coverages are also designed to protect you as the landlord. Be sure to insure your property for its proper usage. You will benefit the most by having the proper form of insurance. The worry is having a loss that may not be covered because the proper form of insurance is not being used.

You will find in order to close on a loan for an investment property, the lender will require the proper form of insurance. An important example would be a covered fire at a home you rent out. Lets assume it will take 10 months to rebuild and your tenants are no longer paying rent. With the proper form of insurance, you may receive loss of rental income to assist you in paying the mortgage. If you have the property insured as a primary home and you are living at your primary residence at another location already, there may not be assistance for your loss of "rental" income, as this coverage is not part of a primary home policy.

Generally

The categories of coverage for this type of policy are:

A – Building Property or Dwelling – This is the same as Dwelling above in the Primary Residence Policy.

B – Other Structures – This is the same as Separate Structures in the Primary Residence Policy.

C – Personal Property – The coverage limits are generally designed to be much lower assuming that a landlord does not have personal items in a rental property. A landlord property may have a refrigerator, washer/dryer or a few other items. So your maximum coverage amount should be much lower than a primary home policy and landlord package policies are generally designed with lower personal property limits for this reason.

D – Loss of Rents – This is similar to the Loss of Use in a Primary Residence Policy and will help assist you for your loss of rental income due to a covered loss. This is a very important coverage to have as a Landlord and many lenders look for this clause in the contract in order to close on a loan for a rental property.

E – Personal Liability – This is similar to the Primary Residence Policy and protects you for lawsuits from your negligence. As landlords, we recommend maxing out this coverage as the cost is minimal for the extra protection. A personal umbrella policy would also cover a single family rental home.

F – Liability – Medical Payments to Others or Guest Medical-same as Primary.

Building Ordinance or Law – Same items to consider as a primary home policy.

Sometimes landlord package policies have coverage for burglary and vandalism, or they may be add-on coverages that you will want to discuss with your agent.

Review the covered perils and ask the agent to review all important details and limitations of the policy. Again earthquake and natural disaster flood are separate policies in order to have coverage for this peril.

CONDOMINIUM/CO-OP INTERIOR POLICY (HO-6): For shared structure ownership

Used as a PRIMARY RESIDENCE or LANDLORD/rented to others POLICY
Insurance for a condo can be tricky, but it is relatively simple if you know what to look for. If you are buying a condo, here is what we would recommend prior to the purchase. Find out what the HOA covers and what your obligations and options are for your condo unit.

A very common situation that occurs in shared structures are water losses that involve multiple parties due to the shared ownership of the structure. These are important tips for you as a buyer. If you prepare in advance, it will help to alleviate some of the stress of the loss situation.

1. Obtain a copy of the master HOA insurance policy from the HOA. Contact the insurance agent and review the policy and common loss situations with the agent to educate yourself on what you need to know.

2.   Obtain a copy of the master HOA CC&Rs: this is a large document of rules and regulations of the association. Read the document and ask questions.

3.   Master HOA: The HOA insures the common areas and the walls and roof of the building structures. It is possible for your HOA to have over 3 master insurance policies for fire, earthquake and flood. Find out what types of policies the HOA has in force so you have that understanding of any gaps in coverage. Many do not have earthquake and flood coverage – might not be needed.

4.   Purchase an interior HO-6 policy to protect your interior condo investment. The policy is typically very reasonably priced for some excellent coverage. Until recently banks that were financing condominiums did not require an owner to get these interior HO-6 policies and often owners skipped this important and reasonably priced insurance. We are all lucky that banks now typically require this insurance. This is because there is a LOT of risk that can happen inside the unit that can cause severe financial loss to the owner of the unit if they don't have an interior coverage policy. Even if you pay cash for your condo and you do not have a requirement to purchase an HO-6 interior policy, we personally would not buy a condo without this coverage – the risk of loss is simply too high.

HO-6 Interior Primary policy: From the walls in of the condo unit. It is also possible to have an HO-6 interior condo policy that protects you from fire, and separate policies for interior earthquake and natural disaster flood. These are your options to consider for your condo unit.

HO-6 Interior Condo <u>Rented to others</u>: This policy is for when you are renting the condo and provides you with the valuable loss of rental income coverage. If the lender knows the purpose of the loan is to rent the condo, they will look for the specific loss of rental income clause on the insurance policy prior to closing on your loan.

What if there is a water damage loss? The ideal situation would be that every condo unit owner has an interior HO6 insurance. If there a loss, each condo unit owner can have their insurance carrier represent them to work out if the loss is covered and who is responsible for the damage. We can guarantee that if you do not have an interior HO6 policy there is no-one in your corner to help you. This is a common and very frustrating situation as the HOA will always tell you that you are responsible for all damages. Water losses can be tricky on determining who is responsible.

Did the loss occur within the walls of the condo such as a washing machine hose bursting which may fall on the interior HO6 policy. Or did the loss occur within the walls of the structure, possible an HOA master policy issue? This HO-6 policy may also cover costs if you or your tenant cause damages to other units. For example, if your washing machine hose breaks and floods other units and causes damage, you may be covered up to your policy limits. Additionally, if your neighbor's washing machine hose breaks and floods your unit, you may be covered up to your policy limits.

If you do not carry an HO-6, we highly recommend that you obtain an interior unit insurance policy to protect yourself whether it is a Primary Residence or Landlord Rental property. A few examples of why these policies are important:

A – Building Property or Dwelling – This is the same as Dwelling above in the Primary Residence Policy but it should be a much smaller amount because the HOA insurance covers the majority of the building structure so the condominium owner does not need to cover the cost of what the HOA covers. This effectively covers the kitchen cabinets, flooring, and inside structure items that are permanently attached.

C – Personal Property – This is the same as in the Primary Residence Policy for owners but you would need less coverage if it is a rental property per above.

D – Fair Rental Value –(if a rented condo) This is similar to the Loss of Use in a Primary Residence Policy and will help you financially for your loss of rental income due to a covered loss while your tenants are most likely not going to be paying rent due to repairs that make the condo temporarily unlivable.
– Additional Living Expenses – (if your primary residence) covers your additional expenses to live if you are not able to live in your condo due to a covered loss.

E – Personal Liability or Family Liability Protection – This is similar to the Primary Residence Policy and protects you for lawsuits from outside parties where you are found negligent in your personal life.

F – Liability – Medical Payments to Others or Guest Medical-same

K – Loss Assessments – This covers costs related to assessments made by the HOA for gaps in coverage by the HOAs insurance for a covered peril like a fire. This is not for maintenance assessments or specials assessments related to maintenance of the building. Example may be a fire in a pool house. If the HOA did not have enough insurance to rebuild the common pool house, they may assess the owners for the difference. If you have loss assessment coverage, you could then submit a claim to your HO-6 policy. Know your coverage limits.

RENTERS INSURANCE – Landlords might want to require tenants to carry this coverage. The tenant would be required, per the lease, to pay and carry this coverage.

Purpose: to protect tenant's loose personal property and liability and loss of use. Renter's coverage may be purchased if you rent an apartment, a house, or a condo and other types of structures-check with your agent to see what is available.

Sometimes required coverage by the Landlord: many apartment complexes now require tenants carry renters insurance. The main reason apartment complexes require this insurance is to protect their liability. Apartment complex owners know if something happens in the unit, where a guest may be injured and sue, that each tenant is protected because it is a requirement to rent the space.

Other uses: if you are a landlord, your tenant will contact you if there is a problem, such as a theft or fire to help take care of them. After all you are the landlord. We would recommend the lease include wording that you are renting the space to the tenant, but you in no way provide coverage for their items from theft or fire. Just like some apartment complexes, We do recommend that you require your tenant carry renters insurance as a lease condition.

Increased coverage options: within company guidelines, it is possible to add extra coverage for items such as wedding rings, sports equipment, musical instruments and artwork.
Cost: minimal cost per month for a basic policy.

Common coverages:

C – Personal Property – This is the same as in the Primary Residence Policy for owners but you would most likely need less coverage if it is a rental property per above.

D – Additional Living Expenses – (if your primary residence) covers your additional expenses to live if you are not able to live in your rental due to a covered loss.

E – Personal Liability or Family Liability Protection – This is similar to the Primary Residence Policy and protects you for lawsuits from outside parties where you are found negligent in your personal life.

F – Liability – Medical Payments to Others or Guest Medical-same

Many people rent and most of us have a lot of stuff. Some companies estimate the basic renter has over $30,000 in personal property. Many of us cannot afford NOT to have this policy. This policy is well worth the minimal monthly fee.

PERSONAL UMBRELLA POLICY

Purpose: stacks excess liability on top of your current auto and property policy(s) to provide excess liability coverage. So your typical homeowners policies have the Family Liability lawsuit protection of up to $300,000 if you are sued. This policy allows you to increase it by $1,000,000 to $1.3M, or $2.3M, or $3.3M depending on the value of your assets that you need to protect.

Who needs a personal umbrella policy: someone that has assets to protect, a new driver in the household, owner of single family rental properties, high value home or high value of investments, swimming pool in back yard.

If you are sued and found negligent, the other party can go after your assets to cover their loss. The goal is to eliminate gaps in coverage for the unforeseen events that can happen.

Special umbrella benefit: this one policy stacks excess liability on many of the things you own such as your autos, properties, boat, RV or motorcycle(s).
Coverage limits of liability: umbrella policies a start at $1 million and typically increase by a million up to $5 million in coverage, or more depending on the carrier and need of customer. Customer would need to meet the underwriting requirements of the carrier.

EARTHQUAKE INSURANCE

Purpose: to protect your property from the peril of earthquake which is an excluded peril coverage on home owners insurance. This policy is not required by lenders at this time. If an earthquake were to occur and do major damage to your home structure you would not have any coverage without this policy. If you have a big mortgage to pay and an earthquake were to destroy your home, you would still owe the money to the bank. We would recommend researching the location of your property to see if you are near an earthquake fault and research your options.

You could contact the California Earthquake Authority with questions or your states insurance agency regulator. The closer you are to an earthquake fault, the more expensive the coverage for obvious reasons. Even if you are not close to a fault, we have seen earthquakes cause major damage in other states and countries.

You should ask yourself, what is the monthly cost to insure my property which is valued at $ _____ dollars – and does it make sense to have that coverage? Would I feel better by purchasing this coverage? Is this home/property my biggest asset to protect?

Available for primary home, landlord properties, condo, mobile home and even renters.

Typical Coverage selections from the Ca earthquake authority website:
Coverage
Dwelling Coverage (Coverage A)
Dwelling coverage helps protect the investment you have made in your home. It will help pay to repair or, (up to the policy limit) replace, an insured home when structural damage exceeds the policy deductible. You may select a 10% or 15% deductible for your Dwelling coverage.

The insured value of your home, as stated on the declarations page of your companion homeowners insurance policy, determines the Dwelling-coverage limit of your CEA earthquake policy. If your home's insured value changes in your homeowners policy, the insured value for your earthquake coverage will change, too, and that will affect your earthquake-policy premium.

Personal Property Coverage (Coverage C)

Personal Property coverage protects many items in the typical home, including furniture, TVs, audio and video equipment, household appliances, bedding, and clothing.

A base policy provides up to $5,000 to replace personal property, but you can increase your Personal Property coverage to as much as $100,000.
Items Not Covered
Dwelling-Related Items

Your CEA policy excludes some items from dwelling coverage. A partial list of items that are not covered includes:

- Detached garages and most other structures that are not part of the dwelling
- Land damage (other than $10,000 in coverage for land stabilization)
- Swimming pools and spas
- Awnings and patio coverings
- Fences, landscaping, and irrigation systems
- Antennas and satellite dishes
- Patios and decks
- Walkways and driveways not needed for pedestrian or disabled access to your home
- Certain decorative or artistic items such as mirrors, chandeliers, stained glass, or mosaics

FLOOD INSURANCE
What is a natural disaster flood?

Flood

– A general and temporary condition of partial or complete inundation of two or more acres of normally dry land area or of two or more properties (at least one of which is the policyholder's property) from:
– Overflow of inland or tidal waters; or
– Unusual and rapid accumulation or runoff of surface waters from any source; or
– Mudflow; or Collapse or subsidence of land along the shore of a lake or similar body of water as a result of erosion or undermining caused by waves or currents of water exceeding anticipated cyclical levels that result in a flood as defined above.

If a property you own or are considering purchasing is in a high risk flood zone your lender will require you purchase flood insurance to close on a loan. When a property is in a high risk flood zone and you have a loan, the flood insurance policy may not be cancelled, unless the flood zone changes from a high risk area to a preferred area, which hardly ever happens, ever. Even properties in a preferred area may purchase flood insurance. The cost is much less assuming the risk is much less too. Review the definition of a flood above to determine if this policy applies to your property.

INSURANCE DISCOUNTS

Review your discount options with your agent. Some common discounts are:

Home & Auto, Age of Home, Monitored Alarm, Interior Sprinklers, Retired, Professional, Type of Roof, Renovated

MAKING CLAIMS

Your insurance policy is a specific contract for specified perils. If you suffer a covered loss, it is in your contract to file a claim and have the covered loss damage repaired up to your policy limits less your deductible. Some items to consider that may affect your good standing with insurance companies are the severity of claims and how many claims a person files in a short period of time.

When purchasing a new property, your claim history is reviewed and can increase your insurance cost and cause a few temporary problems with meeting current underwriting guidelines. If you file a claim on a rental property, this is actually viewed more favorably than a claim on your primary home. In that, we mean some carriers will not surcharge your rental property policy for a claim like they would on a primary residence.

Many policies have significant claim free discounts as a benefit to policy holders if there is no claim activity. So the caution is this, lets assume a fence blows down in the wind and the cost is $1200 to repair. Wind is a covered peril and lets assume you have a $1000 deductible. That would mean insurance would pay out $200. If the claim is filed, you will lose your claim free discount (if provided in your policy), Therefore determine if the discount savings lost is greater than the $200 insurance payout. So the caution is filing very small claims.

The major covered losses are paid without question and homeowners do not usually worry about a premium increase as insurance covered them for so much. So if there is a major loss of course that is what insurance is for and make the claim, but be cautious about making very small claims

Tip: during the claims process, work with your adjuster and discuss everything that is happening. Let the insurance company do their job for you and consult your adjuster before making any monetary decisions related to the loss.

PUBLIC ADJUSTERS - http://en.wikipedia.org/wiki/Public_adjuster

So if you have a loss and insurance is responsible to pay you for that loss, and you do not think the insurance company is making you a fair offer of reimbursement, there is help. You can hire a public adjuster to help you negotiate your claim. They usually charge a percentage of the claim, like 10%.

They can be a good advocate for you on bigger losses, **BUT BEWARE.**

Here is the issue. This is similar to when Bob Dole fell off the stage in 1996 Presidential election and said his phone was ringing during the fall with several lawyers trying to reach him about suing…before he even hit the ground. So if your house catches on fire, the public adjuster may beat the fire department to your house and try to get you to sign on with them to represent you against the insurance company.

DO NOT SIGN. DO NOT RUSH. THEIR CONTRACTS CAN BE VERY VERY FAVORABLE TO THEM AND NOT TO YOU. YOU CAN ALWAYS ENLIST THEIR HELP IF YOU NEED, BUT DO NOT SIGN ANYTHING UNTIL YOU HAVE THOUGHT THROUGH THE ISSUES AND TALKED TO YOUR INSURANCE AGENT AND COMPANY. IF YOU SIGN THE PUBLIC ADJUSTER'S AGREEMENT YOUR HANDS MAY BE TIED AND NOW YOU ARE AN ADVERSARY, EFFECTIVELY IN A DISPUTE, WITH THE INSURANCE COMPANY.

WORK WITH YOUR INSURANCE COMPANY FIRST WITH THEIR PROCESS TO SEE IF YOU CAN GET A FAIR RESOLUTION. YOU CAN ALWAYS ENLIST A PUBLIC ADJUSTER AND IT MAY MAKE SENSE TO DO THAT. BUT FIRST, DO NOT SIGN ANYTHING AND TAKE A DEEP BREATH FOR A FEW DAYS OR WEEKS BEFORE COMMITTING TO ANY CONTRACTS. YOU'LL BE GLAD YOU DID!

UNIQUE INSURANCE NEEDS

Discuss any special insurance need with your agent. A single insurance company may not have a product for every kind of risk or need. You may need to seek the advice of a broker with another carrier to provide special coverage needs. No one carrier will accept every kind of risk, and this can be confusing to the consumer. You may in unique situations need the help from several carriers based on your need. A good agent will help to direct you.

A Few other items to consider:

C.L.U.E Comprehensive Loss and Underwriting Exchange Report – Once you have a property in escrow, have the seller's agent, with the seller's permission, order a C.L.U.E. Report for your review. It is about $20 and shows you any insurance claims made on that property for the past five years. The insurance agent may be able to do this too for you.

Deductibles - A higher deductible gives you a lower premium, so explore this with your agent. Will you really make a claim for a small amount/loss as your future premiums may increase?

Policy Paid for at Closing - Make sure your policy is paid for out of the escrow money at closing so it is in place the second you take ownership.

Get estimate of cost early in the process so no surprises occur, like the policy is very expensive or your unit cannot be insured.

Buying with Cash? Make sure you have the right coverage in place - with mortgage financing, the bank acts as a double check that you have the right insurance by requiring certain coverage. If you are buying cash, the bank's insurance experts are not there to make sure you have the appropriate coverage.

Overinsured? - We note above to make sure you have enough coverage, but also make sure you are not way overinsured either, you pay more for higher maximum coverage limits, so you want to RIGHT size your insurance coverage.

LPB Services LLC © 2010

CHAPTER 11

TITLE INSURANCE AND HOLDING TITLE

Title insurance and holding title are generally low risk items on your list of issues to clear in doing your due diligence. But you still need to understand the issues and take an hour to review your preliminary title insurance binder policy and make sure you are taking title in the most appropriate way for your circumstances. We are going to run you through the main issues in this chapter and make sure to ask questions to your title insurance company officer or an attorney if you do not understand anything.

As noted, there is low risk of an issue related to title, however when there is an issue, it is usually a large dollar amount – so protect yourself and reduce your risk by understanding the process.

Title insurance - This is a policy that protects you, the owner, from claims on your ownership rights to your property related to the prior owners. Claims of this type are very very rare, but they do occur so you need protection. And the policies are relatively inexpensive relative to the risk. The seller of a property typically pays for the policy that protects you the buyer. You typically pay for a separate policy that protects the mortgage lender who financed your property. The risk is very low but you need to read and understand what is excluded from the policy because if the title company lists an item that they do not cover and you have a loss related to that item, you are on your own.

Holding Title – There are many ways to hold title to your property. You can hold it as the sole owner, with someone else, as husband and wife, in a limited liability company or LLC, or in a Trust and other ways. How you hold title makes a difference as to how it is passed to your spouse, partners or heirs upon your death, or what happens if someone is suing you and can they take the property, or if someone suing your LLC which holds title to the property can try to take your other personal assets. LLC ownership can also impact your financing and insurance rates for single unit properties. We will cover the basics herein but you need to discuss these items with the escrow agent and/or title officer and maybe an attorney. Each state has different laws that govern how title is held and you need to know how it applies in the state within which the property is located.

Deed Types – There are several types of deeds and the most common of which and most protective to you is a "general warranty deed". Most normal real estate transactions are going to have the seller giving the buyer a general warranty deed or grant deed. Sales at the county courthouse by foreclosure, by banks or financial institutions of their real estate owned (REO), depending on state laws, could have a less protective deed conveyed to you as part of the sale. These deeds could be called special warranty deeds or quit claim deeds. If the seller is granting you a general warranty deed or grant deed then you are in good shape. If the seller is only granting you a special warranty deed or quitclaim deed you need to discuss the risks of these less protective deeds with the title insurance representative and possibly an attorney.

You need to carefully review your title policy and make sure you are holding title in a way that is appropriate for your circumstances. The deed type is important to understand too, although the vast majority of deeds in residential transactions are the grant or general warranty deeds that afford you the highest level of protection. Read on to understand the process and issues.

TITLE INSURANCE

Title Insurance protects you, the owner, in cases where there is a defect found in the chain of title from before you took ownership. The title insurance company will examine the past chain of title at the county courthouse and prepare a title "abstract". A review of this should alert a buyer to any issues that might seem strange and be a "cloud" or issue on title.

An example of a title issue would be if you close escrow on a property and six months later the ex-husband of the seller files suit to recover the property claiming that he was a part owner of the property and the seller had no right to sell it to you. The title insurance company would step in and hire a lawyer to defend your title and if there eventually were damages, like a court made you sell the property back to the ex-husband or there was some payment to him, the title insurance policy would pay out those damages instead of your having to pay them.

The title insurance company will review the title abstract and the title officer will note and discuss any issues with the escrow officer. The typical issues are unpaid property taxes or making sure the person selling the property has the right to sell the property. These issues typically get cleared as the process moves along. If there are unpaid taxes, the escrow officer puts those amounts on the closing statement and they get paid out of the seller's proceeds from the sale. The title company also reviews documents to ensure that the right party is signing the deed to transfer the property to you. Almost all issues should be resolved by the time you are ready to close on the property.

BUT THIS DOES NOT MEAN THAT YOU CAN SKIP THE STEP TO READ THE SCHEDULE B POLICY EXCLUSIONS TO YOUR TITLE INSURANCE POLICY. THIS STEP SHOULD TAKE FIFTEEN MINUTES MAXIMUM. By reading the "exclusions" page, you will be able to make sure there isn't anything else "funky" related to the title where you the buyer continues to have the risk of loss related to that issue. Like an easement the neighboring property has to cross over your land.

EXCLUDED TITLE ISSUES -The way the title company would alert you to a title issue before you close escrow is on a document titled "Preliminary Title Policy Schedule "B" Exclusions to the Title Insurance Policy", which is the listed exclusions from the policy that apply to your specific property. That is why you need to review the title policy to see if there are any issues you need to clear that the title company has "excluded" from covering. If the title policy company has excluded an issue on schedule B, that means that they will not insure you for that issue and you are on your own to defend your title if someone files a lawsuit or has a lien that was excluded in Schedule B. Many items listed on Schedule B should not be a problem, like utility company or water company easements, but you had better get an understanding of each item to make sure it will not cause any future issues. The only way you will know of an issue is to closely read the title policy and ask questions of the title insurance agent if you do not understand something.

DO NOT SIGN ANY PRELIMINARY POLICY OR ACKNOWLEDGEMENT OF THE POLICY UNTIL YOU HAVE A CLEAN COPY WITH ANY EXCLUSIONS THAT YOU DO NOT LIKE REMOVED.

You are going to receive, as a part of escrow, a copy of the Preliminary Title Policy and a document to sign where you agree to accept the terms on the preliminary policy. DO NOT sign this. You need to first ensure that any exclusions like #8 on the policy below are removed. If you signoff on the document without all the issues removed, you are taking the liability for that item instead of the Title Insurance Company. So if there is a problem related to this issue years after you close escrow, the Title Insurance Company is going to pull out what you signed and say, "You agreed to exclude that issue so it is your problem not ours". So again, DO NOT sign off until all the items and issues that cause you a concern are removed and a clean copy is forwarded to your for your signature.

DO YOU UNDERSTAND THE ABOVE PARAGRAPH. Here it is, in six years when the cousin of the seller (the Trustee of the Trust in #8 below) knocks on your door and says he wants the house back because his uncle did not get his signature to sell the house and he was an owner, you are now up the creek! It is going to be on your dime to hire an attorney to defend your title, instead of the Title Insurance Company's. It is on your dime to cover any settlement with the cousin, instead of the Title Insurance Company's. Therefore, protect yourself, DO NOT sign any preliminary policy until it is clean and clear of issues.

Schedule B Policy Exclusions or Exceptions - Next is an example Schedule B and let's take a look at some items on this schedule. Remember that if whatever is noted on Schedule B becomes a problem after you close, it is your problem not the title insurance company's problem because they excluded coverage for that item. Click here – the third and fourth pages are the exclusions or exceptions that we have referred to as Schedule B – although it is not referenced that way in this document. You will see "exceptions" at the top of page three – click for the <u>Title Policy Schedule B Exclusions Page</u> so you know what it looks like.

Preliminary Report   **CLTA PRELIMINARY REPORT FORM**

Issued By

Preliminary Report Number:

73710001756

In response to the application for a policy of title insurance referenced herein, **Chicago Title Company** hereby reports that it is prepared to issue, or cause to be issued, as of the date hereof, a policy or policies of title insurance describing the land and the estate of interest therein hereinafter set forth, insuring against loss which may be sustained by reason of any defect, lien or encumbrance not shown or referred to as an exception herein or not excluded from coverage pursuant to the printed Schedules, Conditions and Stipulations or Conditions of said policy forms.

The printed Exceptions and Exclusions from the coverage and Limitations on Covered Risks of said policy or policies are set forth in Attachment One. The policy to be issued may contain an arbitration clause. When the Amount of Insurance is less than that set forth in the arbitration clause, all arbitrable matters shall be arbitrated at the option of either the Company or the Insured as the exclusive remedy of the parties. Limitations on Covered Risks applicable to the CLTA and ALTA Homeowner's Policies of Title Insurance which establish a Deductible Amount and a Maximum Dollar Limit of Liability for certain coverages are also set forth in Attachment One. Copies of the policy forms should be read. They are available from the office which issued this report.

This report (and any supplements or amendments hereto) is issued solely for the purpose of facilitating the issuance of a policy of title insurance and no liability is assumed hereby. If it is desired that liability be assumed prior to the issuance of a policy of title insurance, a Binder or Commitment should be requested.

The policy(ies) of title insurance to be issued hereunder will be policy(ies) of Chicago Title Insurance Company, a Nebraska corporation.

Please read the exceptions shown or referred to herein and the exceptions and exclusions set forth in Attachment One of this report carefully. The exceptions and exclusions are meant to provide you with notice of matters which are not covered under the terms of the title insurance policy and should be carefully considered.

It is important to note that this preliminary report is not a written representation as to the condition of title and may not list all liens, defects and encumbrances affecting title to the land.

Chicago Title Insurance Company   By:

Dated

                                                                    _____
                                                                    President

Countersigned By   Attest:

_____   _____
Authorized Officer or Agent   Secretary

CLTA Preliminary Report Form - Modified   Adopted: 11.17.2006   Printed: 03.30.10 @ 03:28PM
SSCORPD0817 doc / Updated: 03.12.2010   CA---73710001756

At the date hereof, exceptions to coverage in addition to the printed exceptions and exclusions in said policy form would be as follows

1.   Property taxes, which are a lien not yet due and payable, including any assessments collected with taxes to be levied for the fiscal year 2010-2011.

2.   The lien of supplemental taxes, if any, assessed pursuant to the provisions of Chapter 3.5 (Commencing with Section 75) of the Revenue and Taxation Code of the State of California.

3.   Note: Property taxes for the fiscal year shown below are PAID. For proration purposes the amounts were:

        Tax Identification No.:   624-422-24
        Fiscal Year: 2009-2010
        1st Installment: $317.06
        2nd Installment: $317.06
        Exemption: $0.00
        Land: $14,873.00
        Improvements: $38,379.00
        Personal Property: $0.00
        Code Area: 01045

4.   Agreement regarding school district

        Recording Date: July 17, 1974
        Recording No.:   74-192192, Official Records

5.   The matters set forth in the document shown below which, among other things, contains or provides for: certain easements; liens and the subordination thereof; provisions relating to partition; restrictions on severability of component parts; and covenants, conditions and restrictions but omitting any covenants or restrictions, if any, including, but not limited to those based upon race, color, religion, sex, sexual orientation, familial status, marital status, disability, handicap, national origin, ancestry, or source of income, as set forth in applicable state or federal laws, except to the extent that said covenant or restriction is permitted by applicable law.

        Entitled: Declaration of covenants, conditions and restrictions
        Recording Date: December 11, 1974
        Recording No: 74-322115, Official Records

        Said covenants, conditions and restrictions provide that a violation thereof shall not defeat the lien of any mortgage or deed of trust made in good faith and for value.

        Said instrument also provides for the levy of assessments, the lien of which is stated to be subordinate to the lien of certain mortgages or deeds of trust made in good faith and for value.

        Modification(s) of said covenants, conditions and restrictions

        Recording Date: December 27, 1974
        Recording No: 74-335305, Official Records

        Modification(s) of said covenants, conditions and restrictions

        Recording Date: November 17, 1976
        Recording No: 76-384504, Official Records

6.   Cable Access Agreement

Recording Date: December 20, 1975
Recording No.:   75-368736, Official Records

7.   Cable Access Agreement

Recording Date: April 12, 1991
Recording No.:   1991-0165184, Official Records

8.   Any invalidity or defect in the title of the vestees in the event that the trust referred to herein is invalid or fails to grant sufficient powers to the trustee(s) or in the event there is a lack of compliance with the terms and provisions of the trust instrument.

If title is to be insured in the trustee(s) of a trust, (or if their act is to be insured), this Company will require a Trust Certification pursuant to California Probate Code Section 18100.5.

The Company reserves the right to add additional items or make further requirements after review of the requested documentation.

9.   Any rights, interests, or claims of parties in possession of the Land not shown by the public records.

10.   Any rights, interests or claims, which are not shown by the public records but which could be ascertained by an inspection of the Land or which may be asserted by persons in possession thereof.

NOTES

1.   If a county recorder, title insurance company, escrow company, real estate broker, real estate agent or association provides a copy of a declaration, governing document or deed to any person, California law requires that the document provided shall include a statement regarding any unlawful restrictions. Said statement is to be in at least 14-point bold face type and may be stamped on the first page of any document provided or included as a cover page attached to the requested document. Should a party to this transaction request a copy of any document reported herein that fits this category, the statement is to be included in the manner described.

So you can see in this policy that – Available at www.ProfessorBaron.com:

1,2, and 3 - Discusses property taxes and that they are PAID. If they do not say PAID, make sure they will be paid at closing – so alert escrow.

4 – School district agreement from decades ago – probably not an issue.

5 – CC&Rs related to the condominium homeowner's association – you will get these documents as a part of the HOA disclosures – Chapter 8 can help.

6,7 – Cable TV service easements – probably not an issue, BUT MAYBE COULD BE AN ISSUE.

8 – Relates to if the property was owned by a Trust – so this one you need to discuss with the Title Officer and Escrow because you do not understand and get this clause removed before you sign off accepting the Title Insurance Preliminary Title Policy.

9 – Rights of any people living on the property – If no one is living there that isn't a party to the transaction then probably not an issue.

10- Other general exclusion.

We recommend you require the title insurance company to get a a complete copy of whatever is recorded on the property related to

- A lien listed by a contractor.
- A note about an unsatisfied mortgage or deed of trust.
- A lis pendens which alerts you to a lawsuit related to the property – get more info!
- An easement of some type that runs across your property – Private easement of neighbor, or other, or Cable TV, Gas, Sewer, Electric, Phone, etc. You need to review these, what if the city has a sewer line easement right through the middle of your property? You may not be able to build or add on to a property due to this easement. Get the documents and review them.
- Any exclusion or item that you do not understand.

Survey – If you live in an area where they typically do surveys of boundary lines of a parcel or lot, make sure to look at the survey to ensure your fences, driveways, sheds, etc. are not on the adjacent property and the adjacent property owners do not have these items on your property.

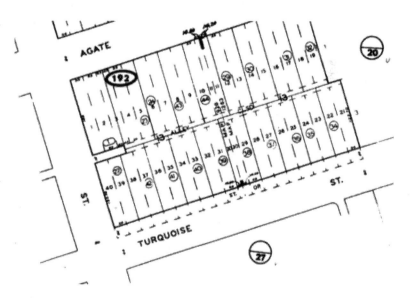

Plat – Many areas have county plats of neighborhoods or properties. You should review the plat and how it applies to your property. It may show easements or other issues you should know about.

The good news again is that title issues are very very rare because most get cleared by the title insurance company. But that doesn't mean you do not have to understand what is covered and what is excluded because you do not want to be one of the rare cases where you lose tens of thousands of dollars or more over a title issue. Take the time to get the documents and to review the exclusions and get any issues you do not understand resolved before you agree to the policy.

Who pays for the policy? The seller will pay for a title policy to insure the title they are giving to you and you pay for an additional lender's policy to protect the lender in case of an unforeseen title issue. Whenever you refinance you will pay for another policy for the new lender.

In having title transferred to you, you will most likely have to fill out a Statement of Identity for the title company so they know who you are. Here is an example of that: <u>Title Company Statement of Identity</u>. We just put one in here just so you know what it is. You may also have to fill out a form to let the county know who you are and pertinent information about the transaction. In California it is the <u>Preliminary Change of Ownership Report (PCOR)</u> and again, just here so you know what it is.

Final note: AGAIN, make sure you take the fifteen minutes to review those policy exclusions!

HOLDING TITLE

Depending on the state within which the property is located, there are many ways to hold title.

For most people, partners and married couples it will be one of the following: Sole and separate property, Tenants in Common, Joint Tenancy, Community Property, Community Property with Right of Survivorship, or in some type of Trust.

Depending on the state laws and how title is held will determine many legal issues related to your ownership and how any joint owners, spouses, or heirs will inherit or not inherit you assets. For example, if you buy a property with a friend and the escrow company titles the property as you and your friend as Joint Tenants, that means there is the right of survivorship. So worst case you buy with a friend, then years later you get married but never know to understand or revise the title. You then unfortunately die – guess who gets the property. It goes to the survivor as filed on the property deed – so your friend who bought the property with you gets it instead of your spouse.

This schedule from Lawyers Title Insurance Corporation can give you a feel for the issues – but you need to discuss this with your Title Insurance Officer or an attorney to make sure you are comfortable with how you hold title. Click here on website: Concurrent Co-Owner Interests Options.

Trusts. There are many many types of trusts that can hold title to property. The most common type for residential unit buyers is the revocable living trust, also called an inter vivos revocable trust. The main reason to do a revocable trust is to skip probate court upon the death of the Trustor, who is the person who creates the trust and titles property into the trust. Other reasons could be to grant a family member or other trusted person the right to control assets if the Trustor becomes incapacitated or the Trustor simply wants someone else to manage their affairs.

Probate is the process of a court executing the will of a person who has passed away and it can get very expensive depending on the value of the assets. For example, in California it is about $30,000 to $40,000 for probate court costs for a $1,000,000 estate. Smaller estates are much less, bigger ones are more expensive. If a inter vivos trust is set up, which costs about $2,000 - $4,000, all the assets in the trust would be passed to the heirs outside of probate and without the large amount of fees. So if there is a larger estate and or the owners are getting older and want someone to help manage their affairs, discussing a revocable living trust with an attorney is probably a good idea.

A Few Notes on Trusts:

- There is no asset protection from Inter vivos trust so it will not shield assets from the reach of a creditor.
- Inter vivos trust assets are not publicly listed in court documents like assets in probate court will be.
- A trust also could include other assets like stocks, bonds, bank accounts which would need to be re-titled into the trust.
- There are many many types of trusts, some get very expensive to protect assets, to legally avoid paying taxes, or to pass assets to certain heirs. Consult an attorney.
- If you finance or refinance a property held in a trust you may have to re-title the property to your personal name and then transfer it back to the trust after closing on the loan. That is not a big deal.

Or, they may require you to sign a personal guarantee – think that one though and the ramifications before you do that – but probably not that big a deal as long as you do not default on the loan.

Title may also be held in a limited liability company or LLC, in an S Corp, in a limited liability partnership LLC. We will discuss these items in the LLCs and Asset Protection chapter but for the average real estate buyer buying single residential units they are not needed. If you have significant wealth outside of the real estate assets, then you would discuss costs and benefits of LLCs, etc. with your attorney.

TYPES OF DEEDS

When you purchase a property the seller, whether an individual, a corporation, the trustee at a trustee sale, or any seller grants you a deed to own the property. There are several types of deeds like grant deeds, general warranty deed, special warranty deed, bargain and sale deed, quitclaim deed.

The laws and types of deeds you are granted as a buyer depends on the state and what the seller is willing to give you. In most deeds for normal property transactions the seller gives a buyer a grant deed or general warranty deed which basically is the seller guaranteeing that they own the property, have the right to sell it, and they warranty the time they owned the property and the prior ownership periods. If that is what you are getting and the title insurance company is insuring the title, you should be fine.

If you are getting less of a deed than a grant or general warranty deed, it may be a special warranty deed that may only warrant for the period the seller owned the property and not for prior ownership periods. Quitclaim deeds only give the buyer whatever rights the seller had in the property and with no other warranties. These may be fine too, in some cases like foreclosure sales or tax deed sales that is all you are going to get. Discuss these with your title insurance officer and make sure you can obtain good title insurance and what exclusions there would be related to not getting a general warranty deed. Then you can make your decision on whether or not you are comfortable with the title for the property you are going to buy. If not, do not buy the property.

LPB Services LLC © 2010

CHAPTER 12

LLCS AND ASSET PROTECTION

Litigation and Lawsuit news is often on TV and in the newspapers these days and of course people want to protect themselves in case another party files a lawsuit against them. One way commonly touted as an asset protection method is filing for a limited liability company, or LLC entity, to hold title to your property. It could also be an S-Corporation or limited

Superior Court of California

County of San Diego — Court Closed Friday, December 31st

| Home | General Info | Civil | Criminal | Family | Probate |

liability partnership, or LLP. They are similar so we will term them LLCs in this chapter. Holding title in an LLC could potentially shield your personal unrelated assets from any legal judgments against the LLC entity that you created to hold the property.

Note: Trusts, Revocable Trusts, Inter Vivos Trusts, etc. are different animals from LLCs and the basic trust information is discussed under Holding Title in Chapter 11. The basic trust affords you no lawsuit protection – they are created to avoid probate court and those costs, keep inheritances information out of the public court record, and more easily transfer assets upon the death of the maker of the Trust. There are also many fancy named trusts that do afford liability protection, like Grantor Retained Annuity Trusts (GRATs) or Qualified Terminable Interest Property Trust (QTip) that have different purposes and can shield assets from liability, reduce taxes, or transfer assets for estate purposes. These complex trusts are expensive to form, $10,000 to $25,000, and are not needed by the typical individual buying properties. If you are very wealthy, hire a good trust attorney to help you through the maze of issues.

LLCs purpose. For example, your tenant sues the LLC owner/Landlord because they fell and got hurt. The Landlord is actually your LLC that holds title to the property, NOT YOU, and so the tenant can generally only sue the LLC entity and not you personally. Let's say they win the lawsuit and get a $75,000 judgment against the LLC. Again, the judgment is against the LLC, not YOU. The tenant who won the lawsuit most likely will only be able to seize any equity you have in that property or any other assets you have titled into the LLC. They generally cannot try to claim your other personal assets like cash, stocks, bonds or your other properties that are not in that specific LLC.

That is the major benefit of an LLC to help you protect your "other" assets from being seized in litigation that you lose related to an entity you own. But there are some significant issues and costs related to holding title in an LLC for one to four unit residential properties and just in general. So we will cover those issues and some common sense strategies on whether or not LLCs make sense.

And so you know where we are going with this chapter the two most common sense items to protect your assets are:

1. Take steps to avoid lawsuits in the first place.
2. Keep liability coverage insurance in place that has enough maximum coverage to defend you against any lawsuits, settlements or judgments against you.

So we will discuss the common sense issues and then some of the costs vs. benefits of LLCs and how to better protect your assets.

AVOID LAWSUITS IF YOU CAN

The best way to protect your assets is to avoid lawsuits if you can. When it comes to property, to avoid lawsuits, you want to keep your property in good shape, quickly tend to any dangerous issues, and treat your tenants with respect. Slips, trips and dog bites seem to be pretty prevalent but so are security deposit or contract dispute issues, housing discrimination in the rental of the units and mold. Evictions are another type of lawsuit and they are covered in Chapter 13 – Renting/Managing Your Property. Some people, but very very few, are the types that just file lawsuits often – you can find out who they are with a public filings search as a part of the credit report review process. Many counties also have free lawsuit look up areas on their websites. If a prospective tenant has previously filed many lawsuits, beware because if you rent to them you may be next.

Generally though people file lawsuits because they are aggravated with some situation. So trying your best to maintain good relations with your tenants and being fair if there are any issues that are your fault, or no one's fault, is a smart move. Even if it is their fault, treat them fairly and professionally. Like if the water pipe breaks and damages their stuff, even if you are not legally obligated to do anything, you might want to make a fair proposal to settle the issue. Taking responsibility quickly if you are at fault and helping to mitigate damages and trying to be fair goes a long way with most people.

If you just cannot come to a resolution with your tenant regarding an issue, try suggesting mediation to your tenants as a first step. Or try to have some other neutral party try to work with them on your behalf. And if it is not a lot of money, you are probably better off to give in to your tenant and be settled with the issue. If you end up going to court, as the litigation proceeds, one claim from a tenant that was small and could have been settled all of a sudden then miraculously turns into several different more expensive issues and becomes much more stressful and time consuming.

You are the landlord, you probably have more money than the tenant, you do not need the time consuming hassle of fighting with them, so step up to the plate and reach out a hand and try to avoid going to court. You might be mad about giving in, but you won't be sorry if it quickly ends the dispute and keeps you out of court, keeps your tenant in place, happy, and paying rent!

Overall lawsuits, whether you win or lose, are time consuming, extremely stressful, expensive to all parties and take away from the important things you should be doing like finding your next property acquisition so you can accumulate more real estate.

INSURANCE

A typical homeowner's or investor insurance policy has $100,000 or $300,000 worth of liability coverage as described in the Chapter 10 – Property and Liability Insurance. This covers you for those slips and falls, dog bites, tenant lawsuits, and other issues as long as you are not negligent. Discuss these with your insurance agent. If your net worth is $1,000,000, then the $300,000 typical policy is not enough to cover you in case of a large judgment. So get an umbrella policy to step up your liability coverage to like $1,000,000 – and they are very cheap, like $275 per year per additional $1,000,000 of coverage. This coverage will pay for hiring a lawyer to defend you or having that attorney try to negotiate a settlement. Or if that doesn't work and you lose the suit, the insurer will pay any judgment against you up to your policy limits.

Good insurance with adequate coverage is one of the smartest things you can do to help protect not only your property but also all of your other assets.

LIMITED LIABILITY COMPANIES, LLCs

So is an LLC still needed if you carry adequate insurance and keep your property in good shape and treat your tenants professionally?

That question is something you need to consider with an attorney depending on your circumstances, but for the vast majority of people the answer is no. Let's talk about some negative issues that LLCs will cause.

Cost. In some states, like California, an LLC costs $800 per year to maintain and you need to file LLC tax returns that could cost a few hundred dollars more. That is a lot of money if you add that $800 plus dollars into your cash flow statement. The commercials from companies that file them tout, "Only $140 to file an LLC for you." However, many people do not realize that is just the filing fee for the private company doing the filing – there is still the $800 annual tax in California. Make sure to find out about all state annual taxes or fees that are required for an LLC. Some states may be minimal costs, but find out early in the process if you are considering filing an LLC entity.

Mortgage Financing. For the most part you are not going to be able to obtain residential mortgage financing for a property held in an LLC – it will have to be held in your personal name or a Trust for financing. For commercial assets it is not an issue due to the way mortgages are structured and sold for commercial assets. But the banks in general will not loan on a residential one to four unit property held in an LLC. Even if they would, you still need to consider the annual costs of maintaining an LLC and insurance may be an issue too as detailed below. You could transfer title to an LLC from your personal name after you close escrow, but you may be violating your mortgage agreement so you need to think though all the costs and issues and talk to an attorney if you believe you need to hold title in an LLC.

Insurance. Many insurance companies will not write policies for smaller residential units that are held in LLCs. Or they may write them but rate them as commercial policies and at a much higher premium. So if you intend to hold title in an LLC, like if you paid cash for the property, or re-title it to an LLC after you close, you should make sure your insurance company is okay with that. And you need to ask how much more, if any, the annual premium will be due to the LLC entity being the one insured. Some insurance carriers are okay with LLC titled property, and may charge the normal rates, but they may charge more, so ask questions and figure out the additional costs related to insurance, if any.

Cash purchase. If you buy with cash, you can title the property in an LLC if you like. However, you still will need to pay state annual fees, if any, and may have the insurance issues noted above. So check those items out to help you make better decisions.

Cash purchase. If you do pay cash and put the property in an LLC, all that equity is at stake if the LLC gets sued – that would be any equity amount above the liability coverage you have in your normal property and liability insurance policy. So if you buy a $300,000 property for all cash and put in an LLC, and you only have a $100,000 liability maximum insurance coverage, the insurance will cover legal costs and judgments up to the $100,000 and then the property equity is now at risk if you lose and get a judgment against the LLC above that $100,000. And that is a lot of money/equity at risk. A better bet may be to have a much higher liability insurance policy in place, like $300,000 or $1,000,000 liability limit, and it probably will only be minimal additional cost. That minimal cost will also most likely a lot less expensive than the annual LLC costs.

Overall, LLCs may be needed if you have significant other assets. But maintaining adequate liability insurance for an amount that covers those other assets is probably less expensive then an LLC and sufficient asset protection for a typical person. Talk to your insurance agent and your attorney on this and what is at risk if you get sued and lose. In general, the higher your net worth, the more you have at risk, and the more critical it is to properly plan your how you hold title to your real estate AND your proper insurance coverage.

LPB Services LLC © 2010

CHAPTER 13

RENTING AND MANAGING YOUR PROPERTY

Preparing to Get Your Acquired Property Ready for Rental

GENERAL ITEMS

Once you get close to closing escrow, which is the date that title and ownership transfer to you, it is time to start the process of getting your property ready for renovations and/or renting the unit. If it is already occupied by a tenant that is great news, you are saving yourself a LOT of time, money and hassle by buying a property that is already rented. See article on Reviewing an Existing Lease and Keeping Your Tenants here.

Article: Reviewing an Existing Lease and Keeping Your Tenants

Keeping Tenants and Reviewing An Existing Lease

If you have purchased a property that already has a tenant in the property you are typically doing yourself a huge favor. Not only do you usually get their security deposit transferred to you at closing, you will probably get some pro-rated rental income, you also will not have to go in and paint, re-carpet, take the extensive time to advertise, have the property vacant during that time, meet prospective tenants to show the property, work up a lease, etc. You will have to do that down the road when they leave and then you will understand the workload involved.

Of course if the existing tenants were/are bad, late with rent, don't take care of the place, etc. then it might make sense to try and work with them on those issues or terminate the lease at the soonest possible date. However, maybe the prior landlord never fixed broken items and the tenants were unhappy but you can try to correct that as the new owner who will keep the property in better shape and respect your tenants.

Short Sale – If it is a short sale you may also want to consider leasing it back to the seller if they have jobs and credit (a good credit profile from before the short sale wrecked their credit) that are fairly good. The bank that agreed to the short sale might not allow you to do this per the sales contract, so make sure you are in compliance with the bank's addendums.

GO MEET TENANTS

If you are taking the property with tenants and especially if you would like to keep the tenants, make sure you get a copy of the existing lease and review it. It helps to see the last few months of cashed rental checks if the owner will provide them so you know the current rental amount, any utilities that are reimbursed, and that tenants are actually paying rent. Plus you need to know whether there is still an existing term left on the lease, like six more months, or if the tenants are month to month at that point. If their lease has a term left you really have to wait until then to make any changes.

Either way, schedule to go meet with the tenants and let them know you would like them to stay as long as they would like and you will offer them a new lease when their existing lease expires. If you plan to raise the rent at that point, make it reasonable depending on the situation and market rents. And know the amount you want to ask for as an increase and be prepared to discuss that with them when you meet them. You do not want them to leave because they do not know whether you will let them stay or raise the rent significantly. People do not like uncertainty, so if you want them to stay give them some certainty.

You might want to ask the tenant if there are any items or issues that need to be fixed or resolved so you know them before you close escrow and you can attend to them – after you close escrow. Hopefully the tenant won't ask for the world, but we've found that reasonableness from a landlord usually gets reasonableness and happiness and good relations from/with a tenant. And good relations are key to making your property management life easier.

And of course, common sense here, let them know where to send the rent checks $$$$$ going forward!!!

LEASE

Review the lease terms from the existing lease. Ask the tenant, diplomatically, to fill out a new rental application, primarily so you can have updated contact information, work information, emergency contact information, etc. You do not need to run a credit report, as they already have possession of the property. You should however, check the local court database for any lawsuits, evictions, bankruptcies, sex offenders database, or criminal charges so you simply are aware of any issues – more information is typically better.

NEW LEASE

When the time comes to renew the lease you can change it to another one, like the state association of Realtors lease if you like. Add in a page of addendums if desired and note the transfer of the old security deposit to the new lease. Sit down and discuss the terms with them, get the lease signed – and any addendums to the lease or lead based paint disclosure - and the longer you keep your tenants, the easier your landlording will be!

End of Article: Reviewing an Existing Lease and Keeping Your Tenants

We primarily discuss an owner who is going to manage the property on their own, but the last portion of this chapter discusses using a management company to handle your property if that is your plan.

ONCE YOU TAKE TITLE IF EMPTY

Plan on spending most nights and weekends at the property until you have it rented and the tenants take occupancy of the unit. If you are doing a renovation, even cosmetic, you need to get a realistic schedule of the timeframe to get the work done. You want to start advertising it for rent at an early but appropriate time due to the fact that a potential tenant will usually need a lead time before the date they can move in. So that realistic conservative timeframe for rehabilitation with some contingency time is best because it usually takes longer than one thinks to get a property rental ready.

There are lots of items and issues you can do to hopefully improve the chances of owning property with a nice consistent rental income stream and tenants who take care of your property and end up staying for many years. That is the best and lowest stress and most financially advantageous way to do it! This chapter will give you some tips and important information to assist you towards that goal!

SUCCESSFUL REAL ESTATE OWNERSHIP

The most important items in successful real estate ownership are:

- To work hard upfront to get good tenants and;
- Work harder to keep those good tenants as long as possible.

And it is always hard work and time consuming to do these tasks – and all tasks in real estate for that matter!

KEEING PROPERTY IN GOOD SHAPE AND ASKING REASONABLE RENT

Putting and keeping your property in good clean shape is one of the more worthwhile tasks you can do towards this effort. People like to live in nice clean places and if your property is in the best shape of the comparable nearby rentals and reasonably priced, more potential renters will want to live in your unit. In conjunction with this, we suggest asking market rent for the unit, not above market.

Both of these will give you a greater pool of applicants to select from. You are much better off financially to rent the property quickly at a reasonable rate than to have it empty for a month or two trying to get a higher rent - because those lost months of rent are never coming back. And if you lose one month, that is like dropping your rent one-twelfth of the monthly rate – so better to ask reasonable prices and get it filled. And vacant units get vandalized too and insurance generally does not cover vacant units – talk to your insurance agent about this!

Doing the above tasks should allow you to quickly attain a good pool of rental applicants so you can review their qualifications and pick the one or two that you feel will be the best the tenants you want living in your property.

KEEP YOUR TENANTS FOR THE LONG TERM - Keeping your tenants as long as possible is also your best long term bet. Every time you have to turn over the property to a new renter you may lose a month of rent. You most likely will have to do some repairs, painting, cleaning that will cost hundreds or thousands of dollars out of your pocket. And the most time consuming part of this is that you will need to advertise the property again, show it again to many potential tenants, make calls, hand out and collect rental applications, run through the process of doing a credit report – maybe do this whole process twice before you find the right tenant. Then you have to schedule to be there for them to move in, solve a few issues, fix a few more items, etc.

Round trip you are talking about 1-2 months of rent plus all your time in re-leasing the property. If you have a regular job then it will be very disruptive to your life. It is still worth it in the long run, but why not do some, but a lot less hard work, keeping your existing tenants.

TO KEEP TENANTS:

- Keep the property in good shape and updated as much as you can afford. Not just fixtures, carpets, etc. but also things like low energy light bulbs, caulking windows and doors, etc. – and make sure potential renters know you are saving them money.
- Fix items and issues when they occur. If you don't take care of your property, neither will your tenants.
- Treat your tenants with respect and work with them to clear outstanding issues. Be responsive and reasonable to their requests.
- Negotiate fairly with them if there are problems. If you treat them fairly, they will probably stay a long time – hence no months with no rental income.

We give our tenants multi-year options in the original lease to renew their leases at very reasonable rental rate increases. This makes them happy that they will not be subject to large rental increases, we find they treat the property better because they know they may and can stay for a long time, and we believe just brings about all over better relations. We can cancel these options if the property is sold or if they tenant is not a good tenant, so think through this carefully – but we think it makes a lot of sense.

We require in a lease addendum that tenants report maintenance issues to us, especially water issues. We also discuss this with them at move in and other times we have contact with them. It is so much easier and less expensive if you tenants alert you so that you can fix small issues before they become big expensive issues. We don't charge them and we let them know that – we just want to be able to fix issues.

Once you have gone through the whole leasing process below you will know how much work it is if you do a good job of it. You will then appreciate the two items noted above of working hard to get and keep good tenants!

NOW YOU HAVE CLOSED ESCROW, CONGRATULATIONS, YOU OWN STICKS, BRICKS AND DIRT!

GETTING YOUR PROPERTY RENTAL READY

If your property needs work to get it rental ready you should already be ready to start work within a few days of taking ownership. You prepare by again reviewing your filled out Home Inspection Checklist – Chapter 9 – that you completed with your home inspector. We are confident you will be adding to this list as you are surveying the property after you take ownership. Hopefully you are buying a property that is in decent shape and the repairs that are needed are not too expensive and can be completed in a relatively short period of time like thirty to sixty days. It probably will take longer than you believe to get it ready so you just want to move the process along as quickly as possible.

You need to be fully involved in this process if property ownership is new to you and you will learn it is time consuming. By being fully involved not only do you learn by watching, talking and listening to the people doing the work, it will assist you in better making decisions about controlling costs. And the more familiar you are with your property issues and problems the better you will be able to handle them as they creep up in the future. If you are not around to watch, review, and comment on the work being done, you will not gain a learning curve to help you better understand the process, what works and what doesn't work, and most importantly control costs as your real estate portfolio expands.

You'll learn some tough and expensive lessons the first time(s) around, but the more time you spend upfront on properties the more you will learn and be able to fine tune as your portfolio starts to accumulate three, then five, then nine properties.

Note: If you are rehabbing the property for a tenant move in, know exactly what you plan to update and be careful to make sure tenants know exactly what they are getting. You don't want to overpromise and then have to come in after they've moved in and continue to do work. We promise you will have to do some work once they move in regardless, but just try to minimize it by being careful of what you promise. Of course you may have to make those promises to get the good tenant that you really want and that probably makes sense, but just be mindful of this issue.

Don't forget to get those 10.0% off coupons for Lowes and Home Depot on the Internet – you can buy multiple ones on Ebay.com – buy from a reputable seller. You may also want to get Home Depot or Lowes consumer credit cards as they sometimes have generous terms of low interest rates or 0.0% interest for the first six to twelve months.

GETTING CLOSE TO RENTAL TIME

When you realistically feel you are getting close to rental ready like thirty days out, you want to start advertising the property for rent. Be careful because construction usually takes longer than one thinks and you want to be conservative on what date you tell a potential renter it will be available for occupancy.

You should already have a good idea of what the market rental rate is for your property because you did this in Chapter 3 to help you pencil out your real estate deal. You can also refresh this analysis as your real estate agent should be able to provide you some current rental comparables, you should call on any signs you see on other nearby properties, call any property management companies with nearby operations and scan Craigslist.org, Zillow.com, Trulia.com, and Hotpads.com for asking prices on properties comparable to yours.

CRAIGSLIST.org - You can also test the market rental rate by advertising your property on Craigslist.org – which is free. It is incredible that this resource exists and since so many people use Craigslist.org to find properties you can get some great market data with a little work. Place good, information filled ads with quality pictures showcasing your property on their website at what you think is the market rental rate. If you get lots of inquiries you will know you are in the ballpark. If it is an overwhelming number of inquires, you are asking too little rent. Few inquiries, you are asking too much. You can immediately change your ad and the price to test the market – it is really incredible!

ADVERTISING

Once you have a fair rental rate in mind you start advertising. In any metropolitan area with Craiglist.org, as we noted above, it is the most viewed website of property listings – and it is FREE and easy to use! Your ads stay live for seven days on Craigslist.org but due to their moving down the list quickly you may just want to post different ads every few days and have a few running at one time.

Your local area may have other services too and your real estate agent can alert you to these sites. The other sites noted above are also good places to list your property – Zillow.com, Trulia.com, etc. You should also put a sign on the property – as long as you do not think it is an area where it could be vandalized – and any other advertising you can do that is reasonably priced. You'll make it up when you get it rented quickly. You could also have an open house where neighbors could come see the place and may know someone who they would like to live near them and may give you a good lead on a tenant.

Make sure you comply with the local, state and federal fair housing laws. Craigslist.org has good information on these laws that you can see here: Craigslist.org Fair Housing Laws. Make sure to check your local city and county laws too.

The ads. We suggest always putting pictures of the property, information on the features, and any special items that make your unit more attractive – like "new carpets" or "updated kitchen". Put the monthly rent, that they pay utilities and name those utilities, the security deposit amount, application or credit check fee, yes or no on pets and what type of pets, one year or month to month lease, and any other good qualities of your unit like near retail or parks. Put your best foot forward!

EMAILS AND CALLS COMING IN

First, if emails and calls are NOT coming in the market is telling you something - you are asking too much rent for your property. So lower your asking rental price after a few days or a week.

Make sure to answer all calls and respond quickly to emails. If their emails have a phone number, try to call the person and if you do not get them then leave them a message that you are following up with an email. And then follow up with an informational email. You do not want to miss any calls as you may lose a good tenant by not quickly responding.

Tell the prospective tenant about the property and ask them open questions and listen. Good questions would be:

- Tell me a little more about you and who will be living in the property with you.
- Tell me a little more about your job and income history, rental history, savings and any evictions, foreclosures or bankruptcies. What negative marks will I find on your credit report?
- Why are you moving?
- What is your moving timeframe based on your existing housing situation?
- Any criminal history of your or anyone that will be living in the property? Explain please.
- Do you have any pets, non-operable cars, noise making music instruments or other machines, RVs, home based businesses, day care, inventory for business, how many cars?
- Smoker? Smoke inside stains walls and ceilings.
- Who are your references and how do you know them, business, rental history or personal references?

You are going to obtain a credit report and criminal history regardless, but asking these questions will help you determine whether or not you think this person is a good fit. If you think they may work, try to schedule a showing of the property right then at their convenience. If you think they probably will not work you could tell them you will get back to them on a property showing day and time or you can just let them know they do not fit your credit or rental profile (if they don't).

After you get a feel for if you think you are interested in their being a tenant you may want to discuss with them about any conditions or concerns you have related to your property. Like you want someone with a certain credit profile, or no evictions, or a certain minimum level of income – maybe two or three times the monthly rental amount. You may also want to let them know in the ad or on the phone that no business is to be operated at the site, pets or no pets (some breeds are not covered by some insurance companies so confirm with your insurance agent and discuss with a potential tenant), recreational vehicles or not in the driveway, working on cars, etc.

And are you looking for a one year lease, a six month lease, or month to month. The longer the lease the better you will learn after going through the entire time consuming leasing process – but what you can secure is going to be somewhat dependent on the local market in which your property is located – so know your market. By going through this information upfront with a potential renter this will avoid your taking the time to show someone the property who you would reject for some reason. You have to be a little negotiable too as you will rarely find the perfect tenant. Maybe their credit is bad due to a short sale but they have good long term jobs – just think about what works for you.

Again, make sure you comply with the local, state and federal fair housing laws. Craigslist.org has good information on these laws that you can see here: Craigslist.org Fair Housing Laws. Make sure to check your local city and county laws too.

RENTAL APPLICATION - For those individuals who you think may be a good fit and you plan to show the property, have a rental application ready that you can email to them so they can fill it out and bring it along if they choose. The best place to get a rental application is from a real estate agent. Every state has an Association of Realtors and they have standardized real estate forms of every type. Those forms are created, reviewed and updated by the association's real estate attorney(s) so they are the most updated and they have strong legal protections for the landlord and tenant based on state laws.

Ask your real estate agent to provide you the standard state association of Realtors rental application and use that application. There may also be a local or state apartment building owners association application and that be similar and as good.

TENANT SCREENING

This is the process of doing your due diligence on your prospective tenant – essentially reviewing the information they provide on the RENTAL APPLICATION and verifying it with independent information to assist you in making a decision on whether or not to rent your property to them.

You can usually charge then tenant for the cost of taking the rental application and credit report – check your local laws on this. We usually collect the cost of screening with their application and tell the prospective tenants that we will not cash their check until and only after we review their application and have decided to proceed to a credit check. We only do a credit check if we have decided that we are ready to rent the property to them, subject to the credit verification. And if the credit check matches their application information, we typically rent the unit to them. You can do it however you like and for us this just seems like a fair way to do it and you want to have good relations with your tenant – and this is a good start.

In assessing whether a potential candidate will make a good renter the main items you want to understand are their:

Income – Do they make enough to pay rent and their other expenses and how solid is their income history, so how long has their current income stream been in place and how does it look going forward? You would verify income and employment history by calling their employer, looking at paystubs they provide, or other documentation like pension statements, government benefits, alimony or child support documentation, or tax returns.

Debt - You would verify estimated debt payments from their credit report – like car, credit card, student loan, or other loan payments, or alimony or child support they pay from their application or credit report.

THE OVERALL PICTURE IS YOU WANT TO DETERMINE: Does their income less their estimated debt payments leave enough money to pay rent and other living expenses?

Assets – Do they have backup or reserve funds to pay rent if their income stream is disrupted? Most renters have few if any reserve funds. You would verify this from their showing you and bank, mutual fund, pension or other asset type of statements that they provide. Do not expect much in reserve funds, but some is better than none.

Rental and Payment History – Have they paid rent in the past and been a good tenant, so check references, and have they generally paid non-housing bills in the past? You would verify this by calling current and prior landlords, looking on their credit report for evictions and on their credit report for overdue bills or non-payment of bills, foreclosures, bankruptcies, or other negative credit marks.

In general better credit and rental history potential tenants are ones with long past rental history and good recommendations, enough income to pay the rent and that rent is a maximum of plus or minus 45.0% of their gross monthly income or less. And maybe a lower rent to income percentage if they have others to support who do not earn an income. They should not have too much credit card or other debt, and have NO history of evictions, and hopefully no foreclosures, or bankruptcies.

Foreclosures and Bankruptcies in the past may be okay depending on their current job situation. Foreclosures especially in today's environment may not be that bad if they have a good job but just let a past property they owned go into foreclosure – again you want someone to take care of your property and pay the rent on time. Bankruptcies can be from medical problems, business problems, etc – if they are in the past and the prospective tenant has decent steady employment now and good recent rental history that may be fine.

Evictions are a different story – this is just our opinion. This probably means that person got into financial trouble and did NOT work with their past landlord to either move out or satisfy the lease. It is time consuming and expensive to evict a tenant, so if the owner went all the way through the hard work to obtain an eviction action – typically called an Unlawful Detainer judgment - it probably means the tenant was not doing their part to try to mitigate the damages to the owner.

And you need to be very cautious because you could be the next owner in this circumstance if you take tenants with evictions. Not to mention that the potential renter didn't have the forethought to consider the significant detrimental ramifications of an eviction mark on their own credit report. There may be reasonable reasons and if the prospective tenant can explain the reasons and you can verify them and they are reasonable to you that may work – but again, caution here.

We cannot really provide more specifics on these as it is your decision on who to select as a renter and you need to gain an understanding of the typical credit profile of the renters that would like to live in your property. Use your best judgment, talk to your real estate agent and/or other property owners that you know. Some of tenant screening services will also give you ratings. You should also look at someone's FICO credit score if that is part of the credit report your order. Generally scores over 700 are pretty good, 600 – 700 are okay, and under 600 are not that good. But do your research online and again talk to your real estate agent or mortgage broker on credit scores.

Keep your selected potential tenant advised of where you are in the process – you do not want someone who you believe would be a good tenant to rent another place because you are taking too long to get back to them. Therefore, you should be moving very quickly to screen the tenant and offer the property for rental – like one to two days at the longest to get back to them.

Low Income Tenants – Section 8 Program

The section 8 program is a Federal Department of Housing and Urban Development program to help lower income families with rental housing assistance. Section 8 participating individuals or families that have applied and been accepted to the program find suitable housing in their local jurisdiction from a property owner who is willing to accept Section 8 participants. The program is administered by the local city or county government and typically a participant pays thirty percent of their income towards housing expense and the Section 8 program pays the rest directly to the landlord via electronic transfer. It is hard for renters to get accepted to this program as there are usually long waiting lists at the agencies that administer them for the city – sometimes five or more years of waiting to be accepted to the program.

Participants can also be kicked out of the program if they do not pay timely rent or damage a property they live in. Many participants in this program know they are fortunate to have the government pay a portion of their rent and take very good care of properties and are great tenants. You as the landlord are required to keep your property in good clean condition or you could get kicked out of the program. Many times county agencies have listings of property owners that will accept Section 8 participants and list them on their website for potential tenants to review. But in general tenants who call may also ask if you take Section 8 tenants. You set the rent and it must be market rent based on comparable properties.

In considering Section 8 tenants, you should do the same due diligence that you would do on a normal tenant. What is their rental history, do they have good recommendations, do they have the income to pay their portion of the rent and other expenses, who will be living at the property and how many people? Let Section 8 tenants know you will consider them and you will have to look at their overall financial and rental history picture – you can find some good tenants here and many landlords love the fact that a healthy portion of their rent is guaranteed and paid directly by the city. Make sure you confirm with the city that they are in good standing in the program and what you as an owner need to do to secure the guaranteed payments from the city.

You can find more information at your local jurisdiction housing agencies and in these two places – Wikipedia and HUD. Make sure to talk to your real estate agent and other property owners in the HUD Section 8 program to learn about their experiences and thoughts related to accepting these tenants.

Again, Make sure you comply with the local, state and federal fair housing laws. Craigslist.org has good information on these laws that you can see here: Craigslist.org Fair Housing Laws. Make sure to check your local city and county laws too.

CREDIT CHECK and CRIMINAL HISTORY CHECK

There are many companies that will provide credit and criminal history checks for individual owners. It is however getting much harder to do credit checks these days. First ask your real estate agent if they can do this check for you on a prospective tenant. If not, there are some services listed below. They will need to verify your information, the purpose of your credit check, and that you have the right to do this credit check – so something signed by the potential renter and maybe some additional documentation from your rental applicant giving you the right to verify their information. A few service providers of these checks are:

1. First American Corporation, one of the largest data providers of real estate information in the country.
2. Transunion, one of the three major US credit bureaus.
3. Experian, this is Experian, also one of the three major US credit bureaus.
4. Citicredit .net

There are lots of others and you may want to discuss with your real estate agent and or search online for other screening companies.

Some of these companies will give you a kind of rating or score for the prospective tenant, so just read through what they have to offer and select the one you think will be best for you. You can also review the report yourself and look at their total debt, their credit score, any evictions, bankruptcies, late payments, etc. It is a complicated document but About.com has some fairly straightforward explanations to help you understand better:

About.com How to Read Your Credit Report – Go to www.about.com and see the credit report information.

GOOGLE, YAHOO and FACEBOOK IT!

Search Google, Yahoo, Facebook – It never hurts to google or yahoo their name and/or email address and maybe check Facebook just to see if there is something out there that may cause a concern.

Court records – Many counties have court records on line and you could check their name there too for any issues.

THE LEASE AND LEASING PROCESS

Now that you have selected the tenant that you would like to rent to it is time to prepare a lease. We suggest to have your real estate agent give you a copy of the state or local real estate association's standard format lease or get the one used by the local or state apartment building owner's association. Again, those documents are vetted by the association's attorney and well tested over time. Even if you are using another lease, it never hurts to review the most commonly used lease to see if there is anything in there that is NOT in the lease you have selected. Take your time to review and understand the lease terms, it will govern your relationship with your tenant for hopefully years to come.

The California Association of Realtors lease is very straightforward and easy to understand, very little legalese to decipher. It is however six pages long but all the language is there to PROTECT YOU, so make sure to read and understand it. It follows California law so if your property is not located in California you want the one that is for your state or local jurisdiction.

We prepare a separate addendum in plain English that covers the following Items that are important to us:

- Lease Options for Additional Years and Landlord Rights to Terminate the Option – especially if the property is sold. This details rental increases going forward.
- No Business, Excessive Noise, Day Care, RV Parking, Repair Work on Equipment, Inoperable Cars or Work Trucks
- Any HOA or city violations and fines are the responsibility of the Tenant.
- No Water Beds, Chemical Storage, Firearms.
- Utility Service Changeover Must be Ordered a Week in Advance by Tenant
- Property not in perfect shape and every property has chips in paint, dings in walls, etc. and Landlord will fix major issues but not minor ones (Note: We always offer to pay for paint and supplies if they want to buy and fix items).
- Service Companies, Phone Numbers, Process Information

You will learn over time what clauses and issues impact you and you will revise your lease and practices over time. That is part of the process of real estate ownership and being a landlord.

We typically email the prepared lease to the tenant with instructions on where to sign and initial, to return the cashier's check security deposit with the lease (if we did not get the security deposit when they filled out their application), and a timeframe for returning the signed lease – three to five days is reasonable and put an exact date in the email. Let them know you are excited to have them as a potential tenant but you are still showing the property and taking applications as you wait for their returned lease and deposit. When they are ready to deliver the documents/money you should meet with them face to face and walk them through the lease terms and get everything in order. Only the timely return of the signed lease and security deposit will secure the unit rental to them. Move quickly to get your signed lease done.

Some Leasing Tips:

- 45-60 days notice of lease termination ALWAYS ending the lease on the last day of the month.
- All utilities to be paid by Tenant – people never conserve unless they have to pay the bills. If multiple units you own, like a duplex, split the water bill for reimbursement by the tenants. Put formula in lease.

- Rent payments to be made via electronic transaction to your bank account – either via online or bank transfer or Tenants depositing it directly into your account.
- Emergency contact information in your lease.
- Report any water issues, overflows, spots on walls or ceiling immediately. Stress that they need to alert you on these so you can fix small issues before they become big and expensive.
- Report any maintenance items to you.
- Landlord to handle and pay for yard and exterior maintenance – the tenant generally will not do it and that causes damage.

MULTIPLE YEAR LEASE OPTIONS - We give our tenants multiple year options with fixed rents. For example, we do a 1 year lease at $1,250 and as long as they are good tenants, pay on time, take care of the property, they have a fixed rental schedule: Year 2 - $1,270, Year 3, $1,295, Year 4 $1,325, Year 5 - $1,360. They just need to let us know near the end of each term if they plan to stay. This gives us small bumps in the rent to cover higher expenses but gives them the comfort that they will not be kicked out or rent increased too much.

In doing this, we feel tenants make the properties their "homes" and better maintain them because they are going to live there a long time, they keep better care of the place, and better relations with the landlord. We keep options to cancel the extensions if they are not good tenants, if we sell the property, or for any reason and in the case we want to cancel for "any reason" we give them some rental reduction on the last month as compensation for terminating their lease.

Remember, you want to keep your tenants as long as possible and the little you give up in not raising rents much - if the market rental rate does in fact increase - is more than made up for by having a 0.0% vacancy rate and not having to take the considerable time and energy to re-lease the property every couple of years.

DAY TENANT TAKES POSSESSION

The first month's rent should be delivered to you a few days before your tenant moves in to the property – the exact date should be noted in the lease agreement and it should be a cashiers check or money order.

You need to do a walk-through of the property with your tenants when you hand them the keys to the property. This is a final chance for you to note anything you need to repair or replace and discuss any tenant issues or concerns. Your lease should give the tenant five days to alert you in writing or email to any items or issues that are not in operable condition at move in – so you can fix them.

Show your tenants where the water shut offs are located and where the electric box is located and how to reset circuit breakers or fuses (including GFCI fuses in the kitchen and bathrooms). Request they be careful on what they send down the house drain pipes from the kitchen sink and other drains – old pipes do clog – and so do new ones. And show them any other items that need attention, door locks, etc. If you know your property you will know what the tenants need to know.

MANAGEMENT OF PROPERTY

Some properties can go a long time with very little interaction by the owner. However, you never know where there will be a tenant, electrical, plumbing, appliance, utility, roof, you fill in the blank: _____ ISSUE. Be prepared have to visit the property or handle an issue three to five times per year. And be prepared to spend between $50 and $150 on average per month on repairs for uninsured issues. So $600 to $1,800 per year is probably a good guess depending on the age, size, condition of the property and your skill in handling those issues and relations with tenants. It makes sense to inspect the property, if you have not, probably once per year and especially look for water issues on the ceiling, attic, behind water using appliances or fixtures.

It doesn't hurt to know what plumbing or electrical service provider you are going to call if there is an issue. So you may want to figure that out and keep it in a place that is easy to access and you may want to give that information to them.

You should also keep a file for your tenant with their lease, lease application, credit and rental documentation, emergency contact numbers, emails, phone number, etc. – everything you used in making the lease and leasing decisions.

Work hard to keep your tenants as noted at the top of this chapter. Once you have gone through the process or leasing a property you will understand why it is much better to keep your tenants in place than to have your tenants vacate the property.

Default by Tenant on Lease – What to Do?

If you do not receive rent on time or your tenant alerts you that they are in financial trouble and will not be able to pay rent what do you do? First give them written notice that they are in default as required by the lease and local law and keep a record of the issues and responses and actions of all parties. You want to do is handle this in a straightforward and professional manner and try to get your tenants to help mitigate the financial damages to all parties. If they cannot pay rent you are probably not going to collect additional monies if you pursue them into court – which is going to cost you at least $500 and probably more like $1,000 – that you will never see again. The goal is to get them to move out in a reasonable timeframe and leave the property clean and damage free. By offering to not chase them into court or damage their credit they will hopefully jump on the opportunity to leave on good terms.

By working with them you may also be able to show the property to prospective tenants during this process and maybe even get the property re-leased from the date they move out. You could consider offering that if your tenants help you towards this effort, again to mitigate financial damages, that you would return some of their security deposit. Remember, they are probably out of money so there is little to be gained by your being unprofessional. Suggest they move in with family or friends or to a less expensive situation. If you can resolve it amicably, it really will be a win-win for everyone – so work hard towards that goal.

HOWEVER, sometimes trying to work with them will not work due to strained relations or unreasonable tenants. If that is the circumstance, you have to make sure you comply with all the laws on eviction and most likely will have to have an attorney handle the process. Keep trying to get them to move out and leave the property in good condition while you continue with the eviction process. Offer to stop the process if they work with you – again, you probably will never collect any of the missed rent payments, attorneys fees, or reimbursements for an property damages - so try hard to work with them to move our responsibly. One property owner we know just offers his tenants money to get out if they leave in a reasonable time and leave the property in good shape. Remember, damaged properties also take time to repair, you lose rent during that period and it takes up your time - so mitigate and negotiate as you can.

If you or your tenants are too involved and upset to be reasonable in dealings with each other, try to enlist a family member or third party mediator, with your tenants' agreement, to help out and make a fair deal with all parties. Do not send hastily drafted angry, destructive, or threatening emails that hinder the situation and may cause you issues if you end up in court. Keep your conversations, offers and promises on the phone and if you work a fair agreement and the tenant wants it in writing, make it short, sweet and to the point. Again, your goal is to get the defaulting tenants out as quickly as possible with little damage to your property as possible. Remember that rarely will people who are ticked off at their landlord be helpful in mitigating damages or leaving the property damage free.

Tenant's Give Notice of Move Out

As long as you have required sixty days notice of termination in your lease (and on the last day of the month) you should have plenty of time to prepare for re-leasing the unit once your receive notice that your tenant is vacating the unit. Request access to determine and request their opinion on what needs to be fixed, replaced, or cleaned upon their move out – they lived there so know they know the items and issues. Get the process in place to handle those issues in an expedient manner as soon as possible. And start advertising the property as soon as possible per the above rental process.

Most new potential renters have to give thirty days notice so they are already looking for their next unit and prefer to have a signed lease as soon as possible. And of course your best bet is to have a tenant lined up for when the existing tenants vacate the unit. It will take a lot of hard work to have just a few or no vacant days, but you can do it.

Make sure to be fair about their security deposit and return it within the specified legal timeframes for your local jurisdiction or sooner.

Management by Third Party Company – This IS **NOT** as Time Consuming – Because You are Paying Someone Else to Do It!

This may be a good choice for you, especially after you learn the time consuming nature of the real estate ownership process. These companies usually charge 8% - 10% of rental income on an ongoing basis and one-half to one month's rent for leasing or re-leasing the property. Interview several management companies that are near the property and make your best decision on which company to hire. We suggest though that you first learn the process of self-management so you know the process and issues – and better know your property – and then hire it out to a company if you so desire. There are many great companies and you can find one. Make sure to obtain copies of their insurance policy, check references, carefully read the management agreement so you know what they will and will not do.

CHAPTER 14

FLIPPING, FIXER UPPERS - BEWARES

Often we hear people talking about making big bucks Flipping Property or doing Fixer Uppers for big profits. We see the TV shows and many are quite fascinating, but are they realistic? Is it really that easy and profitable? Conversely, when was the last time you heard someone bragging about all the money they've lost trying either one of these strategies. But it must happen sometimes....right?

Flipping properties or doing fixer uppers to make a profit is very difficult to do – the financial numbers and unanticipated:

_____ <= you fill in the blank with: cost overruns, unknown repairs, surprises, unforeseen expenses, extra months of holding time before you sell it, buyer demands for additional repairs, selling commissions, lower sales price than projected usually make the projects not work out financially. We would guess that the vast majority of people who try this strategy do not make money – most probably decide to never buy real estate again.

We are not saying that it is not possible to succeed with one of these strategies, but being able to successfully buy a property at a large enough discount to make the process work takes significant time, energy and effort. Unless you are looking at and making lowball offers on tens of properties AND if you actually get one under contract and accurately estimate the repair and transaction costs on that property, and accurately predict the time to repair it, list for sale and close the sale on the property – your chance of losing money is high. So you really have to be doing this full time, and even if you are, you are taking a LOT of risk attempting to do something that has a very low probability of success.

Either way, for Flipping, True Fixer Uppers or Cosmetic Fixer Uppers, use the Home Inspection Checklist from Chapter 9 to help you run through all the items and issues that need repair, work and money at the property. Make sure to do the hard work upfront and take significant time to really investigate the costs and timeframes for completing the tasks that need to be done in order to bring the property up to the condition that you decide is appropriate for your investment strategy.

Overall, while there is the possibility of making money with either strategy, and some people can make it work, there is a very high PROBABILITY that it will be the last time you try flipping or a fixer upper! Let's look at why.

Flipping

Flipping is the process of buying a property and putting some repairs into the property, then reselling it in a short period of time - maybe three to six months. Unless you are making offers all the time on properties, the percentage chance that you are going to be able to buy a property for significantly below its' market value and then sell it for enough money to cover your costs and earn a profit, is a very low percentage.

When you try to Flip, you pay thousands of dollars in transaction costs to buy the property (escrow, title, loan points/fee, etc.), and you pay to do the rehabilitation which always costs more and takes longer than one believes – and yes every attempted Flip also has thousands of dollars in fix up costs – carpets, painting, landscaping, new bath and kitchen fixtures. You have to put money into the property if you want to attempt to maximize your sales price. Then when you sell it you pay another round of transaction costs, plus real estate broker commissions, plus interest on your loan, property taxes, and insurance while you are rehabbing it and holding it for sale. And did you count your time for managing the process?

Guess what, most likely there is not going to be much money left over to cover all your time, energy and effort in doing the whole transaction. In fact, unless you have significant experience doing these and have done a LOT of hard work bidding on those tens of properties just to get one at the right price, you probably are going to lose money. And it probably is going to be a lot of money.

Note: These can be all over the map. The rehabilitation costs usually end up being a lot more than an Inexperienced Flipper (and maybe an Experienced Flipper too) anticipates. If you are going to try this, you had better put together a comprehensive budget with someone who has already done these and has extensive experience flipping properties for a profit – which very few people have. Your budget better include significant miscellaneous costs and reserves in case you overrun your estimates, or you do not get the price you were hoping to get, or it takes significantly longer to sell than you anticipate.

A few years ago people were making money Flipping properties, but that was more of a function of real estate prices increasing at the rate of ten to fifteen percent per year. We all NOW know that those price increases were unsustainable, hence the current foreclosure and economic trouble in the United States. You do not have the luxury of increasing prices in today's market, so you must add value or buy at a significant discount, both of which are very difficult to do even for the most experienced real estate people.

Let's just look at an example where someone purchased a $100,000 townhome that needs cosmetic work and hopes to sell it for $140,000 after three months of rehab and providing an estimated three months to advertise, negotiate and close the sale. Profit of $40,000, or 40.0% in a short period of time, sounds pretty good:

Let's look at the costs of purchase, rehabilitation, and carrying costs during the rehab:

FLIPPING - COSTS OF PROCESS TO GET PROPERTY READY FOR SALE

Subject: 1,100 SF Townhome with Cosmetic Fix Needs
(Note - No exterior work needed due to HOA)

Property Cost	**$100,000**	
Appraisal	$450	
Home Inspection	$250	
TOTAL		$100,700
Loan Fees (on $75,000 Loan)		
Original Fees - 1 Point	$750	
Processing Fee	$695	
Admin Fee	$395	
Underwriting Fee	$750	
Tax Service Fee	$75	
Flood Cert Fee	$26	
Credit Report Fee	$15	
Transaction Coordinator Fee	$350	
TOTAL		$3,056
Escrow and Settlement Fees		
Settlement/Closing Fee	$500	
Document Prep Fee	$75	
Title Insurance	$400	
Title Endorsements	$75	
Recording Fees	$80	
Courier Fees	$40	
Loan Tie in Fee	$175	
Notary Fees	$150	
TOTAL		$1,495
Rehabilitation Fees		
(House would be more due to exterior work)		
Carpets	$2,000	
Painting	$1,500	
Replace Bath/Kitch (some items)		
Lights, Towel Bars, Door Knobs	$1,000	
Vanity, Sink, Faucet	$1,000	
Refrigerator/Appliances	$1,200	
Miscellaneous	$1,500	
TOTAL		$8,200

Continues

Continued

Note: It could be a lot more! And it PROBABLY will be!	
During Rehab and For Sale Period - 6 Months Carrying Costs	
HOA Fees (Varies Widely)	$1,200
Property Taxes (Varies by State)	$600
Insurance	$200
Mortgage Payments	$2,400
Elect/Gas/Water Bills	$600
TOTAL	$5,000
GRAND TOTAL Costs Up to Sale	**$118,451**

So this Flip is up to $118,451 in costs to prepare it for sale. Let's say you get a buyer at your $140,000 gross sales price – great job! What is the net sales price:

SALES PRICE AND COSTS		
Sales Price		140,000
Closing Costs		
Commissions (6.0%)	$8,400	
Escrow, Title, Etc.	$4,000	
Negotiated Add'l Repairs	$1,500	
TOTAL Costs	$13,900	
Net Sales Price		**$126,100**

So you will net sales revenue of $126,100. So how much is your profit?:

PROFIT ON FLIP	
Net Sales Price	**$126,100**
Costs Up to Sale	**$118,451**
NET PROFIT to COVER YOUR TIME AND RISK	**$7,649**

As you can see, even if you could sell the property for $40,000 more (which would probably be an extremely lucky event) than your purchase price, there actually is still not a lot of profit here. And this is not even including your time to be there full time during the rehab and part time during the sales process. And let us guess, you forgot about 80% of the above costs when you first contemplated taking on a Flip. Now you know them, and there will be more, we promise.

You can dissect these numbers and use your own if you believe that you can save costs, do the work yourself, sell it more quickly, or pencil out any better way to do the process. But at the end of the process, with cost and time overruns, it is more likely than not that the numbers are going to be a lot WORSE than the projection above.

And you are taking a huge amount of risk. Is that really the way you want to start of earning your long term real estate fortune. There are easier ways to make money in real estate. We did not say "easy ways", we just said "easier ways" than trying to Flip properties.

We know it sounds exciting and you want to brag to your friends about what you are doing and all the rosy projections and profits you plan to make, but put your pencil to your paper and do not underestimate the costs and time involved in attempting this strategy.

Again, we are NOT saying there is no way that you can make money doing this, but generally there is NO easy money in real estate.

True Fixer Uppers

A true Fixer Upper is a property that needs significant work and is not realistically livable in the current condition. A property in this category would need a new kitchen, baths, windows, flooring, landscaping, maybe electric, plumbing, wall and ceiling repair, etc. These are properties that inexperienced people buy in hopes of enjoying the process and making some money. They usually pay way too much for the properties, based on the costs to rehabilitate it, and DO NOT enjoy the experience.

So one may buy a Fixer Upper property for $175,000 when the market value would be $215,000 if the house was in good clean livable shape. Then the buyer would proceed and in many cases go way over budget and end up spending $75,000 on the rehab with the end result that the house costs $250,000 in total between the purchase price and rehabilitation to put it in good clean livable shape. But the house would still only be worth the $215,000, or maybe a little more, but no where near the total cost of acquisition plus fix up costs.

In doing a Fixer Upper, you will almost definitely add value to the property, but probably NOT more value than it costs you to make those improvements. And if you live in the property while doing the rehab, it will not be fun. It will be downright stressful, disrupting to your life, and not a pleasant experience.

Unless you are a licensed contractor and experienced in doing rehabilitation projects on single family properties, you probably have a 95% chance of losing money attempting this strategy.

Without the experience of past learning how much rehabs cost, you are most likely going to way underestimate the cost and time it takes to successfully take a property from bad shape to sellable shape. And time is money, and money is money too, so realistically you are going to probably lose money. But should you try this to learn and get that experience? **NO, NIL, NOTTA, NOPE, HECK NO! THERE IS A HIGH PROBABILITY YOU WILL NOT MAKE MONEY.**

A cosmetic fixer upper is a much better bet and you can read below about those.
The fact is that rarely do true fixer uppers sell at a large enough discount to value that there would be any profit opportunities available for someone to do a rehab and then sell it at a profit. Those inexperienced buyers have a romantic notion that it would be fun and a great experience to buy a home to fix up to sell – and they will make a profit. We can assure you, it is not fun. It is not cheap. It always takes longer than one believes.

And if you are not there every day watching the contractors and workers, asking questions, reviewing completed work, parts of the rehab will not be done right or in a quality way. You will then put it on the market and buyers will find all kinds of items that still need to be repairs or finished. So do you have from 7 am to 4 pm five to seven days a week for several months to be on site? People and contractors who are in the business of doing these do have that time, and they do have that experience. If you do not, you are asking for trouble and losses.

To add to that, if you buy a fixer upper, let's say for $200,000 and you finance 90% of your purchase, that means you will put down $20,000 plus closing costs to close escrow. Every dollar you spend (after you take title) to fix the property will have to come from your savings or on your credit card. So just be aware while you are stressed out over the rehab and time it is taking, you are also depleting your savings and/or bulking up on your credit card balances.

We advise, at least for the first five or so properties you buy, **purchase properties that are in fairly good shape**, do not need significant work, and can be rented relatively quickly in their current condition with minor repairs. **Pay more for a property in better shape.**

SO...do not bite off more than you can chew! Use the Home Inspection Checklist to help you Budget the fixes the property will need to get it rental ready.

To sum it up, YOU SHOULD NOT BUY FIXER UPPERS unless you have already done enough of them to realize that YOU SHOULD NOT BUY FIXER UPPERS. Of course in that case you will already know that it is not smart to buy Fixer Uppers and hopefully you will follow your own knowledge and advice.

Cosmetic Fixer Uppers

Cosmetic fixers need paint, carpets, maybe new bathroom lights and fixtures or some flooring. We tell people that if they are NOT willing to move into and live in the property pretty much in its current condition for quite a while then they should probably avoid that property. A cosmetic fixer is a property that you are willing to move into AS IS and work on it one project at a time for a year or two. You can better investigate, shop for materials, schedule and budget your single projects, get several bids from contractors on each project, review completed work and do a much better overall job than if you are under stress paying rent in a separate place you are living while also paying the mortgage on a fixer upper where you are rushing to complete many projects at the same time. And in that rush, doing a sloppy job of the rehabilitation.

Cosmetic fixers are also okay for rental property purchases. Buy something in decent shape that may need paint or carpets or a new bathroom vanity and toilet, but not significant work. Most of the time, regardless, it will cost more than you believe. But with Cosmetic Fixers you can close escrow on the property, schedule the work over sixty to ninety days and get the property rented out. Your cash out of pocket will be reasonable and you will start collecting rental income in a shorter period of time. Plus it will not be vacant during a long rehab and a target for theft – that is why insurance does not cover properties that are vacant!

IN SUMMARY – Try to buy properties that do not need too much work – don't worry, it will cost a lot regardless and you will get plenty of chances to use your credit card and rack up frequent flyer miles! If you can't find those, a Cosmetic Fixer that you will move into and work on over time would be the next best option – plus you get the best financing due to your owner occupancy loan type – see Chapter 7 Mortgage Financing.

Skip true Fixer Uppers and leave those to the professionals who do that full time and have the time, energy and experience to deal with these major projects.

A couple of separate items here:

- If you are going to buy a house as a principal residence that has a particular irreplaceable location, lot, views or characteristics that you like, that could modify the analysis a little, just make sure you have a realistic estimate of the costs to put the property in good shape, or:
- If the price is so so cheap on a True Fixer Upper that it seems to make rehabbing sense, that could be worth investigating. BEWARE though - there is usually a major problem if the price is that cheap. If it looks too good to be true it probably is.

Final Notes:

The Home Inspection Checklist in Chapter 9 is really your best tool here. We are confident that if you add up all the repair, transaction costs on the buy-in and the sell-out, and holding costs of either of these strategies, you will see that typically you are going to have to sell the property at much higher price than market value to make a profit. And we wish you the best of luck if your success strategy hinges on selling the property at a much higher price than the market will bear!

CHAPTER 15

SMALL APARTMENT BUILDINGS

This chapter will detail the few differences between buying single family properties between 1 - 4 units and buying apartment buildings that are 5 units and over but not too many units like over 10 or 15.

Overall, apartment buildings are generally the lowest risk type of commercial real estate you can own – with a couple of exceptions like single tenant retail buildings with strong credit quality tenants who have long term guaranteed leases – but there are few of those around at reasonable prices.

So we will stick with real estate that is lower risk and where you can actually acquire property and secure a fair rate of return – Apartment Buildings are the answer.

To "earn" that low risk you need to own properties that are in decent shape, in decent areas, in areas with relatively low vacancy, ones that are moderately priced – hence fairly good cash flows that you verified with leases and general market data – and you need to treat your tenants with respect and maintain your building – JUST LIKE ANY RENTAL PROPERTY.

So let's discuss the differences between residential properties of 1-4 units and commercial apartment properties of 5 units or greater.

Regardless of how many units you plan to purchase, read the entire chapter for all the details and information.

FOUR UNITS OR LESS

These properties need the same due diligence as any other residential single unit property. You need to:

- Pencil out your cash flows with the simple Chapter 3 spreadsheet and maybe the After-tax Chapter 6 spreadsheet to make sure you are comfortable with the pro-forma returns on your cash equity investment. You should probably use Chapter 6 Pre-Tax and After Tax Spreadsheet here.
- Analyze and find a fair deal on the mortgage financing from Chapter 7.
- Do your proper evaluation of the property condition and how much it will cost to bring it up to rental ready quality from Chapter 9.
- Obtain proper property insurance coverage for the risks you need covered in consultation with you agent from Chapter 10.
- Review the title insurance and Title the property as is most advantageous to you Chapter 11 and Chapter 12 LLCs and Asset Protection.
- Make sure you are paying a fair price based on comparable sales Chapter 17.

Those items are with any property and again you are significantly reducing your risk by doing those tasks. There are a few other important items to consider in buying smaller apartment buildings after you complete the above tasks.

In general the more units the better the cash flows, but that depends on a lot of factors like vacancy rates, rental rates, rental rate compared to cost per unit, etc. So you want to pencil out the target property that you may want to offer upon.

Projected Financial Estimates (the pro-forma) - For your pro-forma returns you want to ask the seller for his or her past financial statements and tax returns - you probably will not get either of them – but ask anyhow. Most sellers will also say the rents are below market and can be raised, but you need to verify market rents on your own. Even if they are below market, are you going to raise rents and risk your tenants leaving? Just think that through. In that case you may also lose a month of rent, have to repair or repaint the unit, and do all the work of leasing the unit – so cautious in projecting much higher rents in the very near term. You also need to come up with the amounts for property taxes, insurance, water, repairs and maintenance, and other expenses, etc. to do a proper analysis.

Even if the owner gives you expense numbers, you need to verify they are reasonable for that type and size of property. The seller may have kept expenses low the past few years knowing the property was going to be sold and lower expenses would make the financials look better and hence probably be able to sell the property for a higher price. Then you take title to the property and expenses are much higher than anticipated and you do not make your projected returns. So independent verification and reasonable projections by you of rents and expenses is very important. Put them down on paper or in the spreadsheet and see what type of investment return you can achieve.

Financing Owner Occupied – The financing for four units or less is very similar to single unit residential financing. And can even buy a four unit property as an owner occupant, with really good financing, if you are going to live there for the first year. This is a huge advantage because not only can you be allowed to only put down equity of only 20.0% percent, and maybe less, but you can obtain long term fixed rate financing (apartment building loans for five units or more have a different financing scenario and typically are going to require 30.0% down at least and probably more – explained below). You can also typically count 75.0% of the current market rent or in place rental income from the non-owner occupied units, less expenses, as part of your "income" to help you qualify for the loan. That should help quite a bit.

Financing Investment Property – If you are not planning to live there, you can still typically count that 75.0% of rental income on all the units even though it isn't owner occupied. However, investment property in this case will probably require 25.0% down as any normal investment property in the current marketplace. And the rate or points or both will typically be higher than single family homes or individual condos that are investor units.

Management of Property - You also can manage the property yourself and save a little money and learn the property better by being there on site. This of course has disadvantages too because tenants can always reach you and when there are issues, like water or electrical issues, it can get stressful dealing with your neighbor/tenants. Or if your tenants are constantly asking you to make improvements or causing other issues, you are right there to hear and experience it all – and that may not be fun for long. Alternatively, you can have the property managed by a professional firm and pay 6.0% to 10.0% for their handling that function.

Existing Leases – You also need to review the existing leases of the tenants that already occupy the units and the past several months of the owner's records of bank deposits that correspond to those leases. This will help you determine that tenants are paying rent and the actual current amount. You may also want to try to have the seller get the tenants to sign an Estoppel Certificate. This would be a one page document that details the lease parties, lease terms, unit occupants, security deposit, and termination date. You would ask the seller to have the tenants each sign that document – one for each unit - confirming their rental terms.

The owner may say no, or the tenants may refuse, but if you have some concerns about the actual rental rates or if rent is being collected, then reviewing deposits and getting signed Estoppels will help towards satisfying those concerns. The leases will also tell you who pays for water, trash, etc. so you know what to expect. Note: Always try to push utility costs to your tenants. Water is the biggest issue here, people never conserve unless they have to pay the bills. You could allocate the total water bill by the number of units or number of people per unit – subject to any state or local laws.

Property Inspection Before Purchase – Make sure you do a comprehensive property inspection and make sure to get inside every single inch of the building, closets, utility rooms, attic, crawl space, etc. It is the one closet or area that the seller cannot find the key to that has the leaky roof and mold covered walls….we've seen it before!

Overall multiple units are going to have greater diversification of rental income from several tenants, going to typically have slightly better cash flows, and better returns – but more work because more tenants, more appliances, more toilets, etc. The tenant quality could be as good as single units if you keep the properties in good shape and work hard to get good tenants in the first place – which we always suggest.

FIVE UNITS OR GREATER

These properties need the same due diligence as any other residential single unit property or 4 units or less.. You need to:

- Pencil out your cash flows with the simple Chapter 3 spreadsheet and maybe the After-tax Chapter 6 spreadsheet to make sure you are comfortable with the pro-forma returns on your cash equity investment. You should probably use Chapter 6 Pre-Tax and After Tax Spreadsheet here.
- Analyze and find a fair deal on the mortgage financing from Chapter 7.
- Do your proper evaluation of the property condition and how much it will cost to bring it up to rental ready quality from Chapter 9.
- Obtain proper property insurance coverage for the risks you need covered in consultation with you agent from Chapter 10.
- Review the title insurance and Title the property as is most advantageous to you Chapter 11 and Chapter 12 LLCs and Asset Protection.
- Make sure you are paying a fair price based on comparable sales Chapter 17.

Those items are with any property and again you are significantly reducing your risk by doing those tasks. There are a few other important items to consider in buying smaller apartment buildings after you complete the above tasks.

You also need to do the same pro-forma projections on the property and evaluate your investment returns. You also need to do the same due diligence on the existing tenants and leases and if it is a larger number of units there may be financial statements available for your review. But you still need to independently verify the numbers for reasonableness based on market rents and expenses.

What is Different? A few Main Items – Financing, Management and Insurance

FINANCING

Financing a property with five units or more is commercial financing. This financing is looked at differently by the lenders. They still want strong financials from you, the borrower, but they look more to the property cash flows being able to support the property. This way, if for some reason you do not have an income any longer, the property can still support itself. So the amount of mortgage financing and hence the loan to value (LTV) that you can borrow on a property is limited by the cash flows that the property produces.

We use an analysis called a Debt Coverage Ratio (DCR) to determine the maximum financing. The bank does also look at typical loan to value ratios, like 75.0% LTV, and actually finances a property based on the lower of the minimum required DCR or maximum allowable LTV – which usually means financing is limited by the DCR ratios.

Let's Define –

Net Operating Income (NOI) – This is the rental income from the property minus ALL the expenses, except the mortgage payment – example on left below.

DCR – NOI / Mortgage Payment or minimum multiple that NOI has to be over the calculated Mortgage Payment – example on right. Depending on the financing institution and the type of property, DCRs can be anywhere from 1.15 Times to 1.45 Times – talk to your lender regarding the DCR allowed.

NET OPERATING INCOME ILLUSTRATION			DEBT COVERAGE RATIO	
Purchase Price =	**$2,000,000**		**MINIMUM DCR = 1.25 Times**	
Rental Income		$200,000	DCR = NOI / Mortgage Payment	
Expenses:			NOI =	$125,000
Water	$9,000			
Property Taxes	$17,000		Divide by the allowed X Times	**1.25**
Insurance	$5,000			
			Calculates the Maximum	
Gardening	$3,000		Allowed	
Repairs/				
Maintenance	$9,000		Mortgage Payment =	$100,000
Miscellaneous	$7,000			
TOTAL Expenses		$75,000	**Recalculation:**	
Expense Ratio = 37.50%			**NOI / Mortgage Payment**	
				1.25
			$125,000 / $100,000 =	**Times**
Net Operating Income		**$125,000**		

So our NOI in this example is $125,000 – and this is based on actual results, NOT pro-forma projections – banks require actual numbers these days. So the bank will lend you money, but they want a cushion over the mortgage payment. If they lend you an amount that equates into a $125,000 Mortgage Payment (the same amount as your NOI) and several tenants move out or don't pay rent, you will not have enough cash flow/NOI to pay the Mortgage Payment. So they calculate a cushion called the DCR by requiring that the NOI is something like 1.25 times the Mortgage Payment.

On the right side above the DCR, being required a minimum of 1.25 Times for this loan at this bank, you can see that if the NOI is $125,000, the maximum allowed Mortgage Payment (just principal and interest) would be $100,000 annualized. So the next question is how large of a loan does that $100,000 allowed Mortgage Payment equate to at the interest rate the bank will lend you money at based on the property and your credit profile. Let's say that the bank will lend you money at 6.0% annual interest with a 30 year amortizing loan.

MORTGAGE PAYMENT CALCULATON		LOAN, EQUITY, LTV CALCULATIONS	
ANNUALIZED PAYMENT $	**$100,000**	**Recall the Price**	$2,000,000
ANNUAL INTEREST RATE	6.00%	Loan Calculated (Left)	$1,376,483
AMORTIZATION YEARS	$30	**Equity Cash To Buy**	**$623,517**
MORTGAGE LOAN AMT	**$1,376,483**	DOWNPAYMENT	31.18%
MS Excel Calculation			
Formula =PV(rate,periods,payment)		**LOAN TO VALUE -LTV**	**68.824%**

LOAN AMOUNT – On the left side we used a spreadsheet with the $100,000 annualized loan payment at 6.0% with a 30 year amortizing loan term and the program calculated that equated to a loan size of $1,376,483. On the right side we used the above purchase price of $2,000,000 and subtracted out the now calculated mortgage amount to get the amount of cash equity we would need to as a downpayment to buy this property - $623,517. That equates to a 31.18% downpayment and the loan is 68.82% LTV.

So on individual properties up to 4 units recall that you may be able to borrow 75.0%, so a downpayment of 25.0%. But since five and over units are commercial properties the loans are different and it is based on cash flows – and for this property, with these rents, expenses and NOI, based on the bank's required minimum DCR for this type of property and your interest rate for the property and your credit profile – the maximum loan that you could get is the $1,376,483.

As you can see you need to put down 31.18% to buy this property. A better cash flow property relative to the cost might allow you a smaller downpayment like 27.5%, a worse cash flow property relative to the cost might require up to 40.0% downpayment or more.

The banks actually do also have maximum LTVs allowed on commercial properties like 75.0% - similar as to what you would see in residential loans. But the bank lending officer will do the DCR calculation to come up with a maximum loan amount, 68.82% in this case. Then he or she will look at the bank's lending criteria for the maximum allowed LTV on this type of property, which may be 75.0%. You can borrow the LOWER of the two – so 68.82% in this case is the maximum LTV, not the 75% LTV.

In almost all cases, unless you have lucked into an incredibly healthy cash flow deal, your maximum amount of mortgage borrowing is going to be based on the DCR calculation. Restated, if you calculate that your DCR allows you to borrow 90.0% of the purchase price, the bank will still have LTV limits based on the lower of the appraised value or purchase price and that LTV limit will probably be 75.0% or less – so that 75.0% will be the maximum you can borrow. But great job finding a great deal….if it really is that great a deal!

CASH ON CASH RETURNS - Now you can do a quick first year calculation of your cash on cash if you would like. You would take your NOI and subtract out your Annualized Mortgage Payment to get your Net Cash Flows. Divide this number by your Equity (Downpayment, Closing Costs, Rehab Costs) to get a simple feel for your Cash on Cash Returns. You really need to do this in one of the Spreadsheet Analysis Tools, but here you could simply do a quick calculation.

Pricing and Valuation of Income Producing Commercial Assets – We show how to value income producing commercial real estate assets in Chapter 17 in a separate article - Appraisal – Property Valuation – under the Income Approach section.

MANAGEMENT

Management of multiple units. Once you start to acquire properties with a larger number of units, depending on your employment situation, you probably will have to hire an outside company to manage the property. This is because you now may own 10 refrigerators, 20 toilets, 50 windows and doors – and things break. And when they break someone needs to be responsible for making calls to repairmen, opening the units for the repairs to occur, reviewing the work, paying the bills. Is that going to be you? If not, then find a good management company and pay them fairly to do a great job.

Management Fees, Review, Contract - The larger the number of units, the lower the management fees. Fees should be in the 3.5% to 8.0% range depending on a lot of factors. Some companies include re-leasing of the units fees in that management fee, some collect separate amounts. Managing property is time consuming and stressful – especially when there are major problems – so try to always work with your management company because they are handling these issues so you do not have to. Read the contract carefully, check their references, check their insurance, check out some other properties they manage. Make sure to understand what they do for their fees and what you are responsible for doing. Read their management contract carefully and particularly the insurance and cancellation provisions. You may want to have an experienced real estate attorney review the contract to make sure you are well protected.

INSURANCE and LLCs

Insurance is going to be a commercial policy and make sure to review your insurance coverage, limits, liability coverage, deductibles, and consider an umbrella policy if you have significant other assets.

Note: Your insurance costs and premiums may be very different from the prior owner's costs. That owner may have a long term great insurance record or lots of properties that are insured by the same company. It is vital to get your own bids to make sure what it will cost you.

You also can and may want to title a larger asset like this in an LLC depending on the costs and benefits to doing that. Banks should be fine with your ownership in an LLC for these commercial assets. See the Chapter 12 – LLCs and Asset Protection for the basics and talk to a real estate attorney before you make any final decisions.

Overall, multiple unit residential properties can be great long terms assets that provide significant cash flows a few years out. But make sure to properly analyze the property and do your due diligence so you reduce your risk and enhance your returns.

LPB Services LLC © 2010

CHAPTER 16

SECOND HOMES AND VACATION RENTALS

In this chapter we discuss two common real estate ownership and/or investment strategies that are somewhat related:

Buying a second home to simply use and/or maybe renting it out occasionally to earn some extra money.

Investing in a vacation rental property with the primary purpose to rent it out on a weekly or monthly basis.

Neither of these subjects is complicated to understand but running through the numbers should give you pause to really think about whether doing either of these makes sense to you. The reality is that if you want to own real estate, unless you are very wealthy, you should concentrate real estate where you earn fairly good positive cash flows so you can pay the property bills – which is NOT the case with second homes or typically with vacation rentals. If you are wealthy and you can afford to buy whatever you like without regard to the cash flows then by all means do what you like. For the rest of us, there are some important concepts to really think about in this short chapter.

Second Homes used to make more sense when one could count on a few percent annual appreciation each year. Those days are gone so now they are generally a tougher sell as a good place to store or earn value. Nowadays, it is more than likely they will be a drain on finances that probably will not give you much of an investment return. Realize you are not collecting any rental income to offset that you are paying property taxes, repairs and maintenance, insurance, utility bills, HOA fees, and unanticipated costs. The thought was that they value would go up – appreciate - by more than enough to cover all those annual costs and you end up being positive overall. No longer can we count on that.

Vacation rentals are also generally not a very good financial move. Vacation rentals generate the most rental income in stellar locations like the beach areas. But one pays a very high price for a prize property at the beach and therein lies the problem. With a huge mortgage payment each month, your investment returns are going to be very low and probably negative. We've included a spreadsheet below to assist you in this analysis and we believe it will really open your eyes to the less than appealing financial picture.

We are not saying that either of these strategies are guaranteed to fail, but they both have significant hurdles to success and once you put the numbers down on paper you can see what we mean – then make your own decision.

BUYING A SECOND HOME

Many people purchase second homes (or land to eventually build on) to use and enjoy and hope that in the long term it increases in value. It probably will increase in value over time, but are you earning a fair return on your invested capital for the risk you are taking? For example, one may buy a $200,000 second home, investing $50,000 cash equity and borrowing a $150,000 mortgage. Now in addition to the $50,000 cash equity, you need to pay the monthly mortgage, property taxes, insurance, maintenance upkeep for years and years without any cash inflow coming from the property.

Let's take a quick look at a cash flow forecast for this purchase. Below is a simple spreadsheet but one should really put their numbers in the original Chapter 3 Spreadsheet - InvestmentPropertyAnalysis.xls and analyze this the same way they analyze any property. However, here are the simple numbers – the important thing to note is that with no rental income you are always negative on cash flows and it keeps adding up even higher, in a negative way, each year:

	Purchase	Year 1	Year 2	Year 3	Year 4	Year 5
TOTAL NET CASH FLOWS OVER LIFE OF INVESTMENT						
THE "FORECAST" OR "PROFORMA"						
CASH Equity at Purchase	$(50,000)					
Rental Income Monthly		$0	$0	$0	$0	$0
Monthly Expenses/PITI		$(1,150)	$(1,170)	$(1,195)	$(1,230)	$(1,250)
Monthly Net Cash Flow		$(1,150)	$(1,170)	$(1,195)	$(1,230)	$(1,250)
Annual NET Cash Flow		**$(13,800)**	**$(14,040)**	**$(14,340)**	**$(14,760)**	**$(15,000)**
TOTAL CF	$(50,000)	$(13,800)	$(14,040)	$(14,340)	$(14,760)	$(15,000)
Cumulative Negative CF	$(50,000)	$(63,800)	$(77,840)	$(92,180)	$(106,940)	$(121,939)

As you can see, you put down a large amount of cash equity capital AND keep paying more money on a monthly basis for the life of your ownership. The cash equity you invest increases, in a negative way, each year because you have to pay additional monies to cover the negative cash flows/expenses. Also note that it grows quickly to a significant amount. So when you sell the property, you will have to get a high enough price to pay off any remaining mortgage AND provide enough cash left over to give you a fair rate of return on your invested equity capital.

If you calculate out how much the property value needs to increase to give you a fair rate of return, it is going to have to be some pretty healthy annual increases in value to cover all the negative cash flows. And healthy annual increases, while they may occur, are something we should not count upon happening. However, let's calculate what percentage annual increases in value you would need to BREAKEVEN on cash flows.

PROPERTY VALUE IN ORDER TO BREAKEVEN - YEAR 5	
Year 5 Mortgage Balance (Original Balance $150,000)	$136,765
Year 5 Cumulative Negative Cash Flows (Equity Plus Annual Negative Cash Flows)	$121,939
Net Sales Price Needed at Year 5 to Breakeven	$258,704
Sales Costs on Sale 8.00%	$20,696
Gross Sales Price Needed to Break Even at Year 5	$279,401
Annual Increases in Value to Breakeven on Cash Flow	**6.920%**

So even in the unlikely event that the value of your property goes up **6.92**% per year for five years, you still are only breaking even on the $121,939 of cash equity you have in the property.

As you can see, it is highly unlikely you will get a fair return on your invested capital – especially for high risk real estate. It would probably make better sense to invest your cash into other investments so you earn some income on those investments. This could include income producing real estate or financial assets like bonds or stocks. The main point is that as an "investment" a second home will probably not end up being a very good long term financial investment. This is due to the fact that you have expenses during ownership but no revenue/rental income during ownership.

So before you go and buy a second home, pencil out how much total money you are going to have to invest to acquire the property and invest over the years to cover annual expenses for your ownership period. There is no way to pencil out a good deal with no revenue coming into your bank account. So again, if you are wealthy and cash flows do not matter, then buy whatever you like. If cash flows and investments matter, it might make better sense to put that money into something that produces income. You can always rent someone else's vacation home when you go on vacation and save yourself a lot of money, hassle and effort that you would most likely incur by owning your own second home.

OWN A SECOND HOME ALREADY? If you do already own a second home, do not run out and sell it. You may owe little on it and are happy to keep it and/or you can afford it and you just want to keep that asset. However, you may want to also consider how much cash equity you have tied up in that asset and if it might be worth considering trading that equity to another asset.

To do this you would find the current market value of the property, reduce that amount by approximately eight (8.0%) percent for costs of selling the property, and subtract out the current mortgage balance (if any). You may have to pay taxes too if you do not trade to another real property asset with a 1031 exchange (see Chapter 6 Taxes). So then you have a good idea of how much cash equity you have in the property. And if you know the annual net after tax operating costs (interest and taxes may be deductible so you want to figure out the after tax cost) you can divide that amount by your cash equity to find out a rate of return you are earning – it will be negative.

So you would compare that negative return to how much of a rate of return (or just simply cash flow) you could earn if you invested that cash equity into CDs, bonds, mutual funds, stocks, income producing real estate or any other type of asset. Just something to think about when you are considering the best way to deploy your scarce equity capital. At least penciling out some numbers will give you some basis to consider the most advantageous use of your hard earned money. And…just something to think about here…how often do you use it and how much would it cost to rent a similar property when you go on vacation if you did not own the second home?

VACATION RENTALS

Vacation Rental properties as investments are so poorly understood and there is such a lack of independent useful information on their finances that we created a separate spreadsheet to assist you in your analysis efforts. These properties and their financial picture can be all over the map, so you may be able to make one work, but it probably is not going to be a very good financial investment.

For one thing, you need to generally have a stellar location, like on the beach, to be able to rent a large portion of the weeks out to vacation guests. And when we want to own that prize and stellar location property we will be paying a large sum of money for that real estate. That means we will either invest a large amount of cash and/or take out a large mortgage. So we better be able to generate a pretty hefty amount of NET cash flow, that is NET cash flow, to give us a fair rate of return on our money.

As a side note, these properties also need about twenty times the management time, energy and effort as a regular rental property, so you cannot manage these yourself if you have a regular employment schedule. The management companies charge 20% to 33% fees to manage them for owners, and those are reasonable amounts for the amount of work that goes along with managing a vacation rental property.

Let's get back to NET cash flow being the important item here. We always hear about the big weekly rents the owners receive, but how much of that rental revenue goes to paying the bills. Similar to a hotel, about 50-75% of your revenue goes to operating expenses of the property. And that is before paying the mortgage. So those big weekly rents are sliced to half or one-quarter after expenses are taken out, then when you take out your mortgage payment you end up way negative on cash flows.

And what happens when the economy slows down like in the current environment, just like at a hotel, the revenues/rental income can grind to a halt. Vacation owners had significantly decreased bookings and revenue over the 2008 and 2009 seasons, but they still had to pay the mortgage, taxes, utilities, HOA fees and other expenses. Very unstable revenues in these properties, and that means high risk.

Realize, these properties can be all over the map, but our spreadsheet gives an illustration of a three bedroom townhome/condominium in a typical beach location in California. Our students know to pencil out their own market research and projected financial statements to validate or dispute any spreadsheet they are given in class…and we encourage you to do the same. Independent information on the actual rental amounts that you will achieve and how many weeks you actually get rented are very hard to attain, however you had better be conservative in penciling out your deal.

And, the management companies that also sell the properties are not an independent source of unbiased information because they have commissions and management fees coming to them if you purchase the property. Do your own research and fill in the categories on the spreadsheet. The bottom of the spreadsheet details the websites listing vacation rentals so you can try to analyze rental rates on these sites, but as to how many weeks get rented per year, especially in the offseason, that is tough to estimate. Again, be very very conservative.

You can try to figure out independent estimates of weekly rental income on www.vrbo.com,www.homeaway.com,www.craigslist.org,www.vacationrentals.com.

Good luck with the attached spreadsheet and make sure to read the NOTES at the bottom of it.

<u>Vacation Rentals Spreadsheet</u>

LPB Services LLC © 2010

ProfessorBaron.com

Vacation Rental Property Investment Analysis
Single Year Annual Cash Flow Analysis

BOX 1 - ACQUISITION INFORMATION

BOLD BLUE NUMBERS YOU MODIFY FOR YOUR PROPERTY SPECIFICS
ALL INPUT NUMBERS ARE POSITIVE (+)

Property - 3BR 2BA Newer Oceanfront Condo in Mission Beach $ 1,000,000

Downpayment Amount =		25.00%	$ 250,000
Mortgage Amount =	$ 750,000		
Closing Costs - Loan Points/Escrow/Title Fees/Inspection Etc.			$ 12,000
Rehabilitation/Make Property Ready Budget - Do Not Underestimate			$ 5,000
Total Equity (Downpayment + Closing Costs + Rehab) - **THIS IS YOUR CASH OUT OF POCKET**			$ 267,000

BOX 2 - PROPERTY OPERATIONS STATEMENT   Year 1

	Weeks Rented	Weekly Rate	
Summer Rentals 13 Weeks	12	**$3,600**	$43,200
Offseason 39 Weeks	15	**$1,750**	$26,250
TOTAL RENT	27		$ 69,450

Operating Expenses

Advertising - Mgt. co includes in fee		-
Auto & Travel		
Cleaning & Maint	$150 per clean	4,050
Commission		
Insurance		1,000
Legal		
Management (25% for 3rd Party Co.)		17,363
Repairs - Could be much more		1,000
Supplies (Sheets, Towels, Toys, Books, Pillows, etc.)		1,500
Property Taxes		11,000
Credit Card Charge Expense (3.00%) on Half the rented weeks		1,042
Utilities (Cable $120 - Electric/Gas $200 Avg.) - Could be much MUCH more		3,840
HOA Fees ?? - Could be much more		3,000
Miscellaneous		2,000
Other Furniture Replacement - Could be much more		3,500
Total Operating Expenses (TOE)		$ 49,294

Net Operating Income (NOI) = EGR minus TOE $ 20,156

BOX 3 - MORTGAGE PAYMENT AND CASH FLOWS

Mortgage Payment - Annual	Jumbo Interest Rate =	6.250%	$ 55,952
(Interest Rate depends on your credit/incor Amortization Years =		30	
Annual Cash Flow (COULD BE NEGATIVE)			$ (35,796)
Cash on Cash (Annual Cash Flow / Total Equity) - COULD BE NEGATIVE			-13.41%

BOX 4 - INVESTMENT RETURNS SUMMARY

Year 1 Cash on Cash Return (Compare to Bank CD or Bond) - Except real estate can have much higher risk.	-13.41%
Annual Cash Flow	$ (35,796)

DEAL METER says: Whew whee, somethin' stinks....And I think it is your Negative Cash Flow deal!

CHAPTER 17

APPRAISAL AND PROPERTY VALUATION

Valuation of real estate. As you are shopping for properties to buy you will see the seller's asking or listing price for a particular property from your real estate agent and the MLS listings. But how do you know if that price is a fair price and in line with the current market value for similar properties? You are going to have to do some type of property valuation based on similar comparative market sales and listings with information provided by your agent, the tax records and online information.

Uniform Residential Appraisal Report

FEATURE	SUBJECT	COMPARABLE SALE # 1		COMPARABLE SALE # 2	
There are 53 comparable properties currently offered for sale in the subject neighborhood ranging in price from $ 165,000					
There are 64 comparable sales in the subject neighborhood within the past twelve months ranging in sale price from $ 175,00(					
Address	SAN DIEGO, CA 92115	SAN DIEGO, CA 92115		SAN DIEGO, CA 92115	
Proximity to Subject		0.18 miles NE		0.38 miles W	
Sale Price	$ 220,000	$ 235,000		$ 165,000	
Sale Price/Gross Liv. Area	$ 162.84 sq.ft.	$ 186.51 sq.ft.		$ 158.05 sq.ft.	
Data Source(s)		MLS DOM 107 DAYS		MLS DOM 6 DAYS	
Verification Source(s)		COUNTY REC. DOC# 478801		COUNTY REC. DOC# 462691	
VALUE ADJUSTMENTS	DESCRIPTION	DESCRIPTION	+(-) $ Adjustment	DESCRIPTION	+(-) $ Adjustment
Sales or Financing Concessions		CONV., NONE KNOWN		CONV., NONE KNOWN	
Date of Sale/Time		09/08/08 COE		08/28/08 COE	
Location	GOOD	GOOD		GOOD	

Additionally, after you have a property under contract you will pay for a professional appraiser to prepare a report for your mortgage lender attesting to his or her expert opinion or the appraised value of the property. This purpose of a professional appraisal is to give the lender a good feel for the market value of the collateral - the property - upon which they are relying on to secure their mortgage loan to you.

You are basically going to do a comparative market analysis (CMA) of other properties that have recently sold that are similar to the one you are interested in buying. Your real estate agent will supply listings and may be able to provide a computer generated CMA that shows how your property compares to others. This CMA is essentially what the appraiser will do as a part of the lending process, but your analysis will be much less formal and will take into account your personal preferences with respect to characteristics you would like in the property you are interested in acquiring.

Of course that approximate market valuation of your targeted property is a key determinant that you want to ascertain as you negotiate the price on your target property. Depending on how many properties you have looked at, whether via MLS listings, online, or viewing properties with your agent, you may have a general feel for the value of a target property you want to acquire as soon as you see the listing come out. But there is still work to do based on the square footage, the lot square footage, site characteristics interior condition, deferred maintenance, and any mechanical issues.

There are three different generally accepted valuation methodologies for real estate to determine the Fair Market Value (FMV):

1. Comparable Market Sales Approach – More for residential properties.
2. Income Approach – More for commercial properties.
3. Replacement Value Approach – More for properties with few or no comparables.

And a FOURTH important one that relates residential rental property cash flows and investment returns to what you are willing to pay for a property:

4. Healthy Rate of Returns Approach – Use this in conjunction with Chapter 3 – Cash Flow Analysis Simplified.

Residential properties are typically valued by the Comparative Market Sales Approach and that is what we primarily cover in this chapter. We will also cover the Healthy Rate of Returns Approach and briefly touch on the Income and Replacement Value Approaches.

The price you pay for a property, in an optimal scenario, would be below FAIR MARKET VALUE - (FMV). Realistically, as long as your are close to FMV and not way overpaying you should be in good shape because small pricing differences will even out over long term holding periods.

FMV is an estimate of the market value of a property, based on what a knowledgeable, willing, and unpressured buyer would probably pay to a knowledgeable, willing, and unpressured seller in the real estate market, according to Wikipedia.

COMPARABLE MARKET SALES APPROACH – The "Comps Method" is the primary valuation method for 1-4 unit residential properties.

The economic theory here is that a buyer will not pay more for a property than what it costs to obtain a similar property with similar location, size, condition, and utility or usefulness. Since no two properties are alike, there are adjustments that will need to be made between recent sales (the comparables) and your target property. In many cases there will be many adjustments that one needs to consider. In other cases there are few adjustments. The more homogeneous the population of comparable properties and the larger the population of recently sold properties, the less adjustments that will need to be done to ascertain an approximate fair market value.

Your job is to make sure that the overall price, terms, rents, cash flows make your deal a fair investment for your purposes – whether a personal residence or investment property.

The "Comps" method of estimating FMV relies on recently sold comparable properties that were transacted in an arm's length transaction. An arm's length transaction is a sale between two unrelated parties where the property was sufficiently advertised and marketed over a reasonable amount of time in a market with many buyers and sellers and the two parties came to a meeting of the minds on value.

REMEMBER THAT Nothing can supplement your own common sense review and analysis of the recent property sales in the nearby vicinity, comparable house size and house condition, lot premium (size, views, landscaping, etc.) reviewed against the target property you are considering buying. BUT YOU HAVE TO TAKE THE TIME, ENERGY AND EFFORT TO ACTUALLY DO A REVIEW.

Luckily there are the two additional reports that will be able to assist you in those efforts.

Comparable Market Analysis Report – Your real estate agent should do a Comparative Market Analysis on your target property versus other recent sales or listings in the near vicinity. It may be computer generated fancy report or it may be a simple and informal list of the "sold" properties and their vital statistics. This should be done as you are shopping and get more focused on the exact properties you desire to purchase. Or it could be done as you make an offer on a property you are confident you will get into escrow and are confident you will buy. Do not drive your agent crazy requesting CMA reports on every property you see, be reasonable. When the RIGHT property comes along, get your offer submitted first and then do the time consuming and hard work to shore up your personal belief that your offer is in line with the market pricing.

This report should detail all the recent comparable sales, their locations preferably on a map, prices, square footage of buildings and lot size, bedrooms, bathrooms, condition, pictures, amenities, etc. Make sure that this analysis includes ALL the properties sold and listed recently, not just the ones that are the most comparable and/or the closest matches to your target property. Then you need to review these comparables yourself and determine how they measure up to your target and hence what is a fair price for you to pay for the property you would like to acquire.

By reviewing closely matching comparable sales of properties you will get a good feel for how much the property you are considering purchasing is worth. You will have to adjust the price for differences in condition, size, location etc., but if you look at enough properties, which you should, you will hopefully get a warm fuzzy feeling that the price you are offering is fair. And you may have to bid over that price if you really want the property as others will probably be offering on the property too. That is perfectly fine as long as it is within reason. It is hard to find the RIGHT property for you and if the property is "the one" for ALL the right reasons, paying a little extra is something we've done many a time.

However, if you are financing the property, the bank is going to finance a certain percentage, like 80.0% of the LOWER of the contract price OR the appraised value so there may be some financing issues if it does not appraise at the contracted price. More on this after the appraisal information.

Appraisal – Once you have a property under contract, if you are borrowing mortgage money, you will pay to have an appraisal done by a licensed appraiser. Appraisals cost between $300 - $1,000 for residential properties – depending on size, type, units, etc. Even though you pay for the appraisal, you never get to talk to the appraiser as they are hired directly by the lending institution.

The appraiser is an experienced professional who will do the same type of review that you should do to determine the value of the property. They will look at all the recent comparable sales, listings, adjust your target property value to be comparable to the "comps" to come up with a value that they certify for the lender. Adjustments would be like adding $10,000 to the estimated value of your property because it has one additional bathroom as compared to the other comparable sales.

The appraiser's job includes doing a site visit to the property, inspecting the inside and outside, looking for obvious defect issues, driving the neighborhood, pulling comparable market sales of comparable recently sold properties and using all those facts and the appraiser's expertise and historical knowledge to determine the fair market value of the property. This Uniform Residential Appraisal Report (Note: not for commercial properties) summarizes his findings and his opinion of value - Appraisal Report.

See appraisal Report at www.ProfessorBaron.com

The appraiser is an INDEPENDENT source of unbiased information, which is what you need to help make better decisions. If their value is very different from yours, then you need to look at how they came to their value estimate and see if you, or they, missed something important that impacts the value.

Here is a copy of a standardized appraisal for lender – Appraisal Report that was done on a residential property for sale in an outlying area of the city of San Diego, California in September 2008. Again, the appraisal was ordered to determine the value for the bank who was providing mortgage financing of the purchase.

The pages one through three of the actual "Uniform Residential Appraisal Report" are the most important pages of information that summarize: Page 1. The specifics of the property being appraised; Page 2. The Comparable Properties, Sales Comparison Approach, Reconciliation of the Comparables to the target property and his Conclusion on the Value of the Property; Page 3. Other Information, Cost Approach to Valuation and Income Approach to Valuation.

Page 1 - This page summarizes:

Subject – Information about the Target Property, Owner, Listing Information
Contract – Sales Contract and Contract Price and Date Information
Neighborhood – Characteristics and Location
Site – Information related to the Property Site
Improvements – General Information about the Physical Building(s) on the Site

Page 2 – This is the IMPORTANT page that you need to review:

Sales Comparison Approach – This page has four columns. The first column on the left is the Subject or Target Property and then there are three columns listing the properties that are the most comparable recent sales to the subject property. Page 6 typically has additional comparable market sales and there is usually a map showing all the comparable sales and/or listings to the subject property.
Reconciliation – This is where the appraiser gives his or her value for the property.
Page 3 – This page has additional Information you should review.
Overall the Uniform Residential Appraisal Report is are somewhat confusing and you will need to study the format if you want to fully understand the appraisers report. However, the important issue to note is what price did the expert appraise the property at and how does that compare to your contracted price. The appraiser's report also shows you the properties that he or she believes are comparable so you need to look at those in addition to the properties provided by your real estate agent and ones that you found and reviewed on line.

You the buyer need to look at all this information and analyze whether your offering and/or accepted contract price is in line with the market. You ultimately will own the property, not your real estate agent or the appraiser, so make sure you are comfortable with the price in which you are paying.

AGAIN, MAKE SURE YOU UNDERSTAND THAT YOU WILL NEVER FIND THE PERFECT PROPERTY. BUT WITH A LOT OF HARD WORK YOU CAN FIND ONE THAT IS CLOSE TO WHAT YOU WANT AND THAT IS THE "RIGHT" ONE FOR YOU FOR THE RIGHT PRICE. NEVER WALK AWAY FROM THE "RIGHT" PROPERTY OVER A FEW THOUSAND DOLLARS, YOU MAY NOT FIND ANOTHER "RIGHT" ONE FOR QUITE A WHILE AND YOU WILL HAVE TO DO ALL THE TIME CONSUMING AND HARD WORK OVER AGAIN!

HEALTHY RATE OF RETURNS APPROACH

Another way we look at investment properties, not personal residences unless you are planning to turn them into rental properties in the next few years, is termed the HEALTHY RETURNS APPROACH. Sometimes, as in the current market, pricing can jump all over the map in relatively short periods of time. In these cases, one may reject a property because the pricing is well above very comparable properties that recently sold. However, this theory says that it makes sense to look at the investment returns (Chapter 3) that one can earn if they acquire a particular asset.

For example, in one complex where we recently bought a property for $105,000 the pricing on almost identical units ranged from $85,000 to $115,000 in a six month period of time. The swing in pricing herein was about 50% of the value – which would obviously bring up red flags if the analysis were done solely based on comparable sales. But what if the property had healthy investment returns even at the pricing at the higher end of the spectrum. Let's look at this example.

Rents on these properties that sold between $85,000 and $115,000 are almost identical at approximately $1,250 per month. The newest property on the market is listed at $120,000 and there are plenty of offers so you need to offer market value or above, let's say you offer **$125,000**. If you get the property under contract, are your investment returns good enough so that you should buy the property?

HEALTHY RATE OF RETURNS APPROACH THIS CHART GIVES US SEVERAL DIFFERENT INVESTMENT RETURN SCENARIOS BASED ON THE FLUCTUATING PRICES IN THE CURRENT MARKETPLACE					
DATE SOLD	12/31/09	10/19/09	4/9/10	2/14/10	YOUR OFFER
PRICE PAID	$85,000	$95,000	$105,000	$115,000	$125,000
Mortgage 75.0%	$63,750	$71,250	$78,750	$86,250	$93,750
Equity Cash	$21,250	$23,750	$26,250	$28,750	$31,250
MONTHLY NUMBERS					
Rent	$1,250	$1,250	$1,250	$1,250	$1,250
Expenses	$(335)	$(345)	$(355)	$(365)	$(375)
NOI	$915	$905	$895	$885	$875
Mortgage Payment	$(382)	$(427)	$(472)	$(517)	$(562)
Monthly Cash Flow	$533	$478	$423	$368	$313
ANNUAL CF	$6,393	$5,734	$5,074	$4,415	$3,755
Cash on Cash Returns	30.09%	24.14%	19.33%	15.36%	12.02%
(Annual CF / Equity Cash)					

So as you can see, swings in pricing were severe. But if you are a long term holder, would you turn away 12.02% cash on cash returns? Think it through, where else are you going to get those returns and that does not include pay down of your mortgage principal, nor increases in value. Those 12.02% returns sound pretty good to us as long as we are comfortable with the rental and expense estimates. However, there may be some financing issues if the appraisal comes in lower than your contracted price.

APPRAISAL LOWER THAN CONTRACTED PRICE

In both cases related to (1) personal residences where you might fight for a property and pay more than the comparable market sales indicate the value stands or (2) investment properties where you are willing to pay more than what the current comparable properties suggest because you can still earn healthy rates of return - you may have an issue with the mortgage financing. Let's say you contract upon the property above at $125,000 which gives you a healthy 12.02% return. That is a great return to us. You will pay for an appraisal and let's say the appraiser deems the property is worth $115,000 based on current market comparables. The bank is going to finance the property based on the lower of contract price or appraisal.

The first thing you should do is go back to the seller and ask them to reduce the price down to the $115,000. A bank selling the property is more likely to do this than a private seller, but you should try either way. Have your agent ask verbally because if you offer that in writing it may be a counteroffer which may allow the seller to cancel your deal. Maybe you negotiate to somewhere in the middle like $120,000 as a fair meeting price. The seller may also just say no take it at $125,000 or leave it.

Since the bank finances based on the lower of contract price or appraisal, they are going to offer to loan you $86,250 – which is 75.0% of the $115,000 appraised value. So you are going to have to come up with the equity cash of not only the $28,750 – the 25.0% equity plus closing costs, but also the additional cash that you are willing to pay above the appraised value. In this case it will be an additional $5,000 if you negotiated the price down to $120,000 but the property only appraised for $115,000.

This is the problem you will have if it does not appraise for at least the contract price. You need to come up with the difference in cash if the seller will not renegotiate to the appraised value. Therefore, if it is a very fair deal see if you can get that additional funding somewhere to complete the purchase – relatives, friends, other savings you have - NOT on credit cards because they will show up on your credit report that is pulled just days before you close and that could cause the mortgage loan to be declined at the last minute. This is just part of the real estate game and this happens occasionally in the current marketplace – so be prepared to come up with extra cash if the appraisal comes in low but you still decide to buy the property because it makes the RIGHT sense to you for all the RIGHT reasons.

INCOME APPROACH TO VALUATION – For Commercial Income Producing Real Estate – Apartment Buildings, Retail Centers, Office Buildings, etc.

The income approach to valuation is a mechanically quick and simple valuation method that allows us to determine an approximate value for commercial income producing real estate assets. It is the most widely used valuation method among commercial real estate brokers, appraisers and investors. It is based on actual sales transactions that have recently occurred and the Net Operating Income (NOI) of those related properties.

The income approach uses something called a Capitalization Rate, or Cap Rate for short. It takes an income stream from a property and effectively Capitalizes that income stream based on a market (for actual sales) or desired (for real estate buyers) rate of return.

Since this valuation approach does not apply to residential values, we are going to do a separate ARTICLE at www.ProfessorBaron.com - Cap Rate Income Approach to Valuation.

REPLACEMENT VALUE APPROACH – This is the final valuation approach and it is typically used for hard to value assets – like wineries or special purpose buildings. It basically tries to separate the value of the land as one component of overall value and adds the current cost to replace any structures on the property for a total value. Land plus Replacement Cost of Building equals total value. This approach really does not apply to many residential properties so that is just a simple and quick explanation.

OVERALL – Take the time to come up with a reasonable valuation of your target property. The bank appraisal will help you confirm you are in line with market values. If the bank appraisal is significantly lower than your CMA, you need to review the appraisal in detail and consider whether the contracted price is too much. If you believe it is, try to negotiate down the price using the appraisal or it may make sense to cancel the purchase.

Chapter 18

Land and Building a Home

In this chapter we will discuss two real estate strategies that you generally want to avoid in life. We are not saying that you cannot be successful at and possibly make money with either of these strategies, but there are some significant bewares for each of them. SO LEAVE THESE TWO REAL ESTATE TYPE INVESTMENTS TO THE EXPERTS WHO HAVE THE TIME AND KNOWLEDGE TO DO THESE.

Land is the first item we will discuss and the important item to ask yourself here is: How much cash am I putting down, how much am I paying along the way to carry this land, and when do I realistically expect to get my money back from this investment. And what rate of return am I going to earn on this investment?

Building a Home, for a person who is not an experienced builder, is probably one of the riskiest and most stressful and potentially financially ruinous things you can do in life. You will most likely go over budget, probably by a LOT, it will most likely take much longer than anticipated, probably by a LOT, and it will not be fun. And we are not talking about your building it yourself, we mean your hiring a builder and just overseeing the project and construction. An individual who has the time and resources to handle a project like this might consider it, but you had better have significant back up resources when costs go over budget.

So we will give some basic information and advice on what we have seen related to these two issues. Again, you can make money doing either of these so we are just throwing out some items to consider in your decision making process.

This chapter is also very very short because it does not take much explaining to realize the major risks with either of these.

LAND

Let's see here, we typically have to pay cash for land. That cash was probably sitting in a financial asset that paid some interest or dividends. We also could liquidate that financial asset relatively quickly if we needed. Now we buy land and are investing the money into a very illiquid asset where our money may be stuck for years or decades. That land also does not pay any interest or dividends, in fact we have to pay property taxes on it and maybe insurance and other costs. But down the road we hope to build a retirement home on the property or sell it for more than we paid for it to make our investment returns.

So you have all money going out the door to buy the land, going out the door during ownership and with the hope that the value will increase and it will pay off down the road. You are buying a very speculative asset that earns no income for you. And how do you know it will go up in value? And more importantly, will it go up in value enough to afford you a fair rate of return on your invested equity cash?

That is going take a lot of speculation on how much it will go up in value. Many a person has speculated before that they could earn money in land – and many have lost. Many have won too, but do you want to take those significant risks? Have you ever even talked to anyone who did verifiably earn money, and a fair return, on a land investment? You might want to consider keeping your money in something that pays interest or dividends or buying real estate that pays cash flows.

Retirement options - If you are thinking you will buy the land and build on it for retirement down the road…are you sure you will actually retire there and build a home. What if life changes and those plans change. We do not recommend building a home either as you will read below, but we definitely do not recommend buying land until very near the time you are ready to build on it. Way too many things change in life and you can do better financially by earning a fair return on your money and buying or building something when you are ready to occupy it.

Invest in Land Deal - If someone is asking you to put money into a land deal, you had been make sure they have a proven track record and a solid plan to turn your investment back into cash in a relatively short period of time. Proven means you were able to separately verify that it was factually correct, not just taking their word for it. And what is the plan, how much does it cost, what are the estimated sales prices of the finished lots or buildings and do those estimates seem realistic? Can you verify separately with someone with extensive experience in land development that the plan is sound? Real estate people historically "embellish" their credentials and it is up to you to verify their claims to protect yourself.

In any of the above land items, simply hoping the land you are buying will go up in value, or even hold its' value, is not a really sound investment strategy.

Lastly, as with other real estate investment types, if you are wealthy than it may not be an issue about investment returns or costs of holding property. For the rest of us it probably is a good idea to avoid land and focus on assets with lower risk characteristics and some potential cash flows.

BUILDING A HOME – Leave this to the Homebuilding Companies!

Building a Home – and what we mean is working with an architect to design the home and hiring a general contractor or residential custom developer to build it for you. This is one of the highest risk strategies you can undertake in real estate and in life. This is whether you are building a personal residence for yourself or building a residence to sell. It is extremely stressful, time consuming, and prone to cost overruns and lengthy delays.

Consider that you have probably never built anything, managed a project this size, made these significant financial decisions, or done anything like this before. It is probably a six to twelve month build out, hundreds of hours of your time and hundreds of thousands of dollars of your money. If you have a full time job, that only makes it worse.

Your best bet here is to try and buy a home that is being built by a home building company or buy a home that is already built. Every single story we've ever heard about someone having a custom home built starts out with:

- We can't believe it cost so much more than we thought.
- We can't believe it took so much more time that we thought.
- We can't believe how stressful it was building the home.
- We did save the marriage but it sure did take a lot of couples counseling. Alternatively, one said, "I did get the best divorce attorney in town".
- We do love it, but we'd never do that again as there are easier ways to get a nice home.
- "I wouldn't wish that on my mother-in-law".

Building a home is for wealthy people who can absorb the typically massive cost overruns and delays. Do yourself a favor and try to find a home that someone else has already built and fits close to what you would like in a home. Maybe something you can rehab over time to make it perfect for you.

In all seriousness, make sure you really think it through and explore all the options before you decide to build a home. And talk to some other people who built their own homes to see what experience they had with the process – or at least talk to their marriage counselor!

LPB Services LLC © 2010

CHAPTER 19

MEDIATION, ARBITRATION AND LIQUIDATED DAMAGES

Let's talk about several other clauses that appear in most standard residential purchase contracts – mediation, arbitration and liquidated damages. These provisions appear in the California Association of Realtors (CAR) contracts, as well as the Realtor's Association contracts for most states. Thus, you need to be aware of and understand the basics on what you are signing.

Our attorney and investor contributor, Gary Laturno, Esq., has been a mediator and arbitrator with the American Arbitration Association and the San Diego Superior Court since 2000. www.GaryLaturnoMediations.com. Information here is straight from his web site. Gary is a strong believer, along with several other authors, that "failure to talk seldom produces results" and that one should always agree to try mediation first before going to arbitration or litigation. Mediation will cost less, be less stressful and hopefully give you a fair outcome early in the process.

In his experience, 90% of the disputes he mediates are resolved the day of the mediation or shortly thereafter. A key to success: be willing to listen to the other party's opinion and claims and go to the mediation with an open mind. Failure to listen does not produce results. So, be a listening participant in what may be stressful and uncomfortable circumstances.

In a small percentage of disputes, trying to work with the other party will NOT work due to a variety of reasons, anger, frustration, unreasonableness, hatred, etc. – and that may be YOU not them, but hopefully not. In those cases the Mediation process may ultimately fail. But it makes sense, regardless, to try and work things out as soon as possible.

Mediation

Mediation, as defined by Wikipedia, is a form of alternative dispute resolution (ADR), a way of resolving disputes between two or more parties. A neutral third party, the mediator, assists the parties to negotiate their own settlement. The parties are the decision makers - not the mediator.

So, assume you get into a dispute with another party and both parties are "fluffing their feathers" and threatening to sue. First, calm down. Lawsuits are expensive and stressful, and it would be preferable to resolve the issue in a fair way, expedited way. So, mediation can help you resolve the dispute – before it gets too serious.

Mediation is an informal, non - binding process in which the mediator facilitates communication between disputants and assists the parties in reaching a mutually acceptable resolution of the dispute. In this process, the mediator explores the underlying facts, the relevant evidence and the law, as well as the parties underlying interest, needs and priorities.
Mediation is a flexible and confidential process that is less stressful than a formal trial. It can also save time and money, allow for greater client participation and more flexibility in creating a resolution.

Here are some strong reasons why you should work to a resolution of the dispute in mediation:

1. Mediation is private, confidential and cost effective.
2. Mediation opens lines of communication. Parties are able to be heard and to vent.
3. Parties can structure a resolution that they may not achieve in court.

4.   Parties and their counsel receive a neutral evaluation of their case. Each side learns something.
5.   75% to 90% of all cases that are mediated settle the day of the mediation or shortly thereafter (the success rate depends on the skill of the mediator you select; each party must agree on the mediator.)
6.   Clients are relieved of the burden of the dispute and can go on with their lives.

Typical Mediation Session

Pre mediation:

Legal briefs are not required, but it is helpful for the mediator to at least know the facts of the dispute prior to the mediation. If a brief is prepared, it is recommended that parties exchange briefs. A brief is a written document setting forth the facts and establishing the legal arguments for the party.

Each side should also communicate their opening settlement position prior to the mediation. What is plaintiff's demand? What is the defendant's position on settlement? Let the other party know your opening settlement position before the mediation. You will save time, avoid misunderstandings and increase the likelihood of settlement if this information is communicated before the mediation.

The mediation:

Who should attend? Disputes are more likely to be resolved if decision makers attend. By decision makers, we mean the parties and each individual who will be consulted by the parties to make a decision, e.g., spouses, partners, significant others, insurance adjustors and the like.

Each decision maker should be available to work the entire day. If a decision maker will not be available the entire day, please let the mediator and opposing counsel know prior to mediation.

Prior to the joint session, the mediator may meet privately with each party and their counsel. The purpose of these meetings is to give parties an opportunity to ask questions and to say what is on their mind. The mediator will listen and answer questions.

The joint session which follows is typically more constructive if the mediator has met privately with each party prior to that meeting.

Each attendee is required to sign in acknowledging:

- Attendance at the mediation is voluntary;
- The mediator is a neutral;
- The mediator is not an advocate for any party;
- The mediator does not represent any party;
- Nothing the mediator may say shall be considered legal advice;
- Written conflicts and ethics disclosures were furnished to counsel and the parties;
- Discussions at the mediation are confidential;
- Nothing the mediator, counsel or parties say may be used in arbitration or litigation.

The joint session: The joint session is informal and relaxed. The joint session is not a trial. Parties have an opportunity to be heard and to vent. Mediation should open lines of communication. Effective negotiators not only talk but are good listeners.

Plaintiff typically starts. Talk about the facts, the claims, the damages and whatever else you and/or your client want to say. Use demonstrative evidence if you feel it will help your case. But the mediator should encourage the parties to speak. Every person who attends may speak and tell their story.

After the plaintiff and his/her counsel have had an opportunity to present their case, defense counsel and his/her client have the opportunity to present their position.

After each side has presented their case, the mediator may allow for each side to comment on the other party's presentation.

Joint sessions typically last approximately one hour. Thus, each presentation should take no more than approximately 30 minutes.

The mediator's job at the joint session is to listen, ask questions and to ensure that every person present has had an opportunity to speak.

Separate caucuses. Following the joint session, the mediator will meet privately with each party and their counsel. They will evaluate the strengths and shortcomings of the case, discuss ranges of outcomes at trial, talk about costs and explore settlement options.

Most disputes are about money. But do not overlook the fact that disputes can be about other issues as well. Be creative! Think outside the box! The parties may structure a resolution that they may not achieve in court. The mediator should continue to caucus until settlement is reached or until such time as it is concluded that settlement is not possible at the mediation.

Practice tip: Be patient. The more time that is invested, the more likely it is that the parties will come together with a resolution to the dispute.

Overall - Settlement is seldom easy. Do not give up.

On many occasions, parties and counsel state that settlement is not possible. The mediator should show empathy to these comments but insist that the parties keep talking. What happens? Most cases settle. In fact, 75% to 90% of cases that are mediated settle. Most settle the day of the mediation or shortly thereafter.

Recommendation: If the parties reach a settlement, put the agreement in writing. Get all parties and counsel to sign the document that day.

If the case does not settle, do not give up. The mediator will most likely follow up with phone calls or email to counsel and hopefully a resolution can be agreed upon by the parties shortly thereafter.

Arbitration

Ok, so if you haven't resolved your issue via mediation, the next step is arbitration, which has some advantages and disadvantages, pros and cons, over going to court. If your standard real estate contract provides for the option of arbitration, consult with your attorney before agreeing to the option. He or she can guide you in making a decision. If you do not agree to arbitration, keep in mind that you will be agreeing to litigation as your form of dispute resolution.

Definition: In arbitration the parties present their case to an arbitrator or a panel of arbitrators. In a large case, it is possible to use a panel of three arbitrators. The arbitrator(s) examines the evidence and makes a decision; the decision is usually binding. Arbitration is generally not as formal as litigation in court; the rules of evidence can be altered to meet the parties' needs.

Pros: Arbitration is private and confidential; arbitration can be conducted in a more expedited manner than litigation; the parties can select an arbitrator based on subject matter expertise;

Cons: Arbitration is expensive; arbitrators charge by the day or the hour; the arbitrator is the decision maker; parties typically have no right to appeal.

Again, work hard to settle your dispute via Mediation, you will be glad you did.

Liquidated Damages

One other item in the California Association of Realtors contract and many other state contracts is a liquidated damages clause.

The liquidated damages clause states that if the buyer of the property fails to complete the purchase due to the Buyer's default, the Seller shall retain any earnest money deposit actually paid, into escrow, as a part of the transaction. So, recall that when you make an offer on a property you typically put down an earnest money deposit – typically 1% but up to 3% for a residential purchase. If you sign this clause, you are agreeing that if you back out of the contract, or it fails for any reason related to you that is not covered by a contingency clause, you will forfeit this deposit to the seller as damages. You generally will not be liable for any other damages to the seller as long as they too agreed to this clause and parties generally acted in good faith.

You of course are out your EMD, but that is the risk you take playing in the real estate game. We don't advise herein whether or not to sign this clause, but this does generally limit your losses and risk of being sued in case you breach the contract. Most people find that very appealing. Additionally, the seller may not accept your purchase offer without a signed liquidated damages clause, so just keep that in mind when making your decision in making your offer.

In California the CAR Residential Purchase Agreement is buyer friendly because CAR wants to encourage people to make offers. Due to this, buyers seldom lose their earnest money deposit and that is typically best for all parties involved.

SELECTING A MEDIATOR OR ARBITRATOR

How do you go about selecting a mediator or arbitrator? You have several options. If you are represented by counsel, ask your attorney. She or he will be able to give you a number of recommendations. In fact, if you are represented by counsel, your attorney will play a major role in selecting the mediator. If you are not represented by counsel, you may find it challenging to find a good mediator.

Suggestion: Contact the local office of the American Arbitration Association (AAA). AAA is the oldest provider of private dispute resolution services in the world. They will have a panel of experienced mediators to pick from. Interview several of their mediators.

Questions to ask them: What are your areas of expertise? Do you mediate real estate disputes? What is your background? Did you practice real estate law? How many mediations have you done? How many have you done successfully? What advice do you have for successfully resolving a dispute?

Once you have talked to several mediators you should be in a better position to make a selection, move forward and resolve your dispute.   Good luck!

FINAL THOUGHTS AND SPECIAL THANKS

SO THAT IS IT FOR YOUR REAL ESTATE DUE DILIGENCE LESSON.

REAL ESTATE IS BUYER BEWARE AND YOU NOW HAVE THE TOOLS TO SIGNIFICANTLY REDUCE YOUR RISK...NOT ELIMINATE IT...BUT REDUCE IT. USE THESE TOOLS ALONG WITH YOUR OWN KNOWLEDGE AND RESEARCH AND MAKE SMART, CASH FLOWING REAL ESTATE PURCHASES FOR THE LONG HAUL!

THANK YOU

I WOULD LIKE TO THANK EVERYONE WHO HAS HELPED IN SOME FORM OR FASHION WITH THE PRODUCTION OF MY WORK, ECOURSE AND BOOK:

- THE **INDUSTRY EXPERTS** OF COURSE
- AND MY STILL CANNOT BE PUBLICLY NAMED: **INSURANCE CONTRIBUTOR** AND **WEBSITE PROGRAMMER.**
- **MISS LINDSEY GOOD** – "MY LOVELY AND TALENTED ASSISTANT"
- **JULIA TOCK** – "FOR HER ENDLESS SUPPORT"
- **YET UNDISCLOSED** – THE "VIDEOGRAPHER EXTRAORDINAIRE"
- **BRETT WITHYCOMBE** – "FOR HIS HELP"
- **GILBERT GODOY** – "THE CRAFTSMAN"
- **JEFF CARTER** – "AD GUY"
- **MY FOLKS – CAL AND HELENE** – Who Accept me - AS IS
- **GRANMAMA WEEZIE** - MY NEIGHBOR EXTRAORDINAIRE
- **ALL MY PAST STUDENTS** - THANKS FOR THE A+ EVALS AT SDSU
- **THE WALL STREET JOURNAL** – THANKS FOR THE GREAT EDUCATION OVER THE PAST YEARS!
- **MR. LINDNER** – MY JUNIOR HIGH VICE PRINCIPAL WHO KEPT ME ON TRACK AND OUT OF TROUBLE!

THANKS TO ALL OF YOU AND LET'S HOPE EVERYONE WORKS HARD TO REDUCE THEIR RISK AND PROTECT THEMSELVES ON THEIR REAL ESTATE PURCHASES.

Again...

Real Estate is Buyer Beware…..

Take the Time, Energy and Effort to Protect Yourself on the Largest Purchase you Will Ever Make….

When Things DO NOT Go Wrong, You Won't Forget to Thank Yourself for Doing a Great Job on Your Due Diligence Tasks!

Good Luck!

Leonard P. Baron

APPENDIX
PROPERTY HOME
INSPECTION CHECKLIST

THE ENTIRE CHECKLIST CAN BE DOWNLOADED AT PROFESSORBARON.COM

Property Home Inspection Checklist

ProfessorBaron.com

Buying Real Estate is the largest and riskiest purchase you will ever make in life.
Experienced buyers do their homework to protect themselves from the inherent risks.
You can also protect yourself, you just need to know what to do and how to do it.

Download the latest version of the checklist at www.ProfessorBaron.com to
Use for your Home Inspection and All Your Due Diligence Tasks.

PRINT THIS CHECKLIST IN COLOR IF YOU CAN

Property Address: _____

Home Inspector Name/Number: _____

READ ALL THE ITEMS BELOW CAREFULLY AND IN DETAIL

1   Again, we are not trying to convince you not to buy property. We just want you to have a
fair idea of the costs related to fixing issues with the property you want to buy.

2   In a perfect world, all the issues you find will be replaced/fixed/updated...but realistically you
just need to be aware of the items and current or future costs so you can make better
decisions today!

3   Note: In using this checklist, you may come up with a huge list of expenses/desired upgrades.
You could make this list for any and every property and probably REJECT every property -
but all properties need repairs/upgrades. Just use your common sense o

4   <u>Make sure your Inspector has a copy of this BEFORE the inspection. He/She will not be used</u>
<u>to this kind of detail and you need to make sure he/she knows what you expect and AGREES</u>
<u>to help you answer these questions.</u>

5   Did the Listing Agent make sure and did your Agent Confirm (A week before the Inspection) that the
Water, Electric, Gas and all other Utilities are ON for the Inspection?
Are you Sure that the Key is available to enter the property?

6   Talk to your Inspector and your Experienced Real Estate Agent on Whether
or Not you need any other inspections like - Termite, Mold, Seismic, Radon,
Structural, etc.

7   Plan on spending two to three hours at the property with the Inspector to adequately run
through this checklist. Could be more oR less depending on the square footage of the

8   Every item in this checklist is to make you think about whether or not it is an issue for your
property, so to bring it to your attention, and the cost to correct that issue or item.

9   Discuss your questions with your Inspector - He is the Expert! For unresolved issues, try contractors, Home Improvement Stores or the City Building Department Personnel (Careful Contacting City, See Note on Envelope & Exterior Checklist Page).

10   THIS CHECKLIST DOES NOT HAVE BOXES TO CHECK OFF BECAUSE MANY ISSUES WILL NEED YOU TO MAKE NOTES, SO JUST WRITE ALL OVER THIS CHECKLIST WHEREEVER YOU NEED.

     This is the Riskiest and Most Expensive thing you will ever Buy, Make sure to do your Due Diligence! Every Property needs work, we are just trying to help you avoid a Financial

OTHER THOUGHTS AND CONSIDERATIONS

Energy efficiency of house and potential improvements? Should I do an Energy Efficiency Audit?

        Things like Caulking Windowns, Weather Proofing Doors and Installing Water Heater Blankets are some of LEAST
        Expensive and most Financially Worthwhile Things to Do. Doing them Upfront May Save You Lots of Money During your

REPAIRS TIMEFRAME - I have a realistic timeframe for doing the repairs?
Other Costs to Consider If You are Rehabbing a Home:
While the House is Empty - Utilities, Property Taxes, Insurance, Mortgage Payments, etc.

Drive by Property Day/Night/Weekend - Introduce Yourself to neighbors

Any of These Apply:

Architectural Fees?
City Fees/Permits?
Construction Debris Disposal Costs?

THIS HOME INSPECTION CHECKLIST HAS THE FOLLOWING PARTS:

THESE INTRODUCTION PAGES, EXTERIOR AND ENVELOPE CHECKLIST, KITCHEN AND BATH CHECKLIST, COSTMETIC ITEMS CHECKLIST, PLUMBING AND WATER CHECKLIST, MECHANICAL CHECKLIST, HOA CHECKLIST

Property Home
Inspection Checklist

ProfessorBaron.com

EXTERIOR AND ENVELOPE

**Download the latest version of the checklist at www.ProfessorBaron.com to
Use for your Home Inspection and All Your Due Diligence Tasks.**

**There may be other issues that need to be reviewed, consult/question your
home inspector regarding other potential issues.**

Envelop and Exterior covers all kinds of items that are on the lot, on the exterior of the house, in the attic, underneath
and door and windows. Each one of these items could cost thousands or tens of thousands to repair or replace.
You should gain and understanding of the condition and costs before you purchase your property.

LAND AND LOT ISSUES (Some may not apply to your site)   COST?

Landscaping and Sprinkler Systems?

Condition of Landscaping? Fix, Add To, Replace Bushes, Planter Pots, Grass, Trim Trees/Bushes, etc. What changes,
        additions or clean up is needed...and how much does that cost?
Sprinkler Systems? - Were these tested, do they work? Do you need to install one?

Slope of Lot - Earth Movement Issues? Landslide? - Beware - These are probably not covered by Insurance! Talk to Your Agent!
        Water drainage issues? French Drain Outside? Basement Flooding?

Hardscaping Condition? Concrete Plant Boxes, Decorative Walls, etc.

        What is in property, how old, issues, if needed, cost to replace or repair - your inspector says:

NOTES:

_____   _____

Exterior Structures (Some may not apply to your site) - Each one is very expensive if you need to repair/replace.

Driveway Condition? Sidewalks?
Retaining Walls?
Fencing on Lot?
Sheds or Garages? Garage Doors?
Patios, Decks, Awnings, Trellises, Stairwells, Porches?
Pools, Hot Tubs, Jacuzzis, BBQ Islands?

Do any of the above needs to be repaired, replaced or removed? Possibly/Probably thousands of dollars per item?

        What is in property, how old, issues, if needed, cost to replace or repair - your inspector says:

NOTES:

_____   _____

<u>House Structure Items</u>

Roof Condition, Age, Remaining Useful Life, Cost to Replace?
       Composition Shingle Roof, Tile, Ceramic, Stones/Pebbles, Flat, Pitched?
       Roofs may need Just the Shingles Replaces, or Maybe all the Plywood structure too? Steep pitched roofs can be Expensive.
       If it appears there is an issue, it is easy to call and obtain a few bids to replace the roof.
       Skylights or Other Roof Penetrations - Water Proofed? Flat roof- where Water Puddles?
Exterior Walls - Siding, Stucco, Brick, Painting Needed? Condition, Repairs? Replacement?
Basement - Water Issues? Mold/Mildew Smells? Source of Smell? Water Marks on Walls? Waterproofed?
Exterior Doors? Age, Weatherproofed? Condition?
Windows - Double Pane? Single Pane? Age, Condition, Air Tight? Cost to Replace? Higher Heating & A/C Costs?
Door Locks or Window Locks - Replace? Window/Door Security Bars - Do They Open if Fire?
Rain Gutters? Down Spouts? Condition?

Foundation or Foundation Pier Issues?
Slab Cracks that Should Concern You?
Earthquake Retrofitting? Needed?

Unpermitted Additions? Outstanding Property Building Code Violations? Unsafe Looking Items?
       Consider Asking the City Questions: See Below.

CONTACTING THE CITY - POTENTIALLY REGARDING ISSUES. Call the city ANONYMOUSLY if you have concerns.
Generally they are there to help and are very helpful, but be careful on disclosing the property - some jurisdictions may not
be as "helpful" as others a

       What is in property, how old, issues, if needed, cost to replace or repair - your inspector says:

NOTES:

EXTERIOR AND ENVELOPE

<u>Interior Walls, Attic, Flooring</u>

Insulation in Attic, Walls, Crawl Spaces to keep utility bills low?
Ceiling and Floor Joists Sagging or Sinking Piers in Crawl Space?
Fire Sprinklers Interior - Condition, Local Known Issues?
Wall Cracks, Flooring Warped or Cracked Tile Grout or Tiles - Could be Water or Earth Movement Issue?
Slab Cracks under Carpet - Any evidence of major issues?
Termite Droppings or Damage? Termite Types in Your Local Area?

Detectors - Smoke, Carbon Dioxide, Radon - In house? Needed in local area?

What is in property, how old, issues, if needed, cost to replace or repair - your inspector says:

NOTES:

Made in the USA
Middletown, DE
21 January 2018